A Portrait of

The University of Manchester

A Portrait of
The University of Manchester

Historical Consultant
Professor Brian Pullan

III THIRD MILLENNIUM
PUBLISHING, LONDON

Part 1

Historical Overview

Part 2

Academic Achievements and Developments

Part 3

Student Life

Part 4

List of Contributors

Michele Abendstern is a specialist in oral history who has worked on several projects at the University and collaborated with Brian Pullan (see below) on two volumes on its recent history. She is now a Research Associate in the School of Medicine / **John Arnold** is Director of the Manchester Business School and KPMG Professor of Accounting and Financial Management / **Ken Green** is Professor in and Academic Dean of the Manchester Business School. He specialises in technology and innovation management and has a strong interest in environmental issues / **Sheila Griffiths**, an Honorary Companion of the University of Manchester, is Honorary Archivist of Ashburne Hall and Secretary of the Ashburne Association of Past and Present Students / **Harold Hankins** was Principal, later Vice-Chancellor, of UMIST from 1984 to 1995. He graduated in electrical engineering from the Tech in 1955 and after some years working for Metropolitan Vickers and for Associated Engineering Industries joined the staff of UMIST in 1968 / **Sir Martin Harris**, formerly Vice-Chancellor of the University of Essex, was Vice-Chancellor of the University of Manchester and Professor of Romance Linguistics from 1992 to 2004 / **Chris Humphrey** is Professor of Accounting and Head of the Manchester Accounting and Finance Group (a division of the Business School) / **Hilary Kahn** is Professor of Computer Science and has long been concerned with computer aided design and software engineering. In 1997-8 she was heavily involved in organising the celebrations of the fiftieth anniversary of the world's first stored-programme computer / **Colin Lees** is a member of the School of Education, where he is now Programme Director of the B.A. (Hons) in Education (part-time). He has collaborated with Alex B. Robertson (see below) on several articles on the history of Owens College and with Eric Rowley (see below) on a book about the experiences of members of the University during the Second World War / **Gerard McKenna** was tutor and later vice-warden of Allen Hall from 1967 to 1978. From 1982 to 1997 he was Assistant Registrar in charge of the Accommodation Office of the Victoria University of Manchester / **Arthur Mawby**, an expert on South Africa who lectured in history from 1972 until his retirement in 2005, was associated for more than thirty years with St Anselm Hall. He was warden from 1992 to 2005 / **Sam (Stuart Alfred) Moore,** an econometrician, began his career as a computer assistant and part-time student in the Faculty of Economic and Social Studies in the early 1960s. He became Dean of the Faculty in the early 1980s and was Acting Vice-Chancellor from 1990 to 1992. From 1992 to 1997 he was Robert Ottley Professor of Quantitive Studies / **Maureen Mulholland** is a legal historian, has helped to edit *Clerk and Lindsell on Tort*, and has interests in law and medicine. A graduate of the Victoria University of Manchester, she began her career as a lecturer in the Faculty of Law in 1964 / **Alison Odell** is Director of Sport in the administrative division of Sport, Trading and Residential Services / **John V. Pickstone** was the founding Director of the Centre for the History of Science, Technology and Medicine and the Wellcome Unit for the History of Medicine. He is now Wellcome Research Professor in the Faculty of Life Sciences. His many books include *Medicine and Industrial Society. A History of Hospital Development in Manchester and its Region, 1752-1946* (1985) / **Anne Pullan** has a first degree in English from Manchester Metropolitan University and an MA in Arts and Heritage Management (specialising in Theatre Management) from the University of Sheffield / **Brian Pullan,** a specialist in Italian social history, was Professor of Modern History from 1973 to 1998. He has written two volumes on the recent history of the Victoria University of Manchester from 1951 to 1990, with the collaboration of Michele Abendstern (see above) / **Bernard Richards** is Professor of Medical Informatics and Occasional Consultant in the School of Informatics / **Alex B. Robertson** taught for many years in the Faculty (later School) of Education. He is the author of *A Century of Change. The Study of Education in the University of Manchester* (1990) and of several articles on the early history of Owens College, some of them in collaboration with Colin Lees (see above) / **Alex J. Robertson** joined the economic history section of the History Department in 1966 and was seconded in 1991 to the International Office of the Registrar's Department. He retired in 2001 / **Eric Rowley** is an educationist and economic historian who retired from the University in 1997. He compiled *The University of Manchester at War 1939–1946* (2001) for the celebrations of the 150th anniversary of Owens College, with the collaboration of Colin Lees (above) and contributions from alumni / **Auriol Stevens** is an author and journalist specialising in education issues and was Editor of *Times Higher Education Supplement* from 1992 to 2002. She remains closely involved in higher education and became Pro-Chancellor of the University of Essex in 2005 / **Alison Utley** is a freelance journalist based in Manchester who writes regularly for the *Times Higher Education Supplement* / **Tim Yates** graduated from Owens in 1962 with BA in English Literature and Language (MA 1963). He later became Director of Communications at UMIST, where he set up the alumni magazine *Mainstream*

Foreword

ANNA FORD AND SIR TERRY LEAHY

CO-CHANCELLORS, THE UNIVERSITY OF MANCHESTER

Foreword by Anna Ford

Manchester is an extraordinary city, with a history of great influence not only in commerce, engineering, and civic responsibility, but also in music, literature, art, libraries and sport.

There have been, and still are, many great Mancunians, men and women of conscience and energy who have made a profound difference to the lives of others. It was here that John Dalton laid the foundations of modern chemistry, where Manchester radicals agitated for parliamentary reform; where 'The Manchester School' became so influential in economics; where Friedrich Engels gathered material for his great work, 'The condition of the Working Class in England'; where the movement to secure votes for women, with hitherto unheard-of protests and petitions, was organised by Emmeline Pankhurst and her daughter Christabel; where Rutherford meditated on the structure of the atom, and where the world's first stored-programme computer was invented by Freddie Williams and Tom Kilburn.

Mancunians are proud people who have over centuries exhibited a level of creativity and independence of mind rarely found in such concentration. The entrepreneurial streak that runs through their character led to the emergence of Manchester as the world's first industrial city. Its central role in the industrial revolution meant Manchester mills were producing 65 per cent of the world's textile output. There were chemical works, great engineering factories and a canal twice the width of the Suez Canal, with vast ocean-going ships bringing and taking goods direct to the industrial centre.

It's true that wealth at that time did belong to a few leading industrialists, and factory workers and coalminers led wretchedly hard lives. But some of those industrialists went on to dedicate their fortunes to encouraging education and knowledge. The list of privately funded institutions spearheading change in the city is impressive, and all kinds of learning were given a boost by access to Free Public Libraries after 1850. Some working men later became leaders in the emergent trade union movement and, encouraged by educational visionaries such as Albert Mansbridge, strove to better lives by embracing further and life-long education.

And at the very heart of this great city lies a great University.

The University of Manchester, on which Her Majesty the Queen bestowed a new charter in 2004, had humble beginnings. The Manchester Mechanics' Institution opened in 1824, taught the basic principles of science, and was the foundation stone of what later became UMIST, with its extensive collaborations with industry, and its fundamental research of the highest quality.

In 1851 the seed of the future university emerged as Owens College, with just 64 students and eight members of staff. John Owens (1790–1846), a Manchester textile merchant, believed so strongly in the vital importance of education that he left his entire fortune of £97,000 to endow a college dedicated to higher academic education. As a nonconformist Dissenter Owens strongly opposed laws which barred Dissenters from Oxbridge, so Owens College was to be open to anyone of whatever belief, and whatever class and condition in society (although at that stage this meant only men). Thirty years later women too were admitted. That legacy of openness of mind, and the wish to welcome everyone, still endures in our University community and we're proud to have thousands of students and staff from nearly two hundred countries.

Anna Ford and Sir Terry Leahy.

Owens College was a pioneering institution, leading the way in particular with the introduction of evening classes, a practical necessity for many students. With a highly talented teaching staff there was soon talk of creating a full-blown University. Generous bequests began to flow in and by the turn of the new century, a new charter gave the fifty-year-old University, now known as the Victoria University of Manchester, autonomy over all its activities.

As you would expect, more than a century on much has changed, though the entrepreneurial spirit is stronger than ever. When the new University was founded in 2004 I sensed a collective and profound sigh of relief. The eyes of the academic community, the government and higher education institutions around the world had been on us as we navigated our way through the immense complexities of merging two fully fledged institutions, The Victoria University of Manchester and UMIST.

I can only praise and wholeheartedly admire the extraordinarily hard, detailed work, determination and sheer brilliance of the enterprise. We could have failed, but we didn't, and the breathtaking ambition of the transformation laid out in the Manchester 2015 agenda – 'to make The University of Manchester, already an internationally distinguished centre of research, innovation, learning and scholarly inquiry, one of the leading Universities in the World by 2015' – is already beginning to bear fruit.

For students, the University is now the UK's most popular, with more undergraduate applications than any other British university. Our students are academically top-drawer and richly mixed, socially, racially and culturally.

Our relationship with the City of Manchester is as important as ever and just as we rely, as we've always relied, on the involvement and support of major city figures, we're also one of the city's largest employers. We're involved with school and College students around us in the North West through outreach, and widening participation activities, giving many young people their first taste of the possibilities open to them in a University.

I'd say we're more than ever aware of the importance of our alumni community, and are in contact with 198,000 of you who spread across 197 countries, and we want to build upon your support, advice and involvement in the future.

I'm so proud to have been Chancellor of this University, where so many of my own family have studied for four generations, and I feel sure that it is going to achieve its stated ambition to become one of the world's great Universities, undertaking groundbreaking research and teaching at the very highest level.

Anna Ford,
Co-Chancellor of The University of Manchester,
Broadcaster and Journalist

Foreword by Sir Terry Leahy

I am delighted to have an opportunity to warmly welcome and endorse this important new book. The new University of Manchester has drawn from the very best of its two predecessor institutions, and has made startling early progress. The production of this portrait is therefore especially timely – celebrating the outstanding history of two great institutions, while looking ahead to a still greater future for the current University.

What has been so rewarding about being involved in the creation of the new University has been the strength of the 'step-change' agenda developed by President and Vice-Chancellor Alan Gilbert and his colleagues (see page 188). The refusal to accept second-best, the openness to challenging and re-thinking accepted norms within the sector, and not least the entrepreneurial flair being demonstrated on campus remind me of lessons in management I learnt from the great Sir Roland Smith, when he taught me and several generations of Management Science students at UMIST. Sir Roland sadly died in 2003, but I know he would have been proud of what we are now achieving in Manchester, and the bold style with which we are carrying the new combined University forward. My own subsequent experiences in business have taught me the powerful transformative effect of linking audacious goals with vision and values. It is heartening to see the new University very much set on that course.

A great University is fundamentally about its people – the students, teachers and researchers that are its lifeblood. For students, the University teaches the broadest range of courses available at any campus-based University in the UK, and remains top of the popularity league, with more undergraduate applications than any other British university. It has been especially pleasing to see the new University continuing the strong traditions of both VUM and UMIST in doing everything we can to ensure our doors remain open to all with the necessary academic ability and personal motivation to benefit from a Manchester degree programme, irrespective of their financial circumstances or background.

It is that openness to talent from all quarters that continually shines through in this book, and rarely has that been more important. Very few, if any, global institutions draw people together from such diverse social, racial and cultural backgrounds in pursuit of a common purpose as do our universities. In the light of the many current forces working to pull local and national communities apart, it is vital that the world's leading universities continue to draw talent from such an eclectic mix of backgrounds, and promote the values of open-mindedness and tolerance.

The University of Manchester excels in this respect, and is now actively encouraging its home and international students to reflect on their future leadership roles as global citizens through the Manchester Leadership Programme, which involves seminars, group work and rigorous volunteer work with local community groups. This kind of approach, based on an understanding that students learn vital wider lessons on campus beyond the focus of their studies, helps explain why Manchester students remain as highly sought after as ever by graduate recruiters, with a Careers Service that is ranked 1st in the country year after year by employers.

The current research output of the University is of a quality you might expect from a University which can count 23 Nobel laureates amongst its former and current staff and students. The interdisciplinary nature of the University's research teams reflects the complex and inter-related scientific and social issues in society where first-class research can make a real difference. Our early success in attracting 'iconic' and virtuosic researchers to lead and draw together our work in priority areas demonstrates the power of big-picture, ambitious thinking. The entrepreneurial flair that has always been synonymous with the City and its universities continues unabated in the research environment, with outstanding early successes in the commercialization of ideas on campus.

Those of you who have not visited the University campus in recent years are in for a shock; every time you visit the campus these days you can see the physical transformation taking place before your eyes. The extent of the current building programme provides clear evidence of our determination to provide the University's students and staff with outstanding facilities. As with all of our work, this is merely a means to an end; wonderful facilities only serve to accelerate our progress in becoming a magnet for the best regional, national and international talent.

Finally, let me add that as a former President of the UMIST Alumni Association, it has been heartening to see the warm response of alumni of both VUM and UMIST to this important new book, either as contributors to the rich tapestry of university life that it draws together, or as subscribers. As former students, we form the largest single part of the University's global community, and have an important part to play in taking this great University forward to still greater days. I hope that this portrait of the University – past, present and future – will inspire many of us to re-engage with our alma mater, or to deepen our existing involvement.

Sir Terry Leahy,
Co-Chancellor of The University of Manchester,
Chief Executive of Tesco plc

Owens College and the Victoria University, 1851–1903

ALEX B. ROBERTSON AND COLIN LEES

Three institutions combined to form the Victoria University of Manchester: Owens College, which opened in 1851; the Medical School in Pine Street, founded in 1824 by Thomas Turner; the Mechanics' Institution established in the same year.

Owens was the youngest of the three, but the broadest intellectually, and the drive to establish a university originated from the college, which sought to advance learning both in the humanities and in the natural sciences. Two historians from the School of Education, Alex B. Robertson and Colin Lees, describe the early history of Owens College from its beginnings in Quay Street to the foundation of the independent Victoria University of Manchester in 1903.

After years of half-hearted or frustrated effort, the second half of the nineteenth century witnessed the slow emergence of a national system of education. In the most industrially developed regions in the Midlands and North, arguments for education in an industrial society joined the more common social and religious themes as "a regular topic of discussion in literary and scientific societies, mechanics' institutions and a wide range of organisations through which the intelligentsia analysed society". While higher education lacked the urgency given to elementary and secondary schools, it was becoming clear that, in England, the four universities of Oxford, Cambridge, London and Durham were too conservative or hidebound by restrictive statutes to respond readily to modern circumstances.

As was typical of English education in general, impetus for change came from the regions and from prominent men and organisations. Love and Barton's Manchester guide of 1839 provides an impressive list of institutions that spearheaded change in

Previous page: 'Caf', the deconsecrated chapel where the intelligentsia of both sexes met over tea, coffee and snacks to set the world to rights, 1944.

Above: John Owens.

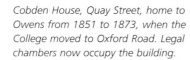

Cobden House, Quay Street, home to Owens from 1851 to 1873, when the College moved to Oxford Road. Legal chambers now occupy the building.

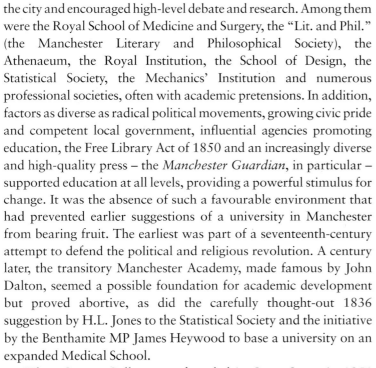

the city and encouraged high-level debate and research. Among them were the Royal School of Medicine and Surgery, the "Lit. and Phil." (the Manchester Literary and Philosophical Society), the Athenaeum, the Royal Institution, the School of Design, the Statistical Society, the Mechanics' Institution and numerous professional societies, often with academic pretensions. In addition, factors as diverse as radical political movements, growing civic pride and competent local government, influential agencies promoting education, the Free Library Act of 1850 and an increasingly diverse and high-quality press – the *Manchester Guardian*, in particular – supported education at all levels, providing a powerful stimulus for change. It was the absence of such a favourable environment that had prevented earlier suggestions of a university in Manchester from bearing fruit. The earliest was part of a seventeenth-century attempt to defend the political and religious revolution. A century later, the transitory Manchester Academy, made famous by John Dalton, seemed a possible foundation for academic development but proved abortive, as did the carefully thought-out 1836 suggestion by H.L. Jones to the Statistical Society and the initiative by the Benthamite MP James Heywood to base a university on an expanded Medical School.

When Owens College was founded in Quay Street in 1851 from the generosity of the Manchester merchant John Owens, few would have forecast its eventual success or that it would draw into its orbit a significant number of institutions in the city. Despite the excellence of its staff from the beginning and a determination to be a genuinely academic institution that never wavered, the first years were extremely testing. While much had changed by 1851, a flow of appropriate students remained uncertain since a post-elementary or secondary tier of education was not in place and the old grammar schools were themselves in need of reform. As the first of the "civic" or "redbrick" colleges by a generation, Owens was in the exciting but uncomfortable position of being a pioneering institution facing an unclear future.

There were some strengths. The short, inspirational leadership of Principal A.J. Scott was followed in 1857 by the thirty-two-year tenure of Joseph G. Greenwood, whose administrative skills and openness to innovation did much to provide steadiness of

purpose in partnership with the University of London – not then seen as an inhibiting force, but as a guarantee of standards and legitimacy. The quality of the early professors ensured that the college was taken seriously in the city and beyond. However, student numbers remained only in double figures for a decade and recourse was made to bold attempts to increase recruitment: evening classes were commenced, at first for teachers, but soon opened to all, and in 1862 the innovative Working Man's College amalgamated with Owens.

These early pragmatic decisions to increase numbers affected the style of the college's development, and links with a wider spectrum of the city than might be expected in so academic an institution encouraged a sense of inclusiveness, a situation strengthened by Owens' refusal to countenance religious tests. A certain lack of formality in relationships and arrangements was encouraged by the cramped conditions in Quay Street as well as by the increasing number of evening students representing the variety of occupations in an industrial city. John Owens' shrewd insistence that his endowment should be used to provide high-quality staff and not buildings meant that the college was housed in unsatisfactory conditions, particularly for the sciences. Until state grants were available from 1889, much of the trustees' and principals' efforts went into raising money.

Considering such constraints, it is striking that in 1865 a decision was made to move to a new site and, despite an economic downturn in the region, £106,000 was raised, the present site on Oxford Road was purchased and a building by Alfred Waterhouse commissioned. Simultaneously, a new constitution was worked out which gained parliamentary support in 1871, and the power of the

trustees passed to a court, council and senate in what became the characteristic government of the "civics". A clause was included in the legislation that set aside the limitation in Owens' will to "young persons of the male sex", but in fact radical attitudes to women were not characteristic of Owens College in the nineteenth century. In 1877 enthusiasts formed a college for women in Brunswick Street which, while linked to the University for some teaching, maintained the "separate spheres" ideology that some senior academics believed necessary. It was the end of the century before all restrictions were removed when, in 1899, women were admitted to the School of Medicine. Had it not been for powerful senior figures such as Alexander, Tout and Wilkins in Arts, and Roscoe in Science, the delay might well have been longer. It is of interest that the largest group of women were training to be teachers, demonstrating how few career opportunities were then open to young women.

Easier to handle than such politically and socially divisive issues were two major advances after 1871. The Manchester Royal School of Medicine amalgamated with Owens College in 1872 and the Manchester Medical Society presented its library. Generous gifts enabled a new medical chair to be founded and a purpose-built building was opened in 1874. This successful re-foundation of the college encouraged local interest, and two prestigious Manchester bodies, the Natural History Society and the Geological Society, presented their collections to the college. When money was raised, the Manchester Museum was opened in 1888 to house them.

These constitutional issues created a necessary framework for growth and stability and, while occupying much time and energy, were never a diversion from the academic work of the college. In an important sense, they further developed the college's relationship with the city through fundraising and links with prominent Mancunians and industry.

Owens' will had encouraged a college philosophy that can be compared to the Scottish system of a community-oriented, broad-access college, aware of the needs of the region it served and

The tower, the Council Chamber and the Manchester Museum (opened in 1888). The Whitworth Hall has not yet been added.

reliant on highly qualified teaching staff led by an actively involved professoriate. The original trustees put together a balanced curriculum of humanities and science, to which medicine was soon added. Working within this academic framework, the able and energetic professorial staff, who in the early days did much of the teaching, acquired a national reputation. They were assisted by the valuable influence of the University of London. The names of Adamson, Alexander, Christie, Core, Delépine, Jevons, Lamb, Marshall, Reynolds, Roscoe, Schorlemmer, Schuster, Theodores, Watson and Williamson bear witness to the talent associated with the college in its first phase. Despite their frequent lack of appropriate school preparation, the students did well and the annual honours lists, proudly read at an annual ceremony and recorded in the *Calendar*, developed a tradition of hard work and high standards. Accompanying this was the emergence of a rudimentary college community with a students' union, magazine, annual sports and, in 1870 and 1876, the first halls of residence, founded by members of the Church of England and of the Society of Friends.

With such positive signs confidence increased and, very soon after the new site had been occupied and the new constitution implemented, the idea of creating an independent Manchester University was canvassed. The city and county were supportive, and in 1877 the Privy Council was petitioned. Opposition came from the emerging Yorkshire College at Leeds, which objected to a territorial title for the university on the grounds that a federation of regional colleges would be advantageous. This idea appealed to the

Victorian buildings today: the Manchester Museum from Oxford Road (top) and the ground floor of its new annexe off Coupland Street (above).

government. In 1880 it approved the idea of a Victoria University with its headquarters in Manchester as the senior member, with the power to affiliate appropriate institutions. In 1884 and 1887 respectively University College, Liverpool, and Yorkshire College joined Owens College in a valuable if rather unwieldy experiment which lasted until 1903. The character of the new university was of great importance. The University of London was, in effect, only an examining board for many associated institutions at home and abroad; the Victoria University was in complete control of its own admissions, teaching, examining and the awarding of degrees.

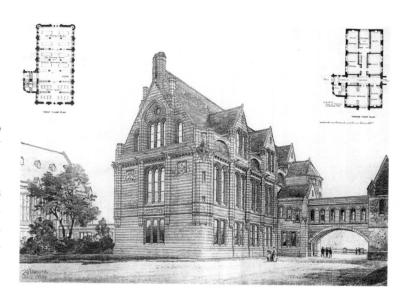

The Christie Bridge that never was – a planned extension to the John Owens Building, dating from the late 1890s.

The final two decades of the century witnessed another spurt in the evolution of higher education at Manchester and in the region. Money became easier to raise and funds for professorial chairs, scholarships and buildings began to flow. The Beyer Bequest in 1875, greater than the original endowment, foreshadowed this financial injection. Further support came from the Whitworth Bequest of 1887 for engineering, medicine and, from 1890, the new study of education; the Christie Bequest, which created the Christie Library, and regular scholarships and grants from the city and widespread local authorities. By 1900 annual income had reached £36,801 in comparison with £4,517 in 1862.

A simple comparison of student numbers is also revealing. By 1900 these had just topped 1,000 – 875 men and 177 women – whereas in 1862 there were 108 men only. Evening classes, which had begun as an expedient, had developed into a major success and gained departmental status. They provided a means for many young men (women were excluded) to follow degree courses or, increasingly, special courses in languages, economics and other skills valued in a commercial and industrial city. By the end of the century, the increasingly formalised university structure, partly encouraged by the federal bureaucracy, began to phase out this admirable experiment. On the positive side, the national movement for adult education found a welcome among some professors and staff. The University Extension movement gained by the appointment of Arthur Milnes Marshall as Professor of

Left: The Christie Library (1895–8) was the gift of the former law professor, historian and bibliophile Richard Copley Christie. For much of the twentieth century the Christie housed the University's principal science library.

Above: Evacuated when science books were moved to the new Library Extension (officially opened by the Queen in 1982), the Christie Library was converted into a restaurant and a clubroom complete with leather armchairs, portraits and bookshelves during the 1990s.

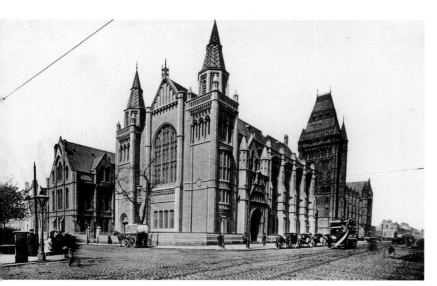

Above: Owens College/Victoria University of Manchester buildings, seen from Oxford Road in the early twentieth century, with the Whitworth Hall in the foreground and the Christie Library to its left.

Right: The cramped University Library as it was in 1897, a year before the Christie Library was erected. The original library was located on the top floor of the main building.

Zoology in 1879 and A.W. Ward, an admirer of Toynbee Hall and a promoter of the Manchester University Settlement in Ancoats, as Principal when Greenwood retired in 1889.

By 1900 a plan of the University reveals that the original Owens College had been enlarged by a range of buildings which created an enclosed quadrangle, of which the last section, the Whitworth Hall – fronting Oxford Road and abutting the Manchester Museum – was in course of construction. Behind and to the north lay purpose-built laboratories for physics, chemistry and engineering, all dominated by the old medical school of 1874 and the massive new structure of 1894. A union building and a small gymnasium were provided as early facilities for students. All of this was encroaching on a warren of small streets and businesses, and segmented by the busy thoroughfares of Coupland Street and Burlington Street. Owens College in the Victoria University was authentically a "civic university" in the physical as well as the philosophical sense.

By 1900 the staff had greatly increased in number and, with the emergence of a hierarchy of lecturers, a fledgling profession was coming into being. In 1900 there were 24 professors, seven lecturers, and 36 assistant lecturers and demonstrators. The status of reader and of senior lecturer was to emerge in the opening decades of the new century. Research and teaching were regarded as central at all levels and, while a master's degree was the usual if still infrequent postgraduate award, the introduction from Germany of the doctorate in 1918 was a major contribution to postgraduate studies. The developing courses and awards in the University greatly affected the emerging secondary schools in the city, none more so than the prestigious honours degree which did so much to create and form the character of the selective sixth forms of the new grammar schools created by local education authorities (LEA) after the legislation of 1902.

The most obvious gap in provision was technology, a serious situation in late nineteenth-century Manchester. The subject was energetically promoted by the influential Arts professor, Samuel Alexander, though it was not yet wholly "respectable" among some conservative academics, or valued by industrialists who distrusted theoretical training. Impetus came from the city itself, where influential businessmen pressured the city council to take action. The obvious candidate for development was the 1824 Mechanics' Institution, which had survived despite the national trend that turned the original radical concept into adult education provision for the middle classes. By the 1880s, as the chapter by Harold Hankins and Tim Yates shows (pages 23–29), it was regaining its earlier values and energy under the influence of its secretary, J.H. Reynolds, and evolving into a technical school with commercial and industrial relevance to the city.

As a result of national as well as local pressure, the idea of replacing increasingly unsuitable Princess Street site began to be discussed, culminating in the opening of the magnificent Sackville Street building, housing the Manchester Municipal School of Technology, in 1902. These developments were watched not

Oxford Road frontage of the Victorian buildings.

Below: The Old Owensian students who remembered Quay Street (1851–73) formed within the alumni a brotherhood which occasionally held its own reunion dinners. At the Jubilee in 1901–2 attempts were made to trace all Old Students, with a view to compiling a register. Two undergraduates commemorated in the John Owens Building are the novelist George Gissing (a prizewinner whose college career ended in disgrace when he was expelled for stealing to support his girlfriend) and the poet Francis Thompson, an absentee medical student whose courses were not to his taste. Hamilton Irving, a medical student with artistic talents, commemorates one of the College's principal social events.

without anxiety at the University, partly from possible overlap with some courses, particularly in the evening classes; partly from concern that advanced technology courses might jeopardise its own science faculty, and alarm at a possible diversion of Manchester Council financial support to its new college. For the first time, the former Mechanics' Institution and Owens College moved into each other's orbit.

The last years of the century were marked by increasing self-confidence. A senior group of professors, led by the new principal from 1898, Alfred Hopkinson, were encouraged to consider independence since the federal arrangement was proving a considerable inhibition to innovation, although independent decision-making since 1880 had provided much valuable experience. These aspirations were encouraged and facilitated by support in the city and the decision of Mason's College, Birmingham, to seek university status, but particularly when University College, Liverpool, petitioned for independence. Auspiciously, in 1901 the college reached its fiftieth anniversary, an event subsequently marked by the completion of the Whitworth Hall, opened by the Prince of Wales among much local celebration. Negotiations with city and government were positive, and a new charter was awarded in 1903 which, although incorporating the old title, the Victoria University, granted Manchester autonomy.

Medicine, Natural History and Owens College, 1824–1903

JOHN V. PICKSTONE

In 1872, the Royal School of Medicine and Surgery (as the school founded by Thomas Turner was now called) joined forces with Owens College, extending the college's academic range and strengthening its claims to university status. John Pickstone, Research Professor of the History of Science, Technology and Medicine, tells the story of the medical school before and after the merger.

In 1824, the civic culture of Manchester was expanding again after the repression of the Napoleonic Wars and the ensuing trade depression. It was regaining something of the liberal vitality which had characterised it in the 1780s when a doctors' dining club had grown into the Manchester Literary and Philosophical Society (known as the Lit. and Phil.), and when some of the same citizens had founded a College of Arts and Science which for a few years provided lectures to the young. The Dissenting members of the group, centered on the Cross Street Unitarian Chapel, had established in 1786 an academy which educated ministers for the Unitarian churches, but which also included young men who would go on to careers in business or the professions. In 1793, John Dalton came from the Lake District to be a tutor there, and he soon established a reputation as the town's leading man of science, working in a laboratory at the Literary and Philosophical Society on George Street. Around 1790, the reform party had taken over the main charity, the Manchester Infirmary, and expanded its services. But from the mid-1790s, under the backlash against the French Revolution, reformers were in retreat, though industry continued to grow apace.

In 1824, as forty years before, science and medicine were central to city culture. In this new generation, several of the

Two sketches by the medical student Hamilton Irving. In 'Tables Turned' (above) the clinicians are in bed and the students (some surprisingly mature) are diagnosing their afflictions. In the bed on the far right is G.A. Wright, Professor of Systematic Surgery 1900–11; in the bed next to him, Julius Dreschfeld, Professor of Medicine 1891–1907. The lower sketch shows Irving himself drawing real patients on the ward.

Students of the Pathology Department at the turn of the century taking a practical class in Morbid Histology. The Old Medical School is now the Coupland III Building.

organisers were businessmen from professional families with philanthropic and scientific interests. The Lit. and Phil. remained their chief meeting place, and Dalton was by this time world famous. In 1821, a Natural History Society was formed which eventually built a large museum on Peter Street. Soon afterwards came a movement to establish an art gallery, which would also offer lectures on the arts and sciences to the middle classes and perhaps to working men – the Royal Manchester Institution was founded in 1823 (it is now the City Art Gallery), providing a meeting space for various scientific groups. In 1824 the Mechanics' Institution was established for the working classes, and a medical school was founded in Pine Street, near the Infirmary.

This was not the first medical school in Manchester – that had been started ten years earlier by Joseph Jordan, who had studied with Charles Bell in Edinburgh and enriched his experience in the Peninsular Wars. He was devoted to anatomy and a very good teacher. But he was not on the staff of the Royal Infirmary, and this disadvantaged him when a competitor school appeared. His new rival, Thomas Turner, came from Cornwall and had been house surgeon at the Infirmary. Turner offered a wider spread of lectures, and built a school in Pine Street; Jordan countered by enlarging his school; and for some years there was also a school in Marsden Street. By the mid-1830s, Turner had won, partly because Jordan was told that if he wanted to be voted on to the Infirmary staff he had to agree to a merger.

Medical education in the English provinces was not then attached to universities (as in Scotland), nor formally to teaching hospitals (as commonly in London); it was conducted by schools owned and run by doctors (as in the USA). The Pine Street School continued until it was absorbed by Owens College in 1872; from 1836 it was known by royal charter as the Royal School of Medicine and Surgery; in 1850, it was challenged by a school in Chatham Street, but a merger was arranged in 1856. The clinical work, however, depended on the hospitals, and in Manchester this was always the Royal Infirmary. After 1872 there were no proprietary medical schools in Manchester, though independent pharmacy schools were begun in the 1840s and continued until the 1920s.

Before 1850, higher education in Manchester was informal, medical or theological. Several denominations had established colleges, but only that of the Unitarians attempted to give much scientific education; it was in York from 1803, but back in Manchester from 1840 to 1853. For the most part, young men went from school to business, to an apprenticeship in medicine, or into engineering. When Owens College was launched in 1851, it chiefly provided the liberal arts plus some mathematics and chemistry. Owens considered linking with the medical schools, but rejected the idea – medical students were lower-class and notoriously rowdy; they would lower the tone.

Much had changed by 1873, when Owens College moved to its new Gothic buildings on Oxford Road. The idea of higher education was taking root across the country, especially when it provided access to degrees of the University of London. The Medical Act of 1858 had led to national oversight of medical qualifications and to pressure for higher standards, especially for more science courses, including practical work. And there was a precedent. At Owens College, Henry Roscoe had established chemistry as a path to an industrial (or teaching) career. He was the grandson of a major figure in the Liverpool Enlightenment and had studied with Professor Bunsen in Heidelberg. He came to Manchester in 1857 and married into the Potter family, one of the richest and most powerful of the liberal, industrial–political dynasties. He was thus very well placed to implant in Britain the central lesson of German universities: that academics should strive not just to teach well, but to create new knowledge and new researchers. The message translated easily into industrial England: research schools, like advanced businesses, would expand by keeping ahead of the competition. In the new buildings opened in 1873, a third of the space was for Roscoe's chemical institute. Now it made sense for Owens to incorporate a medical school, which would bring fees from students requiring science courses. In turn, a college that intended to become a university would lend prestige to local medical education and to its teachers. It was agreed that the Royal School of Medicine would be incorporated into the College, and a new medical school was opened on Coupland Street in 1874, behind the main building. The medical school was enlarged in the 1880s, and in the 1890s a large new block was added to house laboratories; it awarded medical degrees from 1883 (though most students still took the qualifications of the London Royal Colleges).

Even before Owens had moved to the suburbs, the Royal Infirmary had been discussing a similar move, partly for fresh air, and later to take advantage of a site near the university provided from the legacy of the engineer Joseph Whitworth. The issue of the hospital site came to a head in 1902, and the new hospital, opened in 1908, was one of the largest in the country, serving a huge catchment population. In medicine, as in the physical sciences, Manchester could now rival the London colleges.

Around 1900, the major strengths of the Edwardian medical school were in practical subjects. A department of *materia medica* had been developed by Daniel Leech, which educated a few pharmacists as well as doctors; but until the professional requirements were raised after the First World War, the University found it hard to compete with the two private pharmacy schools nearby. The surgery professors were a mixture of local men who had risen through the ranks and high-flyers from the London teaching hospitals who had applied for resident posts there. Some of the obstetricians had national reputations, including William Japp Sinclair who kept abreast of German developments and helped make the Hungarian physician Ignaz Semmelweiss (1818–65) into a byword for obstetric cleanliness. Already in 1873, the leading teacher of clinical medicine, William Roberts, had a reputation for research – he worked in a laboratory at home, where his studies of digestion led to a famous food for invalids, commercialised by a Manchester pharmacist, F.B. Benger. Roberts' successor as Manchester's leading physician, Julius Dreschfeld, was born in Germany, grew up in Manchester, and then studied pathology with the great Rudolph Virchow at Wurzburg. He taught pathology part-time at Owens from 1881, before becoming Professor of Medicine in 1891. That was then a typical British medical career – lab work was for young clinicians.

But the scientists at Owens had in mind another pattern, familiar in Germany from the 1830s: that medical sciences could provide full-time careers in which teaching would be combined with ongoing research programmes. In Manchester the plan worked well in pathology, when Dreschfeld's promotion to professor of medicine made room for a young Swiss pathologist, Sheridan Delépine, who specialised in bacteriology. He developed a laboratory that undertook tests for hospitals, public health authorities and general practitioners. The model worked less well in physiology, where a full-time professor was appointed in 1873 and expected to act as a bridge between chemistry and the new medical school. A similar appointment in Cambridge soon began

Professor Delépine

I was for some thirty-five years involved in teaching and research in bacteriology at the University of Manchester and very much involved in the planning of the then Department of Bacteriology and Virology laboratories in the new medical school, and before that our move into the Williamson Building. When I first arrived, the department was housed in the old Clinical Sciences Building adjacent to the MRI. In my first few weeks there in 1962 I was curious to see an old man staring down from the upper gallery of the foyer at the grand staircase and its half-landing, in the wall of which there was a bust of the first professor, Auguste Sheridan Delépine. When I asked why he did so, regularly on Thursday afternoons, he told me he was paying his respects to his old boss. He went on to say that he was present in 1922 when "they put him in the wall".

Enquiries to the Registrar's office produced no documentation of such an event – which would have been unusual, to say the least! – but the old "lab boy" was quite certain it had happened. To be on the safe side, when the day came to leave the old department prior to its demolition, we enlisted the aid of monumental masons in order to make the most careful retrieval possible, still uncertain as to whether we might find a body or ashes, or maybe just memorabilia.

To cut to the point, Prof. Delépine's ashes *had* been interred in the wall.

Louis B. Quesnel
Manchester

to attract young men to physiological research, building a research school that drew international attention and was to prove hugely seminal for the biomedical sciences in Britain. That did not happen in Manchester. The first physiology professor found the medical students uninterested; they wanted to graduate as doctors, not linger over physiology. He left, and his replacement William Stirling, though appointed for his research, wrote textbooks. Physiology was then less directly useful than pathology, but much also depended on the individuals. Just before the First World War, a new professor of anatomy, the Australian Grafton Elliot Smith, rapidly attracted a research following for surgical anatomy, X-ray studies and anthropological work. He had come from Cairo, as an expert on mummified remains – which was also one of the strengths of the University Museum.

Thomas Turner.

Joseph Jordan.

The Natural History Society, started in the 1820s, opened a museum in 1835 on Peter Street; the first curator and manager was a young geologist, W.C. Williamson, from Scarborough. He later qualified in medicine, but when Owens College opened he was appointed professor of natural history. He taught geology, botany and zoology, and researched on the fossil plants found in coal. When the College moved and linked with the medical school, geology was taken over by William Boyd Dawkins; it was also agreed that the collections of the Natural History Museum would come to Owens. A splendid new building was added for them in the 1880s, and Dawkins became curator.

The zoology teaching was taken over in 1879 by a young embryologist from Cambridge, Arthur Milnes Marshall. He was one of the followers of T.H. Huxley, both in popularising science and in creating a new science of biology focused on functions, tissues and cells rather than on classifications. But like more than one young scientist at the end of the nineteenth century, he was killed in a mountain accident. His successor was Sidney Hickson, an expert on corals, who supported women's education and built up biology as a school subject and as a university degree in its own right.

In 1892, after forty years at Owens, Williamson retired and a full-time botanist was appointed, also an expert on plant fossils. Frederick Ernest Weiss, then aged twenty-six, was born in Huddersfield of a German family and most of his education had been gained on the continent – Manchester University owed much to industrial England's mercantile connections with German learning. For four decades, Weiss and Hickson represented classical botany and zoology, together with W.H. Lang, who was appointed in 1909 to a new Chair in Cryptogamic Botany. He too was an expert on plant fossils, which remained a Manchester specialism. The most famous of the University's fossil-botanists was Marie Stopes, appointed in 1904 and the first woman lecturer in the Faculty of Science; she became better known for her later work as an advocate of birth control.

In the thirty years from 1873, medicine and the life sciences became important parts of the university. That botany and zoology were overshadowed by chemistry was only to be expected – chemistry was the useful science *par excellence*, though a new kind of experimental physics was developing, and the life sciences were becoming important to the economy and especially the Empire. That clinical medicine overshadowed the pre-clinical sciences was again no surprise. Manchester was a scientific medical school – like University College, London, Edinburgh and Cambridge – but it also shared the practical approach of the London hospitals' schools. That balance was to remain a matter of contention until the Second World War.

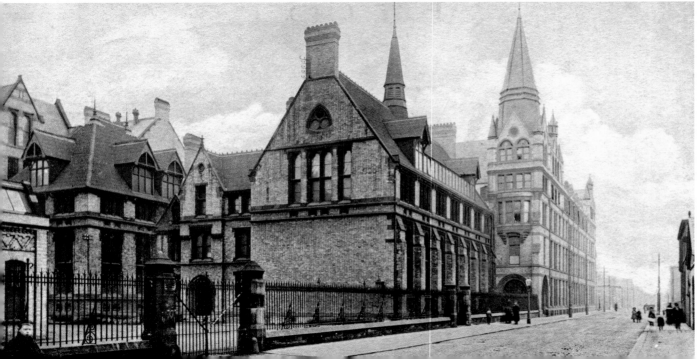

View down Coupland Street, c.1900, showing the Medical School of 1874, with extensions built in 1882–3 and (further down the street, with a corner tower) in 1891–4.

Mechanics' Institution to School of Technology, 1824–1903

HAROLD HANKINS AND TIM YATES

The third partner in the Victoria University of Manchester was the Technical School, which was to be linked to the University from 1905 onwards, although it was owned by the city. The Tech was the ancestor of UMIST and itself grew out of an older establishment, the Mechanics' Institution of 1824 , which was overhauled and renamed in the early 1880s. Harold Hankins, Principal and later Vice-Chancellor of UMIST from 1984 to 1995, and Tim Yates, formerly Director of Communications at UMIST, summarise the history of the Mechanics' Institution and describe its transformation into an English equivalent of a European city technical high school.

The Bridgewater Arms.

UMIST was in its separate existence the direct descendant of the Manchester Mechanics' Institution founded in 1824. In England, few if any colleges other than those of Oxford and Cambridge and Birkbeck College, London (itself descended from a Mechanics' Institute), can claim a longer continuous history. Its development, initially supported by private initiative and finance, and later by the City Council and government funding agencies, has been a continuous one for 180 years. This development, almost always difficult, has been profoundly affected by the prevailing trends in technical education and by the requirements of industry and commerce.

Manchester was the world's first industrial city, deeply affected by changes released by the Industrial Revolution. In 1774 it was a small town of under 25,000 inhabitants; fifty years later, in 1824, due to unprecedented industrial expansion, it exceeded 100,000. There were many who admired Manchester's economic and social growth, but there were many concerned about the utter poverty of its inhabitants. Nevertheless, it had taken the lead in many matters, including education. On 27 April 1824 a public meeting was held in the Bridgewater Arms, a hostelry in Mosley Street, to set up a Mechanics' Institution. It was a period when self-teaching was encouraged, for compulsory elementary education was nearly half a century in the future. The meeting was convened by the cotton manufacturer George William Wood and chaired by Benjamin Heywood, a successful banker and philanthropist. A good-sized audience had assembled, including Peter Ewart, the engineer and millwright; William Henry, son of Thomas Henry, the chemical industry pioneer; and William Fairbairn, the versatile engineer. They were well aware of the economic benefits that such an institution could bring to local business and industry, as well as satisfying the wider educational objectives of the aspiring middle classes. The meeting agreed the Institution's objective:

The Municipal School of Technology at the time of its opening in 1902.

To enable mechanics and artisans, of whatsoever trade they be, to become acquainted with such branches of science as are of practical application in the exercise of that trade.

The strength of local support was such that eleven major shareholders came forward to lend a total of £7,000, which was used to purchase land on Cooper Street and erect a building – of modest appearance, it was the first building for a Mechanics' Institution in England. Inside it had impressive facilities, including classrooms, a library and a reading room. Later a chemical laboratory, a system of gas lighting and ventilation were added. It also had a lecture theatre capable of seating 1,000 people, heated by hot water radiators. The new building was opened by Sir Benjamin Heywood on 14 May 1827. Lectures were arranged in natural philosophy, scientific and technical subjects, as well as history, geography and mechanical and architectural drawing. The library and reading room provided members with borrowing and reading rights. Books and lectures on "political science and controversial theology" were prohibited. The library held books of popular fiction, but it stocked mostly academic books. Subscribers to the Institution paid a life fee of ten guineas or a yearly fee of one guinea.

Elementary classes in the three Rs were offered, but those in attendance did not persevere. Courses in drawing were well attended, and clerks showed great interest in those on bookkeeping and Pitman's phonography. Courses in chemistry and the sciences were poorly attended because they were too advanced, but classes in the performing arts such as dancing and gymnastics attracted large numbers. Most subscribers were clerks and shopkeepers from the middle classes, rather than mechanics or artisans. This state of affairs moved the directors to comment in their annual report for 1828:

It is a subject of surprise and lamentation that persons belonging to the class for which the Institution was designed have not given it the attention which their own interests should have dictated. The mechanics and artisans form but a comparatively small part of the subscribers. Yet they would have found in the education that is offered a means of bettering themselves.

Benjamin Heywood.

William Henry.

Left: William Fairbairn.

Bottom: The Manchester Mechanics' Institution in Cooper Street.

No amount of exhortation from the directors, however, could overcome the long, exhausting hours of labour of the mechanics and artisan class; their poor pay, which left them unable to afford the fees, and the scant means they had of acquiring an elementary education.

The directors, largely drawn from industry, arranged for all loans to be paid off from the profits of exhibitions held in the building between 1838 and 1845. They also arranged activities of a social nature, placing themselves in direct opposition to those subscribers who felt that the objectives of the institution were being compromised. The opposition argued successfully for representation on the directorate and sought to set up a new mechanics' institution, steered towards its original objectives. But this was short-lived, and from then on the Institution offered more social programmes. The library flourished and by 1850 held a stock of 12,000 books, while the reading room took eighty different periodicals. Evening readings, oratorios and Saturday evening musical concerts were organised and well attended; exhibitions attracted very large numbers of paying visitors, and an annual Christmas party organised in the Free Trade Hall attracted over a thousand fee-paying guests.

There were new educational initiatives as well. A boys' day school was started in 1834 to run classes in the three Rs for the sons and brothers of subscribers. In 1835 a girls' day school was set up, offering the three Rs and also classes in sewing and knitting; it continued until 1883, proving so popular that some girls had to be turned away. By 1850, with a programme of social activities in place, membership had grown to 6,282. It was clear, however, despite the considerable efforts of Benjamin Heywood and William Fairbairn, that the Institution had not succeeded in its initial objective of encouraging scientific study for mechanics and artisans. Even lectures in popular science for the general public, which had initially attracted audiences of 1,400, had lost their appeal.

So satisfactorily had the Institution progressed, though hardly along the lines for which it was founded, that the directors decided in 1853 to launch a subscription list for new and more spacious premises. By 1855 a site had been identified at the corner of Major Street and David Street (now Princess Street), and a sum of £20,000 had been subscribed to buy the land and erect a new building designed by John Gregan. The cornerstone was laid on 21 June 1855 by Oliver Heywood, son of Benjamin. This fine building (now home to the Labour History Archive) contained a domed lecture hall, classrooms, and a library and reading room. It was opened in 1857, and its inaugural exhibition of international arts and industry attracted 270,000 visitors. Their entrance fees, together with other liberal donations, freed the building from debt.

In 1858 the Institution showed its willingness to adapt to local educational needs, with its evening classes increasingly shaped by the examination requirements of the Union of Lancashire and Cheshire Institutes and the Society of Arts. In 1859 the Department of Science and Art, recently established by the Government, offered grants to aid science instruction. The Institution took advantage of this from

Oliver Heywood.   *Sir Joseph Whitworth.*

the start, although it has to be said that the response from potential new members was poor. Even the offer of open scholarships from Sir Joseph Whitworth, the successful Manchester engineer, evoked only one successful response. In the meantime, the domed lecture hall was used for popular shows, social gatherings, musical recitals and public lectures, but the need for more commercial classrooms led to a reorganisation of the interior and the loss of the domed space. From 1862 the additional purpose of the Institution was stated to be "to promote social and friendly intercourse". Clubs for gymnastics, chess and billiards, as well as a coffee room and a flourishing library, were available to subscribers. A commercial day school was started, at first with 150 boys, later with as many as 250, taught during both day and evening. Science instruction increased, with students ranging in age from eleven to forty-five, and evening courses in construction and mechanical drawing became very popular.

In 1870 Parliament passed the Elementary Education Act, requiring local authorities to make provision for the elementary education of all social classes. The day departments in the Institution, accounting for over two-thirds of its income, came under threat as private schools supported by public subscriptions and endowments, such as the Manchester High Street School for Girls, as well as schools maintained by the Schools Board out of public local rates, provided stiff competition. Due to these changed circumstances, the number of members began to fall and so did morale. By 1879 the position was becoming desperate, and the Institution was £1,000 in debt. In the same year the directors were required to appoint a new Secretary, as the serving incumbent had left due to "financial irregularities".

In 1879 John Henry Reynolds was appointed Secretary at the age of thirty-seven. He had as profound an effect on technical education in Manchester as Vivian Bowden was to have some

seventy-three years later. Reynolds was the son of a Salford shoemaker, whose trade he followed. Self-taught and without formal education, he devoted all his spare time to improving himself and others. This "intellectual artisan" was ploughing considerable energy into the Lower Mosley Street School, a Unitarian foundation moving into the field of technical education and a challenge to the Institution. The directors knew of his considerable skill as a teacher and administrator.

Reynolds' predecessors had left grave problems. One forged his testimonials; another had poor working relations with his staff; and two had embezzled funds. Reynolds was required to provide a financial surety equal to twice his salary. Not surprisingly, he found the Institution at a low ebb, heavily indebted and with a declining membership. He had a vision of "providing courses relevant to the region's industries and to convert the Institution to a Technical School". Inspired by the establishment of the City and Guilds Institute in London, he cultivated support from local business and industry and the Chamber of Commerce. He received support from Thomas Ashton, a wealthy cotton mill owner; Professor Henry Roscoe, a chemist from Owens College; Sir William Mather, of Mather & Platt; Hans Renold, a chain-maker; and, prominently, Ivan Levinstein, a chemical manufacturer. The turning point came at the Pendleton home of Oliver Heywood where Reynolds persuaded him, and other worthies present, to accept the change.

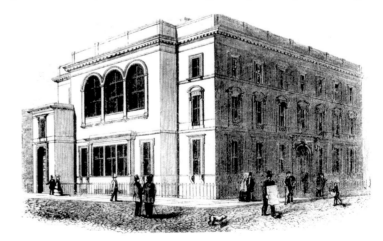

Top: J.H. Reynolds.

Above: J.E. Gregan's Mechanics' Institution (1855–7), now no. 103 Princess Street.

Opposite: The Sculpture Hall in the Municipal School of Technology.

Reception by the Right Honourable the Lord Mayor, Alderman James Hoy, LL.D. (Chairman), the members of the Technical Instruction Committee and the Principal, Mr. J. H. Reynolds, from 7-30 to 8-30.

The Principal, J.H. Reynolds, personally dealt with invitations to the opening ceremonies of the Municipal School of Technology. The edifying Sculpture Hall was, in his view, designed to help students make their spiritual transition from work to study.

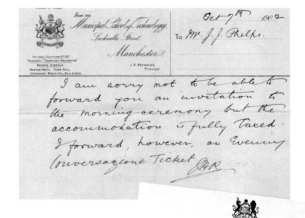

On 27 September 1883 the conversion took place: the Manchester Mechanics' Institution became the Manchester Technical School and the Manchester Mechanics' Institution. A large sum was subscribed by leading firms and individuals, and the governing body passed into representative and influential hands. Reynolds moved to provide the courses that local industries and businesses required. In 1883 day courses were arranged for mechanical engineering, chemistry, bleaching, dyeing and printing. In 1888 he added day courses in spinning and weaving, and in 1891 day courses in electrical and sanitary engineering. By 1891 he had increased the student population from 1,200 to 3,800.

The problem of financing the expansion nevertheless persisted. One way was provided by the legatees of the estate of Sir Joseph Whitworth, who had died in 1887 leaving a vast fortune. They proposed to set up a Whitworth Institute of Art and Industry comprising the Manchester Technical School, the School of Art and a new industrial art museum. It was further proposed to use the land of the former Whitworth Works, bounded by Sackville Street, Whitworth Street and Granby Row, to erect a new building. The directors of the Technical School, seized with the prospect of a new building and by the financial benefits of an amalgamation, entered into purposeful negotiations with the legatees. The legal agreements were obtained in 1891 and the Technical School became part of the proposed Whitworth Institute of Art and Industry.

However, in 1889 Parliament passed the Technical Instruction Act and in 1890 the Local Taxation (Customs and Excise) Act. The former enabled Manchester City Council to establish a Technical Instruction Committee and, by raising a twopenny rate, to fund local technical education; the latter provided additional finance by raising a local tax on alcohol, the so-called "whisky tax". Events then moved rapidly. The legatees, mindful of the increased spending power of the City Council, agreed to abandon their proposal for an Institute of Art and Industry, and to give back the Manchester Technical School. They also generously provided a grant and ownership of the land. The City Council, through the Technical Instruction Committee, agreed to assume responsibility for running both the Technical School and the School of Art and to erect new buildings for them. Further finance

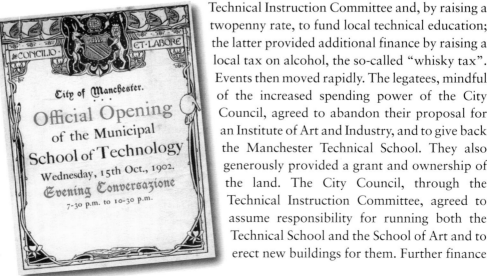

Above: Laying the foundation stone.

Left: The Municipal School of
Technology, as seen shortly
after building completion.

became available by a windfall from the profits of the 1887 Royal Jubilee Exhibition held in Trafford Park. The Technical School's financial problems mercifully appeared to be over. In 1892 the Manchester Technical School was renamed the Manchester Municipal Technical School, with Reynolds still at the helm.

In view of the responsibility for erecting a new building, a deputation from the Council of the School, including Reynolds, visited technical institutes in England, Germany, France and Switzerland, travelling 2,500 miles in two weeks. The plan adopted was based on the Building Trades School in Stuttgart. Further deputations visited the Continent and Reynolds visited institutions in Canada and the USA to observe the means and methods of technical education. Written reports from these visits helped to determine the type of building, its equipment and the structure of taught courses. Architects were invited to submit designs and, with advice from Alfred Waterhouse, the Council of the School selected Spalding & Cross of London as architects, and Neill & Sons of

Manchester as contractors. The first sod was turned by Alderman James Hoy on 26 July 1895, using a silver-plated spade that the University still has. The new building, the finest example of Edwardian brickwork and terracotta in the region, was opened by the Prime Minister, A.J. Balfour, on 15 October 1902. He declared:

> This building is perhaps the greatest of this kind of municipal enterprise in the country … nobody can go over this building, observe its equipment … without feeling that the Corporation of this great city have set an example worthy of the place they hold in Lancashire – and in Great Britain.

What had been achieved, above all, was a lasting testament to the vision and enterprise of John Henry Reynolds, now appointed as Director of Higher Education for the City as well as Principal of the Manchester Municipal School of Technology. In 1902, Owens College awarded him an MSc *honoris causa*.

The Victoria University of Manchester, 1903–39

ALEX B. ROBERTSON AND COLIN LEES

Returning to the former Owens College, Alex B. Robertson and Colin Lees resume their narrative at the point at which Owens ceased to be merely one of the partners in a federal university and became an independent body – a civic university endowed with its own charter and empowered to confer its own degrees. The authors give an overview of the University and its principal academic developments at a time when it was relatively small, impoverished and overcrowded but at the same time intellectually adventurous and academically distinguished.

Between 1903 and 1914, the newly independent University was preoccupied with internal organisation. The former principal, Alfred Hopkinson, was Vice-Chancellor until 1913, creating continuity with the past. The most significant policy was to create new faculties. In 1903, theology gained this status, not without some controversy because of Owens' fear of discrimination; when the century opened, it remained uncertain whether such academic study could take place in a neutral context. A Faculty of Commerce was formed in the same year, bearing witness to many years of distinguished economic and commercially related work. In 1914 the study of education was made a faculty.

Earlier, in 1905, a Faculty of Technology came into being and deserves particular notice. The City and the University were being drawn together by technology. Manchester had high ambitions for its School of Technology and was producing work of degree standard within its large, non-advanced, student body. It had to gain degree status to progress. The Victoria University had no dedicated technology work and could not afford to provide appropriate plant or specialist staff. Since the 1890s, moves towards an accommodation had been made, albeit warily, and the City

supported Owens College in its independence policy with the hope of a more permanent institutional relationship. This arrangement was formalised in 1905, when the teachers of advanced courses in Sackville Street became a faculty in the University, thus giving rise to a long and not always easy relationship which was eventually reshaped when Owens and Tech were unified in 2004. None of the parties involved thought it ideal: the Board of Education disliked it on funding grounds; the University was uncertain of the wisdom of taking responsibility for staff and placing some of them on Senate when they were employed by another body, and the Education Committee increasingly felt that the Principal of the School, who was also Dean of the new Faculty, was sucked into University work at the expense of other responsibilities. If untidy administratively, however, it worked in practice and filled the last great gap in University provision, justifying Samuel Alexander's judgement that it was a major contribution to the ideal of a university for the modern world.

The First World War seriously disrupted the running of the University, and some 370 staff and past and present students were killed. Henry Miers, the first scientist and non-member of staff to be appointed Vice-Chancellor, had a traumatic time from 1915. The end of the war caused its own problems: returning students, often war-hardened veterans, had to be assimilated while income remained static for some years. Despite this, no damage was sustained intellectually, and some unforeseen advances were made due to the war. The new Technology Faculty and Faculty of Science gained considerable reputations from war work, and the Department of Public Health and Bacteriology was a major force in attempts to counter the diseases and infections associated with war. The shocking psychological effects of the conflict led some staff – Stopford, Pear and Elliott-Smith, for example – to develop

An artist's view of Owens College/Victoria University of Manchester buildings seen from Oxford Road at night during during the First World War.

neurological and psychological research. Many more women gained access to courses, including medicine, as well as engaging in war work which many found liberating.

Rutherford was on the staff in 1918, succeeded by Bragg in 1919 – both were Nobel laureates. Among their colleagues were such major scholars as Muir, Unwin and Tout in history; Alexander, Chapman and Findlay in philosophy, economics and education; Lamb in mathematics; Petavel in engineering; Peake in theology and Herford in English. A younger generation was appearing: in 1919 John Stopford gained the Chair of Anatomy and T.H. Pear was promoted to the first Chair of Psychology. Geoffrey Jefferson, the future professor of neurological surgery, was appointed demonstrator in 1926, and high-powered postgraduate groups were built up by the scientists Lapworth and Bragg, and by T.F. Tout in Arts. The years from 1903 saw a steady increase in staff numbers from 73 to 113 after the addition of Technology in 1905; to 152 on the outbreak of war; 165 in 1918; and 219 by the mid-1920s. Of these increases, the greatest expansions were in the lecturer and, especially, the assistant lecturer group, resulting in intense interest in professional issues. A group of senior professors, of whom Tout was the most outspoken, supported claims for increased pay, study leave and promotion opportunities. Manchester played a significant part in the formation of the Association of University Teachers in 1919.

The existence of such talent encouraged the new University to be ambitious after the First World War, despite grave economic problems. Helped by increasingly well-organised fund raising – an appeal in 1919 raised £250,000 – as well as rising government grants, it managed to develop new areas of work. In hindsight, what had been achieved by 1930 under Miers and by his successor from 1936, Walter Moberly, was impressive. Within a year or two of the war ending, chairs in Russian and Italian were created. Pear's Chair of Psychology in 1919 marked the independence of the subject from philosophy. A Chair of Geography for H.J. Fleure in 1930 was important – the subject was still unfamiliar in higher education, and Fleure represented a type of professor increasingly looking outward to encourage his subject locally and nationally in schools and among adults through extra-mural work, and involving students in new types of learning such as field studies. Some lapsed chairs were restored: Comparative Religion in 1923 and Ancient History in 1929. Departments with single chairs were strengthened with a second – for example, French Language in 1919, Political Economy in 1921 and Pure Mathematics in 1923. Already distinguished departments – for example, History – carried their reputations forward in the 1930s by appointing able young staff, A.J.P. Taylor in 1930, C.R. Cheney in 1933 and T.S. Willan in 1935. The two new faculties gained professorships in

The Faculty of Arts Building (1911–19) by Percy Scott Worthington. The University motto, Arduus ad Solem, *seen here as it appears on the classical portico of the Arts Faculty, is taken from Virgil's* Georgics, III, *line 439, about the serpent who "towers towards the sun/Flickering out of his mouth that three-forked tongue" [L.P. Wilkinson's translation of "arduus ad solem et linguis micat ore trisulcis"].*

THE VNIVERSITY OF MANCHESTER
DEVELOPMENT PLAN · OCTOBER 1936

Textile Technology and Commerce and Administration. Most important of the new degrees was the BSc (Tech), achieved after considerable debate and at the insistence of the city against academic conservatives who disliked the subject's association with science. The doctorate, introduced in 1918 to encourage research, was not easy to promote when postgraduate support was so uncommon, but it flourished around eminent professors, particularly in chemistry, physics and history.

These academic developments were paralleled by cautious but real attempts to change the focus of the University and improve internal administration, although the difficulty of doing this in a small, traditional, academic institution should not be minimised. Miers urged that it must become more aware of its local and national responsibilities, a transition eased by the involvement of senior staff in war work and by the introduction of the University Grants Committee (UGC) which indicated lines of development. Tentative relationships were developed with the cotton industry and with government efforts to develop research on agriculture. The School Certificate and a new administrative framework for teacher training colleges also drew the University into national policies. The small but energetic University Press was induced to commission books for sixth forms, and in the inter-war years more systematic attempts were made to recruit students through open days and school lectures. The Manchester Museum greatly increased its educational work with local schools.

A major challenge was how to cope with a sharp increase in students. Most could be considered regional, if no longer local, and there was a small group of overseas students, particularly from the Indian subcontinent. The University had never had money to build up scholarships but, even at a time when local authority student grants were limited, Higher School Certificate students from the multiplying and highly academic sixth forms wanted access, particularly to prestigious honours courses. In 1918 there were 1,031 students, of whom 46 per cent were women. Within a year, on demobilisation, this had risen to 1,649; in 1920 it was 2,899, of whom 22 per cent were women. By 1930 the figures were 2,719, of whom 25 per cent were women, a total increase in a decade of 61 per cent. Growth of this magnitude on a small campus created serious overcrowding. There were large lecture groups and infrequent seminars due to lack of space, a situation that encouraged increasing student complaints during the period. The University made representations to the UGC and drew on its reserves, and some progress was made. Homes for smaller departments were found by taking over houses in the streets around the University as well as adapting older buildings. For example, the Medical School had large-scale internal reconstruction to accommodate such important developments as X-rays, cancer research and enlargement of facilities for anatomy, physiology and pathology. In addition, increasing use was made of the nearby Royal Infirmary for clinical work. Pre-war plans for an

Thanks to Rag: plaque outside Manchester Royal Infirmary, Oxford Road.

Arts building were permitted to continue and the first stage was opened in 1919, although it was by then already inadequate. Lime Grove was gradually acquired by the University, and in 1937 a new Arts Library was completed, the students' Unions were enlarged, and a small Staff House added, creating an attractive enclave in what was an increasingly run-down part of the city. An addition to the physics laboratories was opened by Rutherford in 1932.

Student life in the 1920s and 1930s was still very formal. The stresses of becoming a student, particularly for those from poorer backgrounds, led to a culture of hard work, while a lack of collegiality, a recognised problem of the civic universities, discouraged all but the most active from remaining on campus. A serious attempt was made to develop halls of residence, where possible on the model of traditional university colleges with libraries, tutorial facilities and academic staff on hand to support students. By 1939 there were seven halls intended exclusively for university students, and a few places were provided in three religious institutions with long-established links to the University. Monitoring of attendance, teaching styles, and lack of contact with academic staff at undergraduate level were all matters of discussion in Union debates and student societies, and were of concern to Vice-Chancellor Moberly.

The annual Rag was a significant event, collecting much money for local charities, but was frequently marked by high spirits and occasionally by vulgarity, which caused the authorities much anxiety. Such exuberance was replicated in degree ceremonies, which were noted for dramatic stunts and irreverence leading, on one occasion, to the police being called. A tradition of shielding female students perpetuated separate Unions, and kept women at a distance from all but the formal University celebrations and dances. Only in the late 1930s did Vice-Chancellor Stopford permit the Union to open a bar for informal social gatherings. Sports began to be taken more seriously as a contribution to student wellbeing. More use was made of the Firs estate for teams, and in 1923 a sports pavilion was opened.

There is little evidence, in these intensely political years, of much student engagement. The political parties were represented by student societies, but recruitment was strictly forbidden. Prominent national figures were invited to Union debates. There is evidence that some students intervened during the General Strike of 1926 by supporting transportation of essentials, and there were protests about the presence of the Officers' Training Corps at University commemoration ceremonies. The University Magazine reveals some interest in British and international Fascism by individual student contributors; a Fascist Society briefly existed. As the European situation became more tense, debates in the Union and surveys of student opinion indicated considerable ambivalence about the possibility of war.

Opportunities for staff and students to observe slum life in a great industrial city and engage in social work had existed through the University Settlement in Ancoats since 1895. Between the wars it entered its "golden age", centred on the Round House and Ancoats Hall. This was vividly chronicled by Mary Stocks, whose husband, the professor of philosophy, was an activist, as well as a supporter of the WEA and University adult and extra-mural education which were growing in significance, due mainly to the pioneering work of Waller, Turner and Bibby.

In 1934 John S.B. Stopford became Vice-Chancellor and held office until 1956, guiding the university through war and the remarkable upsurge in higher education that followed. Stopford was a distinguished anatomist whose whole career from undergraduate in the medical school had been in the University. An outstanding administrator, he was noted for his skill in personal relationships and ability to take hard decisions when appropriate. Most important, he was an optimistic reformer who believed that change and growth did not mean a deterioration in rigorous academic standards. In retrospect, it can be seen that a new course was to be charted, but it was not due to Stopford alone. The University contained a number of radical staff, but remained institutionally very conservative. Stopford was fortunate to have a Chancellor, Lord Crawford, whose wide political, industrial and humanistic interests were actively used in support of the University. He was also fortunate in his Treasurer, Sir Ernest Simon, a Manchester industrialist and generous benefactor to the University, who, more than any other individual, was responsible over the next two decades for creating a culture of improvement. Among the many aspects of University life that came under his scrutiny were

Sir John Stopford,
Vice-Chancellor 1934–56

John Stopford retired to Arnside in 1956, after twenty-two years as Vice-Chancellor. The stress of being responsible for the University during the bombing in the Second World War affected his heart and, after at least two heart operations, he died in 1961. He was a delightful man. He and Lord Woolton had been students together and they played football for the University. In later years they went together every year to watch the Cup Final at Wembley. I saw them once, together, at a reunion and they were enjoying themselves like a couple of schoolboys.

Evelyn Duckworth (née Rushton)
BSc Chemistry, 1928

Fancy dress for the Rag procession, Dalton Hall, Shrove Tuesday, 1909.

student and staff welfare; teaching styles; raising money in the American way from alumni; enhancing the environment of the University; linking University and city; urging chairs in new areas and actively head-hunting leading candidates, particularly in science and technology; advocating a campus bookshop and a genuinely competitive Press, and an appointments board.

Stopford's early appointments were notable, maintaining the high standard set by his predecessor (Lewis Namier had joined the History Department in 1931, and the physical chemist Michael Polanyi, who later gained distinction as a philosopher, had been appointed to a chair in 1933). The first woman to hold a chair was Mildred Pope; in French, in 1934. John Jewkes was promoted to a Chair of Social Economics in 1936 and spearheaded Simon's interest in social science research; in 1937 the future Nobel physicist Patrick Blackett joined the staff, and Douglas Hartree transferred from applied mathematics to theoretical physics. Richard Oliver joined education in 1938 and, in the same year, Alexander Todd, famous for his work on Vitamin B1, gained a Chair of Organic Chemistry. Also in that year the very influential electrical engineer, Willis Jackson, joined the staff and did much to cement the University's link with Metropolitan Vickers, part of its growing strategy for cooperation with local industry. In 1939, the last appointments before the war were Harry Platt, internationally famous as a pioneer of orthopaedic surgery, and Geoffrey Jefferson, to a new Chair of Neurological Surgery.

In the 1938–39 Session the University had 2,774 students, its annual income was £295,695 and it had a staff of 288, of whom 43 were professors. Of these, nine were Fellows of the Royal Society and one was a Nobel laureate. Its centenary approached and it was at the height of its prestige and self-confidence. The years since it gained independence had been difficult due to the First World War and years of economic depression, but it had made advances and was accepted as the leading civic university. In this context it remained optimistic even in war and, unlike in 1914–18, detailed plans for the future were made throughout the struggle.

Tech and the Two World Wars, 1903–51

HAROLD HANKINS AND TIM YATES

The Electro-Technics class in 1944, supervised by Dr Raphael Feinberg in the High Vacuum Technique Laboratory.

Attention now switches back to Tech, as the institution on Sackville Street was generally known (it changed its lengthier official name several times). It was at once the partner and the rival of Owens, a name that still clung to the buildings on Oxford Road and their inhabitants. Tech was both within and outside the University – members of its staff who taught degree-giving courses formed the University's Faculty of Technology, but much of the institution answered only to the City of Manchester. Tim Yates and Professor Harold Hankins tell the story of the whole institution and carry it forward to the aftermath of the Second World War.

The newly named Manchester Municipal School of Technology, known as Tech, moved into its new building and work began on providing courses for regional companies. Activities housed in the building ranged from municipal engineering, applied chemistry, physics and mechanical and electrical engineering to baking, brewing and printing; a separate dyehouse was built in 1903 where textiles could be processed and paper manufactured. Francis Godlee, a local cotton manufacturer, financed an observatory located on the roof at the building's northeast corner, which has been used ever since by the Manchester Astronomical Society. In anticipation of further expansion, the city purchased land adjacent to the main building, on a site occupied by St Augustine's Roman Catholic Church and its cemetery. By 1910 the church had been demolished and rebuilt in York Street (it was later transferred to All Saints), and the remains of 6,000 parishioners and thirteen priests were exhumed and reburied in Southern Cemetery.

In 1903 the Manchester Association of Engineers sent forty apprentices, chosen by competitive selection, to study during the

day with their fees and wages paid for, anticipating the national "day release" scheme that became a major activity years later at Tech. Meanwhile, the Victoria University of Manchester, familiarly known as Owens, was constituted by Royal Charter in 1903 with provision for a Faculty of Technology. It was said that Tech needed the degree-awarding powers of Owens, and that Owens needed the industrial reputation of Tech. Serious, and at times difficult, discussions between the city and Owens took place and eventually, in July 1905, it was agreed that the Municipal School of Technology would provide the new Faculty. Under the terms of this concordat, Principal Reynolds became the first Dean of the Faculty, as well as being responsible to the city for Tech's remaining activities. Three professors from Tech took up places on a Senate of twenty-seven members at Owens; and the first cohort of 122 Tech students read for the degrees of Bachelor or Master of Technical Science in the Departments of Mechanical, Electrical, Municipal and Sanitary Engineering, Applied Chemistry and Textiles. Tech retained its own governing body with representation from Owens. It was not until 1923 that Tech students could study for a PhD (introduced at Owens in 1918), and only then if the oral examination took place at Owens. The concordat was the first and only such agreement in the country, and Tech became the first university college whose land and buildings were owned by a city corporation. These were valued in 1905 at £380,218.14s.11d (the City later transferred the land, buildings and mortgages to umist, and on its creation Vivian Bowden declared it was the only university in the land founded on a debt).

In 1912 John Henry Reynolds retired after thirty-three years at the helm. His service had been truly monumental, for in one generation he had taken Tech from a Mechanics' Institution to an institution of university standing. He was succeeded by Maxwell Garnett, a Cambridge mathematician, who had been called to the Bar in 1908 and had worked as an examiner for the Government's Board of Education. He must have found the aesthetic circles of Manchester, if not its culture, a little rough and ready, and he was in every way different from his predecessor, a self-taught former shoemaker from Salford.

Difficult questions as to the future direction of Tech were settled by a rapid expansion in student numbers and by the demands of the First World War, which was to claim the lives of 196 students, including sixty-three who had been members of the Manchester University Officers' Training Corps. Their names are on a memorial, close to the Sculpture Hall, unveiled by Reynolds at a ceremony held on 11 November 1921 when he was nearly eighty years of age. One survivor, gunner 2nd Lieutenant J.D. Cockcroft from Todmorden, returned to complete his BScTech and MScTech degrees with Professor Miles Walker, who then arranged for him to

Below: Sir John Cockcroft, Nobel laureate, who served in the Royal Field Artillery on the Western Front.

Bottom and next page: Woodcuts depicting the Tech's activities (from the programme of the official opening of the Sackville Street building, 15 October 1902).

Far left: The clock that dominates the lobby of the Sackville Street Building.

CHEMISTRY DEPARTMENT.

MECHANICAL ENGINEERING.

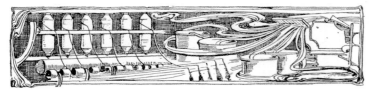

TEXTILE DEPARTMENT.

FLOOR A.

Room SPINNING ROOM. Machinery for the following processes will be in operation in the
11 course of the evening. Cotton mixing, opening, scutching, carding, combing, drawing,
preparing and roving, mule and ring spinning, doubling, preparing and gassing, preparing and spinning waste yarns.

Room WEAVING PREPARATION ROOM. Drum, spindle and pirn winding. Mill and
9 sectional warping, Yorkshire dressing, drawing-in, card-cutting, card lacing.

Room WEAVING ROOM. A variety of cotton and mixed fabrics in grey and coloured yarns
10 in process of manufacture upon plain, twill, satin, dobby, check, and jacquard power
looms will be shown.

work with Rutherford at Cambridge. Here, with Ernest Walton, he developed a very high voltage source to accelerate protons, to disintegrate artificially an atom (of lithium) in 1932. They were the first to do so, and were awarded the Nobel Prize for Physics in 1951, Cockcroft becoming Tech's only Nobel Laureate. Another war survivor was a naval instructor, Frank Bowman, who became Head of Mathematics and author of *Elementary Calculus*, a classic textbook that exercised the minds of generations of Tech students.

During the war, Tech's penchant for technological investigation was used by various ministries and the armed forces, although it had difficulty in meeting the demands placed on it. Electrical and mechanical engineers developed a deep-sea hydrophone to counter the submarine threat to shipping. A high-frequency alternator to power aircraft radios was designed and manufactured, and aircraft fabric materials were routinely tested in the Textiles Department. A new type of gas furnace was designed for the heat treatment of tool steels, thereby increasing the rate at which shells could be machined, while metallurgists produced cast iron of high tensile strength, enabling the range of

gas shells to be doubled. Instruments were developed to measure the permeability of airship fabrics and the envelopes of both the R33 and R34 airships were treated with 'dope' to strengthen the fabric, produced at Tech. The Applied Chemistry Department carried out investigations aimed at improving war materials and the provision of substitutes for materials in short supply; research

PRINTING TRADES.

DEPARTMENT OF PHYSICS & ELECTRICAL ENGINEERING.

MUNICIPAL & SANITARY ENGINEERING.

The main UMIST building in Sackville Street.

New life for a refugee

Dr Abraham Burawoy was a Senior Lecturer in Colouring Matters in the Department of Chemistry in the 1940s and 1950s. Born in the Ukraine, he spent his formative years in Leipzig, attending the university there and being strongly influenced by Professor A. Hantzsch. His career was cut short in Germany, and he arrived as a Jewish refugee in London in 1933. His first position, sponsored by Professor Ian Heilbron of Imperial College, was at Guy's Hospital.

He researched the synthesis of Vitamin A and related substances, increasingly concentrating on molecular structure. In Manchester his comprehensive knowledge of molecular spectroscopy was of great value; his work was eventually published and he received recognition from many leading academics at home and abroad.

Dr Burawoy was held in high esteem by his students, both undergraduate and research, and by staff colleagues in the Chemistry Department. He died in Manchester in April 1959, aged fifty-five.

Dr J.P. Critchely
BSc 1954, PhD 1958

Dr Burawoy (front row, second left) with staff colleagues and research students in c1955.

into a heptachlor derivative of rubber, and work on dyestuffs and pharmaceutical goods. Crucial information was supplied by the Bakery Department to the Food Controller's Office on how to stretch the nation's bread supply by incorporating more brewer's malt into wartime loaves than had been thought possible.

This range of research and development work was eloquent testimony to the commitment of Tech staff working for the national need, as well as servicing courses for part-time students, servicemen and degree students. As a consequence, in 1918, the Manchester Municipal School of Technology was appropriately renamed the Manchester Municipal College of Technology.

The supremacy of German science and technology during the war became only too evident to the government, and so too did the superior technical education that Germany had organised for its workforce. There was no consensus in Britain after the war on how technical education might be developed and improved. Indeed, the economic climate made it very difficult to produce one. The city's Director of Education, Spurley Hey, a no-nonsense Yorkshireman, was committed to the role that vocational education should play in the economic and social life of Manchester and its citizens. He was at odds with Maxwell Garnett, who was seeking to increase the number of university students at Tech. In the event Garnett resigned, and in

Examples of the work of students in the Photography and Printing Department, 1912–13: advertisement for Swindell and Pinder by H.L. Barnwell (first year); for Petaphone by S.T. Stevens (second year).

1920 became Secretary General of the League of Nations Union. He was succeeded by Professor Mouat Jones, a distinguished chemist and mineralogist, who served as Principal until 1938 when he was appointed Vice-Chancellor of Leeds University.

Tech did not stand still. In an appeal for funds it raised £120,000 from industry, and the governing body inaugurated ten research scholarships of £100 each. As early as 1917 lectures had been given in scientific management; in the following year eleven local companies subscribed funds to support a lecturer in Industrial Administration. A department was established in 1926, which by the 1980s had developed to become the Manchester School of Management, arguably the largest and best of its type in Britain and at one stage responsible for teaching 20 per cent of all students at Tech. Many alumni will remember receiving lectures in Industrial Administration in temporary buildings erected alongside the railway viaduct on Granby Row. Under Principal Jones, student numbers increased and by 1927 there were 6,000 evening students, mostly studying for the Ordinary and Higher National Certificates introduced nationwide in 1921. These awards led to the phasing out of the College's certificates, although the highly prized Associateship of the College, AMCT, continued, and was regarded by many industrialists as the best educational award attainable in the city. New courses were developed to meet local and national needs in Librarianship, Health Visiting, Photography, Applied Optics and Motor Mechanics.

This expansion placed a heavy burden on the available accommodation, and Velvet House in Sackville Street was rented as a temporary measure (continuing until 1984). There were three solutions to the problem: build an extension, foster links with other local institutions to avoid duplication of courses, and devolve the so-called "craftsmanship courses" to them. Day-time student numbers increased as more companies supported the day release scheme, reaching more than 1,000 by 1934, including 250 degree students. Industrial Administration and Building were added to departments delivering degree courses, and research flourished more than in other municipal colleges of technology, no doubt because Owens took account of research competence and activity in promoting faculty staff, and because local industries made demands for research.

Nevertheless, in 1936 the city decided to build an extension to the main building on adjacent land it had cleared in 1910, and work began in 1938 with the erection of steelwork. There was no doubt that the economic slow-down before the Second World War, and then the war itself, gave the project a stop-start life, and it suffered from continual postponements. The steelwork remained in place until the 1950s, when work recommenced and the extension was finally opened by HRH The Duke of Edinburgh in 1957. Students of the period will remember the constant hammering of rivet guns as building work continued non-stop during lectures. The cost, estimated at £500,000 in 1936, reached £2m on the building's completion in 1957.

In 1938 Dr (later Sir) James Myers was appointed Principal. He had been the Vice-Chancellor's Assistant, and Tutor to the Faculty of Science at Owens. He was barely in post when the Second World War was declared. Tech once more rose to the national need for war-time training, research and development. Before courses could begin, adequate air-raid shelters had to be built, corridors sandbagged and the entrance to the building barricaded. Lectures in the evening were cancelled because of blackout and safety regulations, and were held instead over the weekend in daylight. The main building was an easy target for the Luftwaffe. In the summer of 1940 it received a direct hit from a bomb that went through the southwest corner of the chemistry laboratory and exploded in the Senior Common Room. But such was the sturdiness of Edwardian construction that, apart from windows being blown out, damage was minimal and quickly repaired.

The government made better use of scientific and technological manpower than in the first war. Although conscription was introduced in the first week of the war, 90 per cent of Tech's part-time students were employed in reserved occupations. The fate of faculty students was determined by the Joint Recruitment Board (JRB), set up by Owens under government decree. The JRB had powers to decide whether students should be allowed to finish their degree courses, be conscripted, or be placed in government research establishments or wartime industry. Tech's full-time students were permitted to complete their degree courses, but such was the need for scientists and technologists that by 1942 'war degree' courses

Rationing, queues and National Service

My year group took higher school certificates in 1946, the year universities were filled with ex-servicemen whose studies had been postponed or interrupted by the war. This made it more difficult for school leavers to get a place – for example, I had been asked by Owens to re-apply after completion of National Service. I thought study after a two-year gap might be difficult, so accepted a place in the Faculty of Technology instead. Friends who did not go to college were called up for eighteen months' National Service, but students were given deferment.

Tech was busy and crowded but seemed to cope very well with the vastly larger numbers of students compared with pre-war days. The major exception was provision of lunch: queues were long and slow-moving, so we often visited a restaurant down the road. We were all accommodated in what is now known as the main building, plus some offices opposite on Sackville Street. Work on the first extension had not yet started.

Student grants had not been introduced, so most students, both ex-service and ex-school, lived at home and commuted to the city centre. Fees were moderate, and there were various grants towards them and the cost of books, in addition to the highly competitive county major awards. Halls of residence were mainly occupied by students from other towns, rural areas and overseas.

Queen Elizabeth, George VI's consort, visits the University as part of the Owens College centenary celebrations in May 1951.

The swimming pool at the McDougall Centre, 1944.

The faculty concentrated largely on engineering, so ladies were very thin on the ground – even the Chemistry Department had only four out of about thirty in the 1946 intake. To some extent, this was balanced by the Saturday evening 'hops' with nursing staff and students, and students from Domski (the College of Domestic Economy).

Several of my schoolfriends were at Owens and we would often meet at their much larger men's union on Oxford Road for lunch (shorter queues!), snooker, billiards or perhaps a swim in the McDougall Centre. Overseas travel was restricted by currency regulations and lack of money, so we spent our vacation time exploring the UK on our bikes, staying at youth hostels.

The Government at that time appeared to be undecided about graduates and National Service. In 1949 they were called up unless accepted for postgraduate research for the Scientific Civil Service, but in 1948 I seem to remember they were not called up. My three years at Tech were followed by two years of National Service.

Alan Leeson
PhD 1956, BSc Tech Applied Chemistry 1949

A Lancaster bomber.

Roy Chadwick of A.V. Roe, congratulating Capt. R.T. Shepherd, the Rolls-Royce test pilot, after his record flight from London to Le Bourget in France.

were introduced for completion within two and a quarter years. Many students were placed in the radar and radio communications industries; others in aircraft, manufacturing and armament. In 1935 Arnold Wilkins, an electrical engineering alumnus, and Watson Watt had conducted the first trials that ushered in the age of radar by using radio beams to detect the presence of aircraft. Roy Chadwick, a mechanical engineering alumnus, became Chief Designer at A.V. Roe in Manchester and designed the Lancaster bomber. Peter MacKay, a Student Union president who graduated with a first in Municipal Engineering, died in the war. His fellow students established an annual prize in his memory, presented by the Principal, for the student who makes the most significant contribution to student life as well as achieving high academic honours.

Special courses were organised for government departments: service personnel took courses in radio technology, production planning, time and motion studies, and quality control. As befitted Manchester's status as a seaport, courses in navigation leading to a Yacht Master's certificate and one in practical navigation were organised. In total over 8,000 service personnel attended courses, and the college workshops manufactured precision mechanical components. The materials testing laboratory played an important role, carrying out 100,000 tests on ropes, webbing, and concrete. The Textiles Department produced special thread, used as a tie band in "sticky bombs". The catalytic synthesis of phenol, the mechanism of nitration in the production of explosives, and the reflection properties of wet fabrics used in camouflage were all investigated. New materials for barrage balloons and parachute harnesses were also developed.

The loss of life during the Second World War was much less among Tech students than in the first war, due to the intelligent use of their scientific and technological skills. Many joined the University Air Squadron, set up by Owens in 1941 to train replacement pilots and crews lost in the air battles of France, Britain and Germany, and many joined the Officers' Training Corps. Twenty-eight Tech students are commemorated on the War Memorial, side by side with their First World War comrades.

After the war, Tech moved quickly to peace-time operation at a time when the government was calling for expansion in scientific and technical education. The 1945 *Percy Report on Higher Education* emphasised the deficiencies in facilities for such an expansion; the 1946 Barlow Committee on Scientific Manpower urged a doubling of the output of graduates in science and technology. Universities and technical colleges were asked to plan the largest possible intake of such students for 1946–47, while Tech was also expected to concentrate on advanced study and research, and to increase the proportion of degree students. By government decree, 95 per cent of these students were to be ex-servicemen and women. They brought a robustness and vitality to Tech life not normally experienced when school-leavers predominated. Staff, however, were well versed in dealing with mature students on the part-time day and evening courses. New courses in textiles, applied physics and electronics were introduced and extra staff recruited to deal with the expansion.

By 1951 Tech had enrolled more than 8,500 part-time students and over 600 degree students, and was poised for more expansion. But it was becoming too big for the City Council to finance. As Professor W.E. (Bill) Morton, sometime Dean of the Faculty, observed, "From beginning to end Manchester did its best for its Faculty and College, and its best was very good." Principal Sir James Myers resigned in September 1951, returning to Owens to take up the newly created post of Director of the School of Education, and Tech began the search for another inspirational leader in the Reynolds mould. Bertram Vivian Bowden's time was about to come.

The University of Manchester During the Second World War

ERIC ROWLEY

Eric Rowley describes the experiences of students, servicemen and conscientious objectors from the University during the Second World War. Dr Rowley is an educationalist and economic historian who retired from the University in 1997. Here he draws on The University of Manchester at War 1939–1946, *a book which he compiled with the collaboration of Colin Lees and contributions from alumni. This work was published by the Development and Alumni Office in 2001 when, as part of the celebration of the 150th anniversary of Owens College, a new war memorial tablet was unveiled in the main quadrangle.*

Following the outbreak of war it seemed, at least for the immediate future, that student numbers at the University would be little affected. H.B. Charlton, the *Manchester Guardian*'s university correspondent, estimated in December 1939 that student numbers for the 1939–40 academic session had fallen by about five per cent compared with the previous session. They were maintained throughout the war at around 2,500, with the exception of the 1940–41 session when they dropped to 2,237 because a number of final-year students had gone into the services.

This did not mean anything like "business as usual". Medically fit male students were required to undertake military training. The Officers' Training Corps was renamed the University of Manchester Senior Training Corps; its purpose was to provide basic training for students to prepare them for military service. This was supplemented by the creation in 1940 of an Air Squadron. The training involved attending parades twice weekly directed towards achieving Certificates "A" and "B", the basic qualifications for military service both for wartime recruits and for those seeking a military career. The "recruit books" of the

Training Corps indicate that long lines of students waited to give their details on enrolment for military training, as if they were queuing to register as undergraduates only with a more deadly intent. A few brave souls have "co" marked alongside their names, indicating a conscientious objection to military service.

The choice of subject to study could, literally, mean life or death. Arts students could, at best, expect to enjoy only limited exemptions and would not normally expect to graduate before entering the forces. Medical students and engineers, however, were able to postpone military service until the completion of their courses. At least one medical student is known to have postponed his studies instead to join the army, much to the chagrin of the Dean of the Medical School. As a result, some courses that started out with a mixed group of male and female students ended with an all-female graduation class. The six-year medical course was reduced in length to permit the group that was scheduled to graduate in the summer of 1945 to receive their degrees six months early, a move more warmly welcomed by the women students than the men: doctors were clearly needed for the advance across Europe into Germany in the closing months of the war.

There were significant losses of staff – so many in all grades that it is remarkable that the institution continued to function. Sixty-two members of the teaching staff were lost from the University, and another ten from the College of Technology. Other lists show over seventy losses of clerical and service staff from the University, and some forty-five from Tech. It is a great tribute to the efforts of those remaining that the University and Tech managed to keep degree programmes going throughout the war, especially since a Government directive in 1942 reduced three-year degree courses to two years and three months. The slow rate

Corporal Francis Ferns gives instruction on the bren gun to fellow cadets in the OTC, 1939.

of demobilisation of staff in 1945 threatened to restrict university expansion for some time after the end of hostilities.

Some members of staff, of German origin, were interned as aliens. The records list Dr Raphael Feinberg, Dr H. Singer, Dr Otto Schutsch and Dr Kurt Mahler. A young refugee, Wolfgang Plessner, had attended Bury Grammar School and obtained a place at the University. He was eventually allowed to continue his studies, and graduated with a first-class degree in 1944 followed by research degrees.

Manchester experienced severe bombing raids on 28 November 1940 and 11 and 12 December 1940, but the most concentrated attack took place on the nights of 22 and 23 December 1940, when Manchester and Salford were blitzed. One student recalls that the raids finished at midnight on 24 December, as if the Germans were acknowledging Christmas. The University escaped relatively lightly, as term had ended on 20 December. Neither the University nor Tech, however, escaped without damage – they were both hit by bombs. Buildings hit included Ashburne Hall and the new centre for physical education and recreation. A landmine exploded some hours later, damaging the wall of Manchester Royal Infirmary on Oxford Road. The damage amounted to £30,000. An unconfirmed report, related by several students, claimed that on one occasion Oxford Road had been machine-gunned by a single German plane flying along its length. Many students recall the difficulties of getting to the University in the aftermath of bombing raids, picking their way through scattered debris and buildings still ablaze. Residents of Dalton Hall recall the red glow in the night sky as the Trafford Park industrial complex blazed under Luftwaffe attack.

The young ladies of Ashburne Hall were "electrified", as one student described it, by the visit of Lyudmila Pavlichenko (1916–74), a Russian sniper credited with the killing of 309 Germans on the Eastern Front. She must have been a formidable speaker at Ashburne Hall and the Students' Union, and led a procession along Oxford Road, demanding the opening of a second front against Germany.

Many of the students were employed as fire watchers, with protection of buildings near the city centre most popular (and most dangerous) as they attracted the best rates of pay. It is a tribute to

their work that the University did not suffer more severely from the air raids. There was humour of a sort in those desperate days. In later recollections, one student remembered a false alarm during the night, which turned out to be a flight of ducks! Another described the centre of Manchester as rather like recent pictures of Kosovo or Chechnya – roofless warehouses had only one or two walls standing and smoke was everywhere. Fire watchers had to be particularly careful in detecting incendiary bombs and putting them out with sand or water – one student even thought of trying to catch them in flight with his lacrosse stick.

When war was declared on Sunday 3 September 1939, it was only twenty years since the end of the previous hostilities. Would those who had declared themselves conscientious objectors and pacifists in earlier years maintain their position in the face of the reality of war, the certainty of having to appear before tribunals and the possibility of prison and ostracism by colleagues, friends and family?

George Arthur Sutherland, born at New Deer, Aberdeenshire on 6 February 1891 and affectionately known to generations of students as "Jock", was Principal of Dalton Hall from 1924 until his retirement in 1958. A major figure in the Society of Friends, locally and nationally, he had served a term of imprisonment as a conscientious objector in the First World War. He gave talks on his convictions and experiences in 1940, when students facing military service had to decide what course of action their faiths and beliefs would oblige them to take.

The treatment of conscientious objectors in the Second World War was less draconian than in the first, but it could still be harsh. Individual objectors from the University reported widely differing

Left: Russian sniper Lyudmila Pavlichenko making a speech during a celebration of the Soviet Union's twenty-fifth anniversary.

Below: The main Debating Hall in the Students' Union, 1944.

responses by tribunals. Their decisions depended on their composition, and the attitudes, bearing and eloquence of the individuals that appeared before them. Some University men reported sympathetic hearings, after which they were required to perform agricultural work or were simply left to continue their studies.

The attitudes of other students towards conscientious objectors varied enormously, from total acceptance to abhorrence, contempt and rejection. Cases of conscientious objectors being "debagged" in Burlington Street are on record, often by engineering students who themselves had the choice of whether to work in industry or volunteer for military service.

Additional educational demands were made on the University during the war. The Department of Education provided a play centre at the University Settlement for children from surrounding areas who had not been evacuated. Sheila McKay, Warden of the Settlement, looked forward to a post-war expansion of educational activities for those whose interests had been stimulated by the relatively limited war time provision.

Under the direction of Ross Waller, the Extra Mural Department of the University widened its work during the war years. Because the university buildings were not blacked out, extension classes were offered in daylight on Saturdays. The department was actively involved in providing educational activities for the armed forces. A programme of lectures was provided for troops stationed at Ardwick and Ringway; by December 1939, these were offered at seventeen of the largest military concentrations in the area. The Vice-Chancellor, Professor John Stopford, and Waller played a major part in their development. By the end of 1940, provision amounted to about forty-five lectures and classes per week. Classes were offered in premises in Bowdon, Mottram Hall near Wilmslow, the Lancashire Independent College and at Whalley Abbey near Clitheroe. The vision of a residential college was realised in 1944 through the opening of Holly Royde College on Palatine Road, the gift of Frank Behrens in memory of his parents. It was officially opened on 24 January 1945 by the Lord Mayor of Manchester.

Wartime memories

The first year of the war (the 'phoney war' period) didn't seem to have a big impact on our university life as far as I was concerned, except that the black-out restricted what could be done in the evenings. The next year was different, as by then air raids had begun in earnest. Again, I don't remember much interruption to the daytime routine, but on quite a few occasions we spent the night, or some part of it, doing our best to sleep in three-tiered bunks in the cellars. I also have memories of fire-watching duty. During night air raid alarms, two students wearing tin hats would patrol together along the dark top corridors of Ashburne Hall, presumably to report the whereabouts of any incendiary bomb that might come down. Luckily, none ever did, and duties were very infrequent as there were a lot of us in Ashburne to share them. Fortunately, from our point of view, Manchester had its worst air raid during the Christmas vac, but it was sad to come back and see one of the oldest and quaintest parts of the city nothing but rubble.

Lilian Smith (née Higham)
TD, 1942, BSc Physics 1941

8 May 1945 – almost Finals time for a student in Ashburne Hall. During the evening many students made their way to the city's heart to celebrate the end of the war in Europe. They wanted to mark the end of a day's National Service in a week. They wanted to mark the end of fire-watching. They wanted to mark the end of learning how to get out of an upstairs window and down an improvised fire escape. They wanted to learn not to look for barrage balloons, or listen for air raid sirens. They wanted to learn how to live in a world nominally at peace. Would lunch tickets, issued by the Halls, still be 10d with a supplement of 1d for 'a healthy life lunch'? Would the imposing Mrs Murray Blair, superintendent of catering, still reign in Caf? Would scrambled dried eggs cooked on a gas ring in Ashburne still taste as good?

Patricia M. Entwistle
1945

I came to Manchester from Halifax in 1946, 'demob' year. Because so many of the fighting forces were to return to civilian life, the University was obliged to take most of its entry from these ex-service people. This meant intake from schools was much reduced, and I was not informed of my admittance until about two weeks before registration. Having quickly resigned from my job as a haberdasher's assistant, I bought a new skirt (no trousers for women then, and I couldn't afford stockings) and travelled over the Pennines on the bus with all my possessions in one large suitcase.

Rationing was still in force and we had powdered reconstituted potato ('pom') for daily lunch in Caf, with ersatz custard on various dubious sweets. Coffee was tuppence a cup. First-year lectures were very overcrowded due to the large post-war intake, and often one had to sit on the steps in theatres or share desks. However, I discovered, to my joy, as a girl science student, that we were outnumbered by men about five to one! I survived my first year, though many were sacked.

Barbara Fawkes (née Henley)
Tcert Education 1950, BSc General Science 1949

I started at Owens in 1945 and stayed until 1950. Of all the seven years, the first was by far the most memorable. It was a time of almost unimaginable transition and turmoil at the University. The war with Japan had ended barely a few weeks earlier, but already members of the armed forces were being enrolled for degree courses; some were already demobilised and wearing 'civvies' while others were still officially on active service and still in uniform. In the first-year chemistry class there were several students in uniform, including at least one from the Polish Army. Some of the lecturers were in the same condition – I remember that Dr Norman Millett, a zoology lecturer, first appeared in his

The Students' Union, 1939.

The Front Quad in the 1940s with the John Owens Building behind – the brick walls on the left-hand-side of the building are probably air-raid shelter facilities.

RAF uniform as he was still waiting for his demob. Another feature of that first year was the number of US servicemen attending lectures while they awaited repatriation; most came from the vast transit camp at Burton Wood between Manchester and Liverpool.

The exam regime was in some turmoil, too. Several of my initial colleagues at Dalton Hall sat their finals in December 1945, finishing the compressed wartime degree courses. One, I remember, having graduated, was immediately drafted into the coal mines as a 'Bevin boy' – a number of young men were compulsorily sent to do their National Service in the mines. Among my other Dalton colleagues in 1945 were several foreign students who had already been there for a year or more – from Iceland, Turkey and Ceylon. Today we think nothing of this – but how (and why?) did foreign students reach Britain during wartime, inevitably over very perilous seas?

Dr Owen Gilbert
MSc 1950, BSc General Science 1948

A prominent feature of university life in 1947 was the large number of ex-servicemen sitting in the lecture theatres. The Medical School was no exception; there must have been about twenty of us returning to study after an interval of several years. After five years in the Navy I found it hard to settle down. It *was* a bit daunting to study alongside youngsters fresh from school, often the brightest of their year, and I imagine it was not easy for them either. In retrospect, staff and fellow students were most generous in accepting this intrusion into their previously peaceful academic lives. Another almost forgotten aspect of those post-war years was the persistence of petrol rationing, food shortages and other

inconveniences. I used to meet up with three or four friends for lunch in the Refectory, and the menu, not very exciting to begin with, was almost always further curtailed by crossed-out items. Needless to say, we survived, and most of us managed to pass the dreaded Finals.

Now retired, I live about as far away from Manchester as it is possible to get, but my address – Rutherford Street, Nelson – is a constant reminder. Ernest Rutherford was born just a few miles away, and round the corner is Nelson College where he started his meteoric rise to fame. The height of that fame and his happiest and most productive years he found, of course, in Manchester.

Brian Prendergast
MD 1961, MBChB 1953

It seems to me quite amazing that there is usually no mention of the tremendous change that occurred at the University after the Labour post-war landslide. The students who came post-1945 would never have stood a chance of attending a university before that. I had the experience of attending for a short time during the war – there were no scholarships, and the majority of students came from middle- or upper-class families who had the money to pay. I remember that the Professor of Zoology, Graham Cannon, said that you couldn't 'do' zoology unless you had a private income, and this went for all the other science degrees. Certainly you could not do medicine unless you were very well-to-do. I was not, and managed to pay the fees by doing fire-watching (which was well paid) and other work.

Dr Lawrence Goldi
MBChB 1953

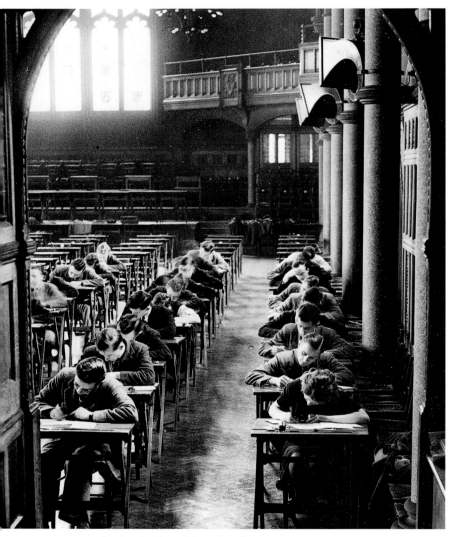

Examinations held in Whitworth Hall, 1939.

and higher school certificate. Recruitment was by nomination by head teachers of suitable pupils of eighteen years of age, or by examination by the Civil Service Commission in the case of those seeking commissions in the Royal Air Force. In some instances, these courses could provide credit towards a future degree course; certainly, many who attended them and survived the war were inspired to go on to do degrees.

Female students made significant contributions to the war effort. In 1941, the Women's University Union had approved a resolution that required them to undertake five hours' war service a week. Male students continued throughout the war to be required to undertake part-time service with the Senior Training Corps, the University Air Squadron or the University Fire Brigade.

As staff levels diminished, so teaching loads increased. This led to a reduction in the options available in certain study areas and to the telescoping of courses. The effects of staff shortages extended into the years immediately following the end of hostilities in Europe and the Far East. Concern was expressed at the likely difficulties in recruiting staff of appropriate experience and qualifications, and in coping with the expected rapid expansion of student numbers after the war.

The effects of the conflict meant that the pre-war situation would never return. Relatively slow demobilisation meant continuing worries about staffing levels, especially in view of the expected increase in student numbers. The student body had changed. Those who had spent years serving all over the world now sat alongside younger students fresh from school. There was some resentment towards those who had not served in the forces, who were now far advanced in their careers compared with those who had been called up and who now, in their mid to late twenties, still had to complete their degrees. Wardens of the halls of residence had to develop new styles of management, since many of their residents had an ex-service background and were often married with children. Many remarked on how strangely different the once-familiar streets around the University now seemed.

In the main quadrangle of the University of Manchester there are two memorials. The First World War Memorial

The University provided intensive six-month training courses in 1940 and 1941 for young men seeking commissions in the Royal Corps of Signals and in the Royal Air Force. The War Office drew up the syllabuses in negotiation with the universities involved, and the teaching was done by university staff supplemented by the technical military services. The level was between school certificate

Sir John Stopford, Vice-Chancellor, chairs a meeting of Senate in November 1944.

commemorates by name over five hundred members of the University who died. For many years, the only commemoration of the later victims was a plaque that simply read "In Memory of those who died in the Second World War, 1939–1945". No individual names were recorded. In 1999, it was decided to research the names of the fallen and list them on a plaque to match the style of the First World War Memorial. Over two hundred names were discovered from all branches of the services, including students from overseas, and of civilians, all members of the University.

The plaque was dedicated on Remembrance Sunday 2001, and also commemorated the 150th anniversary of the University from its foundation as Owens College. Present were a gathering of veterans, relatives of those who died and members of the University currently serving in the Naval Unit, the Officers' Training Corps and the Royal Air Force Squadron.

The University of Manchester, 1951–92

BRIAN PULLAN

By the early 1950s, the veterans who had thronged the post-war University had completed their courses, but Owens was never to return to its modest pre-war numbers. It responded to government demands for the expansion of higher education in the 1960s; had to face growing competition from younger and seemingly less hidebound institutions; and suffered, as did other universities, from restrictions on public funding after 1973. Brian Pullan, Professor of Modern History 1973–98, analyses the consequences of the expansion and contraction of the national system of higher education and the extent to which the University of Manchester was able to maintain its reputation when placed under close public scrutiny.

In the mid-1950s it was almost proverbial that a University would cease to cohere if it had more than 5,000 students – unless it was divided into colleges. Owens, a university founded on faculties and departments and equipped with a few halls of residence, was comfortably within the desirable limit. The institution was intimate enough to be run with a minimum of paperwork by a quartet of oracular administrators who ruled by the force of their personalities and had a strong sense of Manchester's excellence. All had risen from the ranks and matured in the service of the University. Sir John Stopford, a "surgeon's anatomist" (1934–56), and Sir William Mansfield Cooper, a lawyer (1956–70), both Manchester graduates, were the last Vice-Chancellors to be chosen from within. The Registrar Vincent Knowles, the Bursar R.A. Rainford and the Librarian Moses Tyson were accustomed to meet of a morning in Staff House and solve the *Times* crossword together, making themselves available to anyone who cared to approach.

If the University was an academic democracy, a community of scholars, it was a democracy for professors only: with rare exceptions, they occupied all the seats in the Senate, and ran their departments as they chose within the limits imposed by their budgets. A large proportion of the University's income (75–80 per cent) now sprang from the parliamentary grant distributed by the University Grants Committee (UGC), but there was little sense of being exposed to the caprices of politicians. The financial future, guaranteed for five-year stretches, was reasonably secure. Governments seemed to believe in the capacity of universities to

Left: Scientific developments of the 1950s and 1960s: the Williamson and Simon Buildings, by H.M. Fairhurst.

Right: Looking down Oxford Road from the newly erected Mathematics tower, 1968. The coal-black Victorian buildings on the right were sand-blasted a few years later. On the right is the Moberly Tower, a basic residence with minimal facilities for senior students and postgraduates. Arts buildings lie to the right, Science and Social Sciences buildings to the left.

2, Blossom Avenue. Student cultural influences are not always wanted. The seven Miller children live behind the Union and suffer for it. Wednesday and Saturday night hops mean the noise of three bands, drunken, shouting students and cars crammed onto the pavement. Only Robert (far right) likes the music. Harry Miller and his wife will be glad to leave the house they have been in for twelve years although the rent the University takes is under £1. There is no bath and no hot water. The walls are too damp to be papered, and they cannot light a fire in the front room because the wind comes off the Arts Building down the chimney. A few weeks ago the bed came through the sitting room ceiling at 2 a.m.

"If the University don't knock it down soon it'll fall down." They have been told that they will be out by Christmas— "so it's not worth spending a fortune on it."

Above: Terrace houses near Tech.

Left: Problems of the University's neighbours. The Millers of Blossom Avenue.

Right: The new Medical School (Stopford Building) and the church of the Holy Name from the cover painting of the brochure prepared for the opening of the School in 1973.

meet national needs, especially by educating an ample supply of scientists, engineers and technologists who would sharpen the country's competitive edge and enhance its capacity for self-defence.

Young Dr Aylmer, fresh from Oxford, might be depressed by the oligarchy he observed within the professoriate, given to unnecessary secrecy, log-rolling and empire-building. Youngish Professor Flowers, newly arrived from the Atomic Energy establishment at Harwell, might be astonished at the amateurish and informal methods of government. Students might complain of pontifical lecturing and sporadic tutorials, and sometimes of incompetent teaching by academics selected for their prowess at research rather than their powers of exposition or their understanding of slower minds than their own. But many students were conscious of the privilege of being at university, and even – in the wake of world war and cold war – of the privilege of being alive. Manchester could and did boast of recent, spectacular,

pioneering achievements in computer science and radio astronomy; of skill in deciphering and popularising the Dead Sea Scrolls; of the first full-time course in nuclear engineering to be delivered anywhere in Europe. And what other institution outside London could have supplied, simultaneously, the two heads of the Royal Colleges of Surgeons and of Physicians, as Manchester did after 1956?

In the 1960s, the University responded to government demands for the expansion of higher education and in the process lost some of its stability and cosiness. From about 1963, children born shortly after the war (the baby-boomers) would be reaching the age of eighteen and clamouring at the gates of universities. No one of university calibre, argued Lord Robbins' committee, should be refused a university place merely because there were not enough places available. Graduates were vital to the country's prosperity and there was talk of great potential in the social groups unaccustomed to go to universities, which the system of higher education was failing to tap. The burden fell at first on the major civic universities, whose student numbers grew rapidly into the region of 8,000 to 10,000, while the new "green-field" (or "Shakespeare") universities were receiving their first recruits. By 1969–70 there were almost 9,000 students at Owens; by October 1980 they had risen to 11,500, their first high watermark, when some politicians, standing Robbins on his head, complained of an overproduction of graduates. Strenuous efforts were made to plan at high speed – and without benefit of prestigious architects – a functional, utilitarian academic precinct on Oxford Road. The stock of student accommodation increased, much of it in the suburb of Fallowfield, where the Owens Park tower rose above the village like a gigantic robot standing sentinel.

Members of the University responded to Robbins' exhortations to improve the quality of teaching by a more systematic use of seminars and tutorials, to make students less passive and lecturers more approachable. Many Manchester academics strove to establish a system of pastoral care which would treat students as people in the round rather than merely as fledgling intellects requiring examination at suitable intervals. Manchester acquired a Business School, a Faculty of Business Administration placed in slightly uneasy juxtaposition to the rest of the University; it undertook the laborious task of supervising the new Bachelor of Education degree in up to ten teachers' training colleges in the region, and devised with some initial success an ambitious course entitled Liberal Studies in Science. This was designed, in the words of one of its founders, to educate the "speakers, publicists, journalists and civil servants, teachers and industrial managers" who would "interpret a technological society to itself".

The sudden expansion of the university system started a game of General Post throughout the country, and in the session of 1965–6 Manchester received 250 resignations, equivalent to about 30 per cent of its full-time academic staff. Enterprising academics in mid-career were attracted to pioneering institutions which were writing on virgin slates and promising to try educational experiments, to abandon old-fashioned subject divisions, and to set up interdisciplinary schools. Some of these émigrés had become impatient of Manchester's seeming conservatism and complacency, of its slowness to promote and its

reluctance to entrust responsibility to anyone below the rank of professor. The exodus of middle-aged academics tended to widen the gap between generations, by removing the buffer between very senior academics and the very junior, who were being appointed in large numbers and were sometimes inclined to sympathise with their students rather than their professors.

Much-needed efforts were made to liberalise the system of government at Manchester – to create, as the lecturers' union put it, "less a hierarchy of rank and more a community of scholars". From 1963, one-fifth of the Senate was to consist of elected members, and from 1970 a quarter, and they proved to be more regular in their attendance than the blasé professorial majority. Lengthy debate on a new, supplementary charter began in 1963 and the new constitution, blessed with Privy Council approval, came into operation ten years later. Called into question were the authority of the professors and that of the lay members of the University Council. Root-and-branch reformers were disappointed, for the lay majority on Council was reduced but not abolished, and professors retained ultimate responsibility to Senate for their departments. But the constitutional debate established much consultative machinery, in the form of departmental boards and, in response to student demand, staff–student committees, together with student representation on Senate and attendance at Council. Since professors had to live with their colleagues, only the most bloody-minded would totally ignore their recommendations. Principled liberals might accuse the charter of setting up "mere talking-shops without authority" and leaving professors to wield considerable power through their influence over promotions. In time, however, the new charter encouraged better relations between professors and their colleagues, and led to more effective checks on the abuse of authority. Some on both sides of the fence complained of a loss of decisiveness, of a tendency to messy compromise, of a cult of mediocrity, and of unprofitable consumption of time, not in the pursuit of knowledge, but in what students once called "procrascommitteeation".

Behind the scenes, however, the need for decisive top-down management was growing as the competition for resources increased. After five euphoric years from 1962 to 1967, the

The Front Quad, 1960.

government and the UGC were less open-handed, and more inclined to insist that universities account for their expenditure of public money. Hence the need to establish within the University of Manchester a more professional civil service, equipped to make the necessary returns and forecasts. In 1969, the University set up the powerful Joint Committee (of the Senate and Council) for University Development. This body's function was to adjudicate claims for resources – for replacements as well as new undertakings – submitted to it by departments and faculties, and to ensure that victory did not go (as it had been known to, in more egalitarian bodies) just to those who shouted loudest and longest. It operated hierarchically through sub-committees nominated by the deans of faculties, and not until 1982 did these include some elected members.

Between 1973 and 1981 Manchester, with other universities, entered a period of uncertainty in which successive governments declined to protect university incomes fully against steep inflation and drastically reduced the money available for cherished building projects. Opened in 1973, the huge deep-plan Stopford Building on Oxford Road, which housed the Faculty of Medicine, symbolised the passing of the old affluent order; with their high consumption of heat and light, the scientific buildings threw a heavy burden on a University beginning to live in reduced circumstances. Five-year planning became a thing of the past, and staff–student ratios began gently to deteriorate. Under Sir Arthur Armitage, the former President of Queens' College, Cambridge, who proved to be a capable and optimistic Vice-Chancellor, the University did more than merely survive, using the technique of transferring posts from areas of flagging student recruitment to those that were booming. The Faculty of Medicine, which was expanding rather later than were other parts of the University, benefited most from this process of redistribution. Sadly, it became necessary to skimp on the maintenance of buildings and postpone minor works, thus storing up problems for the future and allowing the University to descend into shabbiness. Almost miraculously, however, the University succeeded towards 1980 in obtaining funds from the UGC for a large extension to its overcrowded library buildings on Oxford Road.

There were ominous signs, however, that universities were by this time falling out of favour with politicians and the public. Were they turning out too many graduates in arts and social sciences, producers of paper and arguments, material for an overgrown and burdensome tertiary sector, rather than the hoped-for scientists and engineers? Were they failing to control their radical students? At times of growing economic stringency, should not universities concentrate on vocational subjects? Demographic arguments threatened to turn against universities: it now seemed that the number of eighteen-year-olds in the population would reach a peak in 1983 and thereafter fall away sharply. Surely the system should now be contracted and the burden on the taxpayer reduced.

Determined to cut public spending and disinclined to wait until the peak year, Margaret Thatcher's administration reduced the parliamentary grant to universities in 1981 by some 17 per cent over the next three years. Reluctant to inflict equal misery on all higher education, the UGC applied the cuts selectively and reduced the grants to individual universities by amounts that varied between 6 and 44 per cent. Manchester's cut of 16 per cent implied that the University would face bankruptcy unless it shed about one-seventh of its staff within three years. The new Vice-Chancellor, Mark Richmond, a bacteriologist from Bristol, arrived in summer 1981 and had to tackle the job of slimming down the University before he had formed any relationship with the place or its inhabitants.

To some the prospect of systematic pruning was not unwelcome, for they believed that the University had grown too fast in the 1960s and encumbered itself with too many young academics of modest ability. But permanent academic staff and those deemed to be of equivalent status had rights defined by the revised charter of 1973, and it appeared that the University could not legally dismiss them except on the grounds of proven misconduct, incompetence or incapacity. Trade-union solidarity, respect for the strong collegial sense that had grown since the 1960s, a distaste for governments that incited institutions to break contracts, a reluctance to declare openly that some academics and their departments were worthier than others – all

The Mathematics Building by Scherrer and Hicks (1967–8) (to the left of it is the Computer Building, now the Kilburn Building).

these things stood in the way of compulsory redundancies and planned reductions in the strength of the University. The only feasible solution was to draw on the University's reserves to finance early retirements on generous terms. Of necessity, this process depended on the age structure within departments; its effects were capricious and sometimes defied government intentions. It seemed, to disillusioned observers, that distinguished older scholars had retired, that corporals had taken over from colonels, that the way was blocked to young people, and that the middle-aged heirs of the Robbins expansion were left in possession of the field: Manchester had become no lean

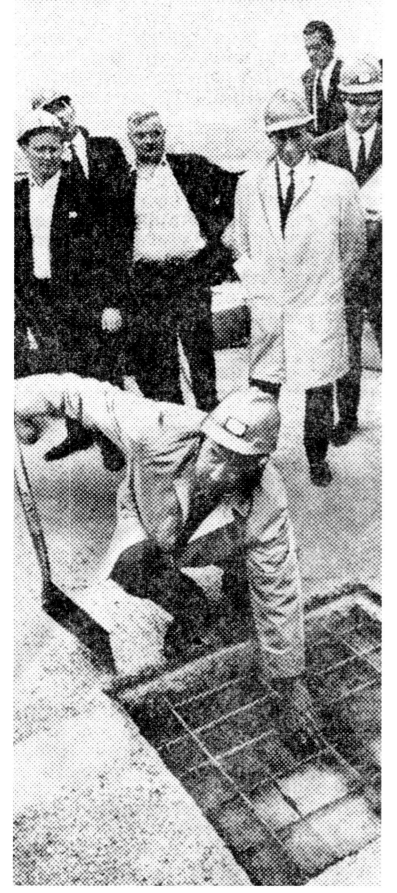

George (later Sir George) Kenyon, then Chairman of the Buildings Committee and afterwards Chairman of Council, takes part in the topping-out ceremony in 1968. The Maths Building was demolished during the session 2005–6.

Professor Sir Mark Richmond, Vice-Chancellor 1981–90.

greyhound, as had been hoped, but a stout and ponderous Labrador retriever. Some of the damage, however, was repaired by Manchester's success in 1982–85 in bidding for posts designed to inject new blood into the system (particularly in science and medicine), and for posts in Information Technology, where the University had long excelled.

Optimistic belief that the cuts of 1981–84 were a unique event did not last for long. It seemed that the government would require further savings of 1.5 per cent a year up to and beyond the end of the 1980s. Academic salaries suffered, since generous settlements might render universities insolvent, and plans to abolish tenure – now seen less as a guarantee of academic freedom and more as an obstacle to rational planning – were soon afoot. From the middle of the decade, however, the government was abandoning the idea of limiting or reducing student numbers and seeking to open universities to more people, but without granting either the institutions or the students commensurate increases in financial support. Allegedly, if universities became more efficient, eliminated waste and mismanagement, adopted economies of scale and looked for other sources of income, they could increase their productivity and do everything required with a much smaller proportion of staff to students. They should adopt – or so the Jarratt Report of 1985 proposed – some of the methods of business corporations and should compete with each other in Darwinian style for limited resources, particularly for the funding of research. The cosy pretence that all departments were of equal calibre should be abandoned and indicators of performance should be sought. In 1986, the UGC began to supply to public consumption some of the most crucial indicators by openly making judgements on the research achievements of departments. In subsequent years, high marks in Research Assessment Exercises became crucial, not only to the reputation of universities but to their finances, and the cry "Publish or your department perishes" was heard in the land.

Manchester in the 1980s shared the common experiences of most universities, which reacted with varying degrees of skill to the moves of a highly *dirigiste* government and the proposals of the UGC for rationalisation. Some things were peculiar to Manchester – for example, the sweeping reorganisation of the biological sciences. Some disciplines, especially Earth Sciences, benefited from schemes to concentrate certain particularly expensive subjects in places of proven excellence. The vigorous liberal tradition within the University which had burgeoned in the 1960s and 1970s took alarm at the advance of executive power and judgemental authority within academia; at government interference with the conduct of university affairs; and at questionable analogies between business corporations bent on profit and universities dedicated to the pursuit of knowledge for its own sake. In 1986 Manchester's first contested election for the office of Chancellor – the University's constitutional monarch, hitherto always an aristocrat or at least a created peer – brought to the throne an outspoken, untitled defender of academic freedom, John Griffith, formerly Professor of Public Law at the London School of Economics. Ingenious constitutionalists began to exploit the power of the University Court – a large body of usually passive governors which nevertheless had ultimate authority under the charter – to question the rule of its executive committee, the University Council. It was hard to avoid the impression that Chancellor and Vice-Chancellor were engaged in minding and checking each other. But the Chancellor presided with impeccable dignity and fairness over the Court, and Richmond, pragmatic rather than idealistic, proved to be a stout defender of academic freedom. As Chairman of the Committee of Vice-Chancellors and Principals in 1987–89, it fell to him to oppose the more extreme clauses of an Education Bill which would have subjected universities to minute and almost unlimited government supervision. He argued in 1988 for three fundamental freedoms – not only to question received wisdom, but also to research on subjects of as yet unrecognised importance, and to be protected from direct and narrow political interference by the government of the day.

Under Richmond's rule Manchester generally held its own in official tables of ranks, without attaining the place in the premier league which it would once have claimed as its right. On its own interpretation it was something like fifth equal in the ranking order of British universities established by the Research Assessment Exercises of 1986 and 1989 – so long as one counted only large, wide-ranging, "full service" universities with at least thirty-five departments. Include more compact and specialised institutions, such as the London School of Economics, and Manchester sank to eleventh place. In 1990 the decision not to pull in great numbers of additional students caused it to descend in the league tables relevant to the distribution of grant money. Sir Mark Richmond thought the University already too large and unwieldy; further growth would make it unmanageable. Other universities, such as Leeds, were soon to expand by as much as 50 per cent and acquire at least a thin financial cushion by not increasing their expenditure at a similar rate.

On the departure of Sir Mark Richmond in 1990 to become Chairman of the Science and Engineering Research Council, Sam Moore, a popular and approachable Acting Vice-Chancellor with a talent for diplomacy and an econometrician's understanding of figures, had the task of steering the University through a two-year interregnum and one major constitutional crisis concerning the relationship of the Manchester Business School to the University. Like the great men of the 1950s, he had risen through the ranks within the University itself, where he had begun in the early 1960s as a part-time degree student and a research assistant. In 1992 the new Vice-Chancellor, Martin Harris, formerly of the University of Salford and most recently Vice-Chancellor of the University of Essex, arrived to take office in Manchester. The changes which followed are best described in his words.

The Last Decade of the Victoria University

MARTIN HARRIS

Sir Martin Harris, Vice-Chancellor of the Victoria University of Manchester 1992–2004, gives the view from the bridge and remembers what happened on his watch. He analyses the reforms that enabled the University to recover and strengthen its position, particularly after 1996, which he identifies as a turning point in its fortunes.

The 1990s were for the (Victoria) University of Manchester a period of uncertainty, of change and ultimately of confident reassertion of its position as one of Britain's very best universities. Both its great appeal to students and its reputation as a leading research university came under challenge in the first half of the decade: both were not just re-established but further enhanced by the time that discussions got seriously underway about the possibility of coming together with UMIST.

Manchester University has always been attractive to students, whether undergraduate or postgraduate, whether from Britain or elsewhere. When I assumed office as Vice-Chancellor in 1992, this situation continued to look unassailable and the annual admissions cycle remained a very relaxed affair, with high-quality applicants continuing to fill the available places. Three things, however, came together in the mid-1990s to disturb this comfortable state of affairs. First, the University had escaped the worst of the cuts imposed on higher education during the 1980s and difficult decisions made elsewhere in the sector had tended not to be made at Manchester. In particular, there had been no impetus for radical revision of the curriculum: in other words, some at least of the offering, particularly to undergraduates, looked rather tired. Secondly, the swing away from mathematics and science in schools began in earnest, which of course reduced

the pool of applicants to a range of key departments, particularly in Science and Engineering. And thirdly, for a brief period, as a result of several high-profile incidents, the negative side of the city's image briefly prevailed over what has generally been very positive from the perspective of potential students, and applications, particularly from the south of England, fell sharply. The second and third of these factors, taken together, were especially serious for science-based courses, given the geographical distribution of schools strong in teaching those disciplines.

Clearly, whatever else a great University is and does, it must be attractive to excellent students. After some hesitation, some reluctance to admit that, without a real effort, applications for undergraduate places in particular might not recover to the point where our traditionally very high quality could be maintained, academic and administrative staff across the University joined together to tackle the issues in a concentrated fashion. Led by the University's immensely able senior Pro Vice-Chancellor, Katherine Perera, student preferences nationally were analysed, the range and content of courses reviewed and recruitment efforts professionalised, with a particular focus on London and the Home Counties.

The overall result was a striking recovery in the University's popularity, which is currently at an all-time high. Particularly gratifying was the notable success in certain fields where recruitment nationally has got steadily more difficult. Let me give just two examples. While undergraduate recruitment for physics has plummeted across the country, concentrated efforts by colleagues in Manchester have ensured that the department's entry is buoyant and remains of a very high quality. In this case,

Previous page: The Beyer Building.

Right: The Nowgen Centre, the multi-million pound, Manchester-based centre for genetics in healthcare and home of the North West Genetics Knowledge Park.

individual attention to applicants, coupled with a broad range of provision including, of course, astronomy, when taken with the long-standing high reputation of physics in Manchester, seem to have been key factors. In quite another part of the University, modern languages have had a dramatic recovery from a low point in the late 1990s. Bucking all the national trends, not only have languages already taught, such as Russian and Italian, been secured, but additional languages such as Japanese and Chinese are being further developed. In this case, determined leadership and the willingness to teach languages in conjunction with a much broader range of other disciplines seem to have been decisive. And there is evidence across the sector that when student numbers are falling and departmental closures are in the air, applicants do tend to concentrate their interest in places where the subject seems totally safe, a trend which has been very much to Manchester's advantage.

So the incipient threat to the number and quality of undergraduate applicants was vigorously and successfully dealt with, helped by the ever-improving and largely accurate perception of Manchester as a dynamic, prosperous and culturally vibrant city. Just as important, however – indeed, in financial terms, more so – is the University's research reputation. Here, too, the story is one of a slight dip in the mid-1990s, followed by a strong recovery which is still visibly accelerating at the present time. When I arrived in 1992, the result of that year's Research Assessment Exercise (RAE) had seemed good – but that wonderful science of hindsight tells us that all was not quite as it appeared. In essence, in a number of important areas of the University, the next RAE in 1996 revealed that the quality of our research, while remaining high, was often not in the very highest category, with adverse consequences, both reputational and financial. This was particularly true in medicine, a subject area vital to the University's success. Looking back, one can see that 1996 was the turning point. The measures to restore undergraduate applications to their traditional strength had not yet had their full effect, and the RAE results were disappointing. This could have marked – and it has happened elsewhere – the beginning of a downward drift which, once established, would have been very hard to reverse. In fact, the opposite happened.

The academic leaders of the University, across all faculties, decided that steps could and should be taken to reassert Manchester's research leadership across the widest possible range of disciplines, and the entire academic community engaged vigorously in the debate as to how this might be achieved. Where appropriate, a full-scale external review took place before a way forward was decided upon; in Medicine, for example, the Pro Vice-Chancellor for Research, Howard Barringer, was assisted by Sir Keith Peters and Sir Colin Dollery, Deans of Medicine in Cambridge and London respectively. Three factors came together to give the emerging research strategy the greatest possible chance of success. First was the determination across the University that, by working together, Manchester's research strength and reputation could be decisively restored; secondly, key staff, the real research leaders, chose to stay and be part of that process; and thirdly, years of prudent housekeeping meant that resources were available for the University to invest its way out of trouble, with the result that although there was inevitably some restructuring and downsizing, including a wide-ranging and generous early retirement scheme, almost every part of the University ended up stronger than before. Suffice it to say that the results of the 2001 RAE strikingly vindicated the decisions made four or five years earlier. Biological Sciences, in particular, progressed

The atrium of the Manchester Incubator Building, a state-of-the-art biotechnology research and development centre, completed prior to the merger between the Victoria University and UMIST.

from an embryonic school under the wing of two other faculties to becoming perhaps the most dynamic academic area of the University. The new millennium started with the University enjoying unparalleled demand for its courses, both undergraduate and postgraduate, and a research reputation demonstrably as high as at any time in the last half century.

Excellence in teaching and research are very properly at the core of what a University is about, and Manchester entered the twenty-first century with an enviable reputation in both and, as a result, in a very healthy financial position. Many aspects of University governance had been addressed during the 1990s. Far more decision-making and associated resources were devolved to faculties, and the deans emerged as senior academic managers,

with particularly marked changes for the better in the Faculty of Arts. The Senate (which had reached 450 members and was still growing) was slimmed down and refocused on its principal task, oversight of the University's academic standards and goals. The ambiguous relationship between the Court, a large biennial gathering, and the Council, the University's legal governing body, was definitively resolved in favour of the latter. Throughout this period, the Council, outstandingly led for most of the period by Christopher Kenyon and latterly by Rodger Pannone, supported radical measures when these were called for – such as the establishment of a strong, unified administration led by Eddie Newcomb – and exercised patience when asked to do so (seeking to change academic practices too quickly can easily be counterproductive!). In short, thanks in large measure to the persistence and determination of Christopher Kenyon, the University started the new century with governance fit for purpose, and this was to prove crucial when, during the last years of my Vice-Chancellorship, the issues surrounding the proposed unification with UMIST, Project Unity, needed to be debated and resolved, a process in which Rodger Pannone played a key role.

There is one final strand to this story of which the University should feel particularly proud. The Victoria University, like UMIST, was created by and within Manchester, to meet the needs of the city and its hinterland. From this developed the world-class university which exists today. What the 1990s showed, among other things, was that being international in vision and aiming at all times for the highest standards is in no way irreconcilable with being a key player in the city and its region; quite the contrary. The Science Park and the Bioscience Incubator, the music and the drama, the Gallery and the Museum, the Clinical Research Faculty and the Genetics Knowledge Park – all of these, whatever else their respective purposes, contribute to the economic, physical and spiritual wellbeing of our fellow citizens, while relations with the city itself have become as warm as they clearly were during the University's first hundred years. The rejuvenation of a great city and a great university went hand and hand. It was indeed a proud legacy that the Victoria University contributed to the new University of Manchester which came into being, as I retired, on 1 October 2004.

The Creation and Development of UMIST, 1951–2004

HAROLD HANKINS

The narrative concentrates again on Tech, which became UMIST in 1966 and thereby experienced the last of "six changes of name, each denoting some subtle or dramatic development" (as a historian of UMIST remarked in 1974). Under its visionary Principal, Vivian Bowden, it changed from a proud city college into an institution of international standing heavily funded by parliamentary grant. Professor Harold Hankins has known Tech for over fifty years and seen it from different angles and elevations – as a student, as Professor of Communication Engineering, as Acting Principal appointed during a crisis, and finally as a very successful head of institution. Drawing on his own special insights, he shows how a Faculty of Technology developed into a famous and successful technological university, capable both of standing on its own and of rejoining Owens on equal terms.

In 1950 I was one of 8,558 part-time students at Tech, the Manchester Municipal College of Technology, and amongst us, in the Faculty of Technology, were 620 students reading for degrees of Owens, the Victoria University of Manchester. Since Tech was geographically north of Owens, we thought of them "as down the road", whilst we fondly hoped they thought of us as "up the road". Either way, Owens and Tech enjoyed a level of cooperation and goodwill that other institutions envied but could never quite replicate or understand. I arrived at the Main Building, an engineering apprentice, to study for a Higher National Certificate and the much coveted Associateship of the College, AMCT. Registration took place in the Great Hall,

accessed through the Sculpture Hall where once, according to John Henry Reynolds, students passing through would experience a spiritual transformation from the world of work to the world of study. Sadly, the neo-classical sculptures had been removed during the war for safe-keeping and never returned.

In 1951 Tech was searching for a new Principal. Sir James Myers had left to direct the School of Education at Owens, and David Cardwell, Vice-Principal and Director of Studies for twenty-seven years, had become Acting Principal. By great good judgement and foresight, the search committee recommended Bertram Vivian Bowden, who had worked with Rutherford at Cambridge, and with Watson Watt on radar during the war. He was Head of Computer Applications at the Ferranti Company. He was *the* man for his time. He had drive, charisma, energy in abundance, all combined with good humour and enthusiasm. He was unconventional, a great

Joe Burgess, Registrar and Secretary of the Tech.

Bertram Vivian Bowden.

Left: The Renold Building, UMIST, a central facility containing lecture theatres of various sizes, by W.A. Gibbon of Cruickshank and Seward (1962).

raconteur and speech-maker often using illogical comparisons to make a point. The Registrar, Joe Burgess, taciturn but astute and highly capable, balanced Vivian Bowden's outward-going nature, and together they made a winning team. Later I became a full-time student in the Faculty of Technology, and Vivian Bowden addressed us in the Great Hall. We knew that we were in the presence of a man with a mission. Bowden lost no time in moving Tech forward, and his vision is described in his highly readable booklet, *Proposals for the Development of Manchester College of Science and Technology*, published in 1956.

After the war the government funded an expansion in the teaching of technology. Manchester now made its rightful claim. The time had come for growth to be facilitated by a constitution and status fit for a national institution. After backing by local and national worthies, Manchester City Council generously agreed to seek an independent governing body for Tech. The City Council and Owens petitioned the Privy Council to establish the Manchester College of Science and Technology, into which the Manchester Municipal College of Technology would be subsumed. Royal Assent was given on 1 August 1955, and the Parliamentary Bill was passed on 1 August 1956. Tech now became an autonomous university college, but one more act had still to be carried out. In 1964 the council built a new technical college on Chester Street, the John Dalton College of Technology, into which by 1966 Tech had transferred its part-time day and evening courses. Vivian Bowden then declared: "The Faculty of Technology of Manchester University, established within the Manchester Municipal College of Technology in 1905, has, in effect, expanded to take over the whole college," although he later mourned the loss of the coexistence of university and part-time industrial students.

The Royal Charter allowed Tech to become a university in its own right, but it chose to remain as the Faculty of Technology. It was not all plain sailing. There existed a pressure group that sought, unsuccessfully, to persuade Tech's Council to declare independence, and there was a great debate in Tech on what it should be called. Eventually, in April 1966, a name was agreed that was to become both the shortest and longest of any university in the realm: UMIST, the University of Manchester Institute of Science and Technology. In Manchester's academe, however, use of the names Tech and Owens persisted in everyday parlance. Explaining to outsiders the origins of these two names, and the relationship between the two institutions, became an industry in its own right. It also created an image problem for UMIST. As Tim Yates, our first Director of Communications, observed: "How do you promote a university which begins with the name of another?"

In 1963 the Robbins Report espoused the ideal that every qualified student should be able to attend university, prompting

Memories of the 1950s

After graduation in Mechanical Engineering from Tech in 1953, I began work as a junior engineer at Simon Handling Engineers in Cheadle Heath, Stockport. Things did not work out well and as a result of a conversation with a fellow undergraduate who had remained at Tech for a research degree, I was encouraged to apply for an M.Sc. research place myself.

I worked in Laboratory D3, a corner room in the Main Building. Working in the lab were three or four research MSc and PhD students, together with several final-year undergraduate project students. One of these was Harold Hankins, later to become the Principal of UMIST. Health and Safety were never mentioned. My work involved using a cathode ray oscilloscope, bereft of its casing and operating at 1000 volts. I recall that I put up a small notice announcing 'Danger 1000 Volts' as a precaution against prying fingers. The sound of a large trolley proceeding down the corridor was the highlight of Thursday afternoons. This was loaded with the latest efforts of the students of the Bakery Department. Loaves and cakes of irregular shapes and unusual colours could be purchased for a trivial sum.

Research supervision was haphazard. Supervisors appeared at odd times, exchanged a few words and disappeared. However they were largely very supportive despite the absence of formal mechanisms such as regular meetings or periodic progress reports. Staff numbers were small and several were in the process of working towards their own Ph.D degrees.

Michael Hartley
MSc Tech 1956, BSc Tech Mechanical Engineering 1953

Kingsley Amis's famous observation "more means worse". The Government accepted the report and announced a rapid increase in the university student population. Bowden had already committed Tech to expansion and Robbins simply invigorated it. By 1960 the number of degree students at Tech had tripled and then doubled again to over 3,500 by 1973. In 1964 Vivian Bowden took up office as Minister of State at the Department of Education and Science during Harold Wilson's "white hot technological revolution". He was elevated to a life peerage as Lord Bowden of Chesterfield. He never came to terms with the formal workings of the Civil Service, and returned to Tech in 1966. While he was in London, Professor Frank Morton, Head of Chemical Engineering, was appointed Acting Principal. He had

Above: Topping out the Chemistry Building at UMIST, 1967. Robert Haszeldine, then Professor of Chemistry, later Principal, appears at the top right.

Right: The Faraday Building (Chemistry), by H.M. Fairhurst (1967).

served as a Pro Vice-Chancellor at Owens, a position held later by another Tech stalwart, Professor Ken Entwistle, from the Manchester Materials Science Centre.

By 1974, when Tech celebrated its 150th anniversary, universities were expanding at a gentler pace. Money was found to clean the outside of the Main Building and open days, special lectures and conferences were held. By then I had joined the academic staff, and in 1974 Bowden promoted me to a Chair in Electrical Engineering. In 1976 he retired as Principal after twenty-three years in the post. He had presided over two decades of remarkable growth, and when he retired he said, "The Government uncorked the horn of cornucopia six months before I came and put the cork back in six months before I left." During his time, twenty-three buildings of all types and sizes were erected, and the academic and administrative staff expanded in proportion to the increasing student population.

In 1976, Professor R.N. Haszeldine FRS, a brilliant fluorine chemist and Head of Chemistry at Tech, was appointed Principal. The last of the UGC's quinquennial grants ended in 1977, to be replaced by an annual block grant. The new system required universities to produce yearly financial and academic plans. Detailed planning in Tech proceeded on a scale and depth not seen before. Comprehensive profiles of academic departments and performance tables were published, and new academic developments had to be funded by making savings from the annual block grant. Tech led the way with two major initiatives in Applied Molecular Biology, and Instrumentation and Analytical Science. With the appointment of three new professors in this latter subject, a new department was created, a rare event in 1979.

By 1980, a new Conservative government declared that the subsidies granted to overseas students were an unacceptable burden on the taxpayer, and those in Science and Engineering were required to pay full economic fees of £3,300. Hitherto, between 1967 and 1975, the fee demanded for all overseas students had been no more than £250. The Government had been elected with a promise to cut public expenditure, including the universities, and in 1981 decided to cut the sum awarded to the UGC by 17 per cent over a period of three years. In July 1981, the UGC decided to apply the cut selectively, and informed each university how much of its grant it was to lose. Owens received a reduction of 16 per cent, Tech one of 24 per cent. A UGC-funded early retirement scheme was established to enable each university to reduce its salary bill.

At Tech, plans were initiated by the Principal to apply the cut differentially across departments. But these proposals were not well received, particularly by departments suffering cuts greater than the average, for after all expansion had been underway for twenty years before. At about this time, a house for the Principal was prepared in Didsbury, a project in which he took a personal interest and over which he established financial control. There were reports in the media of extravagance, and concerns were raised at council about the costs, which were found to have spiralled upwards. These events led to a great deal of controversy in Tech, which now became a focus for national media attention. Following an enquiry into the expenditure on his house, the Principal took early retirement in 1982. I had been selected by my peers to serve as a Vice-Principal from 1979 to 1981, and Council now asked me to act as Deputy Principal with the powers of a Principal. At the same time, a search committee was set up to find an Acting Principal and in October 1982, after interview, I was appointed.

Tech was now in the media spotlight for all the wrong reasons. It needed a period of calm and reflection, but its position had become vulnerable. The UGC and the Research Councils sent representatives to seek assurance about its stability, and the MP for Wythenshawe and the Vice-Chancellor of Salford University publicly proposed a merger between Tech and Salford to form a national university for science and technology. But we had been there before when the Robbins Report suggested the setting up of three such centres including Manchester, Imperial College, London, and the Royal Technical College, Glasgow, to be called SISTERs, "Special Institutions for Science and Technological Education and Research". The Cabinet had declined to accept this concept. Tech now rejected the proposed merger with Salford because of its historical ties with Owens; more importantly, there was no support for it on campus.

The task of restoring trust within Tech and reducing costs now got under way. All were willing to overcome recent difficulties and shared a desire to tackle the problems which now beset us. There was welcome support from the campus unions, and they played a full and responsible role in the recovery. A strict savings regime was introduced. Ceremonial occasions were suspended; vacancies were left unfilled; early retirement was offered; a cheaper gas heating scheme was installed; Velvet House, where Tech had been a tenant for nearly sixty years, was vacated to save the annual rent; and the former Principal's Institute house and car were sold. A key decision was to set up a Budget Committee under the chairmanship of the Vice-Principal for Finance, Professor John Pickering, School of Management. Membership included representation from the campus unions and reflected all the spending areas; its job was to slice up the financial cake. It often engaged in intense periods of debate, and made some very tough decisions. The 24 per cent savings were delivered in three years. Over the next twelve years, the Budget Committee never allowed expenditure to exceed income, bringing stability to Tech both in terms of employment and morale. Much credit was due to the

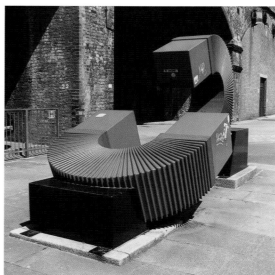

UMIST sculptures with scientific and technological themes (clockwise from top left): railway arch sheltering 'Archimedes' by Thompson W. Dagnall, with the Barnes Wallis Building and the fifteen-storey Wright-Robinson Hall by W.A. Gibbon (1963–6) in the background; monument by Kerry Morrison to the manufacture of Vimto cordial, which began in 1908 in Granby Row; 'Technology Arch' by Axel Wolkenhauer, 1989, 'made possible by North West Arts and British Ropes Ltd.'; close-up of 'Archimedes'; Paul Frank Lewthwaite, 'The Generation of Possibilities', 1999.

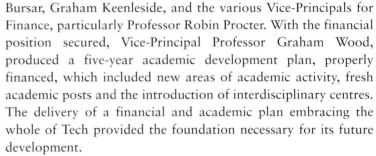

Bursar, Graham Keenleside, and the various Vice-Principals for Finance, particularly Professor Robin Procter. With the financial position secured, Vice-Principal Professor Graham Wood, produced a five-year academic development plan, properly financed, which included new areas of academic activity, fresh academic posts and the introduction of interdisciplinary centres. The delivery of a financial and academic plan embracing the whole of Tech provided the foundation necessary for its future development.

In February 1984 I was shortlisted, interviewed and appointed to the post of Principal. A new Director of Overseas Relations was appointed, Dr Iain Bride, to restore Tech's fortunes via the recruitment of overseas students, and Annette Babchuk, was appointed to set up an alumni organisation.

With a view to enlisting the support of the old universities, the UGC announced plans in 1985 to shift resources from universities judged to be weak in research to those deemed to be strong. In May 1986 it published judgements on the quality of research, classifying departments as outstanding, above average, average and below average. Tech secured enough outstanding and above average awards to suggest that we were among the top ten universities most distinguished in research. It was a morale-

Wine Tasting at UMIST

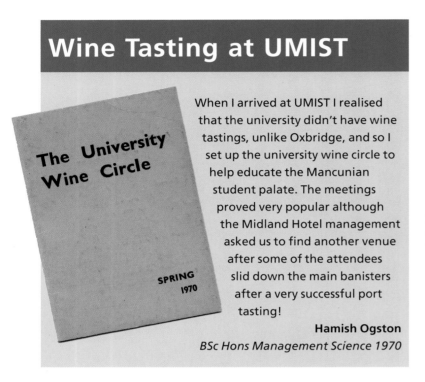

The University Wine Circle

SPRING 1970

When I arrived at UMIST I realised that the university didn't have wine tastings, unlike Oxbridge, and so I set up the university wine circle to help educate the Mancunian student palate. The meetings proved very popular although the Midland Hotel management asked us to find another venue after some of the attendees slid down the main banisters after a very successful port tasting!

Hamish Ogston
BSc Hons Management Science 1970

Work being undertaken on expanding the University campus in 1963.

boosting assessment, particularly when coupled with our success in winning a significant number of information technology and new blood lectureships, as well as a large grant from the UGC to modernise our Joule Library. Tech maintained its position in the top ten for research assessment in 1989, 1992 and 1996, although in 2002 its position fell somewhat. But it ran more postgraduate courses than almost any other university, and led the way in doctoral programmes such as Total Technology, Engineering Doctorate, and Postgraduate Training Partnerships. We received more Science and Engineering Research Council (SERC) studentships than any university other than Oxford, and only Cambridge graduates were more sought after by industry.

In 1992, and again in 1997, Tech was awarded the Queen's Award for Export Achievement. By 2002 it had won the Queen's Anniversary Prize for Higher Education on four occasions, and in 1993 and 1994 the Prince of Wales Award for Innovation. Significant also were honours won by the academic and administrative staff. Over the period 1984–2004 two were elected Fellows of the Royal Society, five were elected both Fellows of the Royal Society and the Royal Academy of Engineering, eighteen were elected Fellows of the Royal Academy of Engineering, five were awarded the CBE and three were awarded the OBE. This total was over four times as many awards as in the previous two decades. A very successful fund-raising campaign was led by Professor Sir Roland Smith, then Chairman of British Aerospace, enabling Tech to make more academic appointments and pump-prime new

building projects, including Ronson Hall, the Weston Centre and premises for the Manchester School of Management as part of the new Federal School of Business and Management with Owens.

In 1988 Parliament passed the Education Reform Act and in 1992 the Higher and Further Education Act, placing the responsibility for all university activities on university councils. It meant that Tech, with its own council, could no longer operate as a Faculty of Owens under the terms of the 1905 concordat. The necessary negotiations with Owens, resulting in a new charter, were led by Professor Graham Wood and Paddy Stephenson, Registrar. One aspect of the new agreement allowed Tech to continue to award degrees of Owens, but this arrangement came to an end in 1997 when Tech awarded its own degrees. In all other matters, Tech became an autonomous university, and celebrated its new charter on 30 November 1994 when Professor Sir John Mason, the distinguished meteorologist who had been President for eight years, was installed as Chancellor.

In August 1995 I retired and Professor Bob Boucher from Sheffield University succeeded me. Later that year Professor Sir Roland Smith was appointed Chancellor. Although the downward pressure on resources continued and students were required by government to pay for their fees, Tech pursued an active programme of development. The 1996 research assessment brought the best-ever grant settlement, and five departments scored 20 points out of 24 for teaching quality. Among the academic developments were those concerned with Life Sciences, to broaden Tech's subject base, and the first 200 graduates completed a pioneering degree course in Financial Services for the Chartered Institute of Banking. Extra

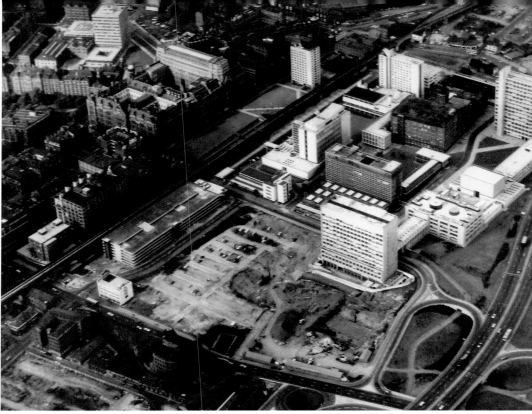

Aerial view of the developing UMIST campus.

resources in the 1998 Government Comprehensive Spending Review compensated only for past underinvestment rather than serving to enhance the annual grant, although Tech won finance for four large joint infrastructure projects, including refurbishment of the Chemical Engineering (the Frank Morton) Pilot Plant. Construction of the swimming pool for the Commonwealth Games held in 2000 began on land owned by Tech.

In 2000 Professor Boucher was appointed Vice-Chancellor of Sheffield University and was succeeded by Professor John Garside from Tech, a distinguished chemical engineer. In the following year, Sir Terry Leahy, Chief Executive of Tesco and an alumnus of the School of Management, succeeded Professor Sir Roland Smith as Chancellor (sadly, Sir Roland died in 2004). Professor Garside conducted a comprehensive strategic review, aiming to increase the student population from 6,500 students to 8,000 with an emphasis on postgraduates. A significant development was initiated for a new £30m Manchester Interdisciplinary Centre, with a contribution of £15m from the Wellcome Foundation, focusing on the interface between biological and physical sciences, and bringing together staff from about half our departments, for completion in 2005.

For nearly forty years UMIST had progressively developed an international reputation as a high-quality, research-intensive university with over 6,000 students, 100 professors, novel degree courses (mostly laboratory-based, for industry and business), and a research income in excess of £25m per year. All are housed on a modern fit-for-purpose campus. In the new millennium, it became apparent that Owens and Tech would be much stronger together if they joined forces, possessing as they did the combined capacity to be a real powerhouse in international higher education. The year 2002 was a momentous one for both. Discussions were initiated between the two institutions as equal partners, under the Project Unity banner, which led to an agreement to dissolve both to form a single new university, logically enough called the University of Manchester, with financial backing from government sources and the Northwest Development Agency. The Vice-Chancellors of Owens and Tech, Professor Sir Martin Harris and Professor John Garside, both retired in September 2004. The following month the new university became a reality when Her Majesty The Queen came to Manchester to present the Royal Charter to Co-Chancellor Anna Ford before a packed assembly in the Whitworth Hall.

Professor Harold Hankins, Principal and then Vice-Chancellor, 1984–95 (left) and Professor Bob Boucher, Vice-Chancellor, 1995–2000 (right).

Project Unity

MICHELE ABENDSTERN

How and why did UMIST and the Victoria University of Manchester form a new relationship after a temporary separation, to create the University of Manchester of 2004? Michele Abendstern, an experienced oral historian and a researcher in social sciences in the University, answers this question by drawing on interviews that she conducted soon after the event with the architects of unification.

On 1 October 2004, two great institutions joined forces to form the largest university in the country on a single site and the first to enjoy an income of over half a billion pounds. The aim of the University of Manchester, however, is not simply to be bigger than any rival, but to become one of the leading universities in the world by 2015. This chapter briefly describes the rationale and execution of the process of uniting UMIST and the Victoria University of Manchester.

At the start of the twenty-first century, the climate proved favourable to the development of a closer working relationship between the two bodies. Martin Harris, Vice-Chancellor of the Victoria University of Manchester from 1992 to 2004, had long recognised the academic and financial opportunities that closer collaboration would offer to both institutions. It was his view that Manchester could not support two universities of the highest international standing, but that it could create a single one by combining the strengths of both. The government of the day was also urging the adoption of economies of scale in higher education as a means of developing Britain's competitiveness on the international stage. John Garside, Professor of Chemical Engineering at UMIST, shared Martin Harris's views; with his appointment as Vice-Chancellor of UMIST in 2000, discussions

Professor John Garside CBE FREng, Vice-Chancellor of UMIST, and Professor Sir Martin Harris CBE, Vice-Chancellor of the Victoria University of Manchester, during the Project Unity negotiations for the merger of the two universities.

The inauguration ceremony for the new University of Manchester was held in Whitworth Hall on Friday 22 October 2004.

about the future relationship between the two universities could proceed. Informal talks between the two Vice-Chancellors resulted in the establishment of a working group to explore the matter further.

This group was made up of ten individuals from the higher echelons of both institutions with wide experience as academics, administrators and managers. It was given the name of the Dalton Group, after John Dalton (1766–1844), the great Quaker chemist and physicist of Manchester who had been involved in the combining of elements, and whose picture looked down on their inaugural meeting. Detailed and intense discussion of several models for collaboration began in September 2001 and culminated in a recommendation to the Vice-Chancellors, early in

2002, that the most promising plan was the most radical of all: double dissolution and the formation of a new University of Manchester. From that point onwards, the idea of Project Unity? (note the question mark!) began to be realised.

The processes of publicising this recommendation and organising consultation were of crucial importance to the success of Project Unity?. The decision was made that all sections of the university community should hear the news simultaneously, and huge effort was invested to achieve this. Emails, internal and external postal deliveries and press releases of identical information were all put out at exactly 11am on Monday 4 March 2002.

Reactions to the announcement varied. The Victoria University of Manchester Council were, by and large, supportive of further talks from the outset. UMIST Council, however, were more cautious, foreseeing losses rather than gains. They feared that the proposed merger might result not only in the dissolution of UMIST but also in its takeover by the Victoria University of Manchester, and they put up a strong fight to defend their interests. The Court was the most resistant body within the Victoria University, not because they opposed unification but because some of them thought that the charter of the new university would significantly reduce their influence. In the end, however, at the decisive meeting in July 2003, only a small minority voted against the proposals.

Between March 2002 and the final announcement that Project Unity? would lose its question mark, an enormous consultation exercise took place at all levels of both universities. This was designed both to listen to the concerns and views of as broad a range of people as possible, and to inform and reassure them that the proposal to unify was aimed at creating a university of high international standing in research, scholarship and teaching; it was not intended to be a device for cutting jobs and saving money. The Vice-Chancellors issued a joint statement to this effect, which helped to calm fears and gain the support of the campus trade unions. To students the proposed merger meant the opportunity to enjoy an even broader prospectus and their voice was wholly supportive of the project. For those promoting Project Unity? the gains to be made from it were clear. Many others, however, experienced real anxieties that had to be allayed if progress was to be achieved. Concern came from many areas, including departments where academic reputations appeared to be threatened or where (as in Chemistry) recruitment was already difficult and where survival became an issue. Some academics within Arts and Humanities feared that a large increase in the proportion of scientists, engineers and technologists would result in their own marginalisation, though most were eventually persuaded of the view that the humanities tend to flourish best in institutions where science and medicine are strongest. The coming together of a largely scientific institution with another whose scientific community was already substantial might appear to have little to do with those who were neither scientists nor

Anna Ford, Co-Chancellor of the new University of Manchester receives the University's Charter from Her Majesty Queen Elizabeth II at the official inauguration ceremony in October 2004.

engineers, and there were some who initially felt that the change, however radical, would have little effect on them. It was soon decided, however, that to focus solely on the development of science, engineering, technology and management would be to waste a unique opportunity to start from first principles throughout. Ideally, Arts and Humanities would become equal partners in developing the new university. Interdisciplinarity became a watchword of the project. Opportunities emerged and were created through the establishment of new interdisciplinary schools designed to bring together subject areas traditionally regarded as having little in common. In the event, every faculty in the Victoria University as well as the Victoria University Senate and UMIST Academic Board strongly supported the proposal.

No project on this scale could hope to succeed without an injection of public money. This was obtained from a mixture of central and regional government sources, which between them provided £82m. Central government support came primarily from the Office of Science and Technology and from the Higher

Education Funding Council of England, who supported it as part of their drive to raise Britain's standing in the knowledge economy. The Northwest Regional Development Agency, the other major donor, provided support inspired by the view that unification would bring increased spending power to the region by attracting more skilled workers and students. The response of industry and local government to the proposed merger was also very favourable, and helped to win the support of sections of both universities not initially comfortable with the idea. Interest in financing research increased when funding bodies no longer had to choose between two universities, and there was a growing expectation that the new University of Manchester would indeed be a centre of excellence.

In considering the new academic structure, two issues were of particular importance. First, it was recognised that if the new university were to make a dramatic improvement in its performance, academics would have to be free to focus on research and teaching. The burden of management and administration which had grown over the years would therefore have to be lifted from their shoulders. Secondly, it was important to ensure that a corporate identity was achieved without overbearing central control, something not easy to impose upon academics, whose loyalty is primarily to their discipline. In creating new boundaries, The University of Manchester also had to break with the past. The rationale behind the four faculties that finally emerged (Engineering and Physical Sciences, Humanities, Life Sciences, and Medical and Human Sciences) is that they should enjoy a certain autonomy, which, it is hoped, will produce a collegiality among their members. However, their deans, who are also Vice-Presidents and members of the senior management team of the university, are directly accountable to the President and Vice-Chancellor. The size of the faculties also enables the economies of scale necessary for the provision of management and administrative support to academics.

The three governing bodies of the university have also undergone an overhaul intended to bring them into line with current practice concerning the management of universities. The Councils have been replaced by a Board of Governors, a smaller

The logo of the new University of Manchester, tracing the University's origins back to the year in which the Mechanics' Institution and Thomas Turner's Medical School were founded.

group with individual accountability for decisions. The Court has become the General Assembly, a body of external stakeholders who act as ambassadors for the University in the outside world and whose role, somewhat like an upper chamber, is also to scrutinise the work of the Board. Finally, the Senate has retained the same title but has become much smaller, the aim being to make it a more effective decision-making body. The University's chief executive is now called not only Vice-Chancellor but also President, a term recognised internationally and therefore in keeping with Manchester's ambition to become known as a university of high international standing.

The University and the City

BRIAN PULLAN

British universities founded between about 1850 and 1950 have been variously described as "provincial", "civic" and "redbrick", to distinguish them from "ancient" universities and those privileged to lie within the golden triangle of Oxford, Cambridge and London. Brian Pullan discusses the different ways in which Owens and Tech were civic institutions: what did the city and its leading citizens give to the University and it to them, through the idealism and practical sense of such organisations as the University Settlement in Ancoats? How did the University come to take over the Manchester Museum, the Whitworth Art Gallery and the John Rylands Library, establishments designed to benefit the people of Manchester and bring prestige to the city? And to what extent did the presence of UMIST and the University and their students, as employers and as consumers of goods and services, act as a stimulus to the city's economy?

Between 1892 and 1956, as other chapters have related, the City of Manchester owned and housed Tech and financed it in large measure from the rates. It was a municipal college which sheltered a university faculty, offering degree courses to a small proportion of its students and vocational training to much larger numbers; it became the largest night school in the north of England for local people, while its reputation, especially in the field of textiles, attracted many students from abroad. The college's governors were a sub-committee of Manchester Education Committee; the college's estimates ascended

The Reading Room of the John Rylands Library in Deansgate.

annually through a hierarchy of committees until they reached the city council and then, suitably pruned and modified, returned to the Principal, who had the job of parcelling out the money. Only in the 1950s did the city hand over control to an independent board of governors. Only then did the main responsibility for Tech's finances pass from the city and the Ministry of Education to the UGC, whose contribution increased dramatically as the Faculty of Technology expanded to fill the whole college and vocational courses found homes in other schools.

Less direct was the city's relationship with Owens College, afterwards the Victoria University of Manchester. From 1892, Owens received a grant from the city, as well as a larger allowance from the Treasury, derived from a sum which the government assigned to provincial university colleges. By the outbreak of the First World War about 30 per cent of the new University's income sprang from regional and national grants – more than £17,000 from central government, a little over £6,000 provided by a combination of the city of Manchester, the counties of Lancashire and Cheshire, and the towns of Salford, Oldham, Bolton, Bury and Stockport. Manchester Corporation, therefore, gave some support to the University but did not own it.

Owens and the University were civic institutions, not in the sense that the city's government possessed or even actively promoted them, but in their dependence on the

Produced in Germany in the late nineteenth century, this decorative plate showing Owens College is a reminder of the long relationship between Manchester and Germany which ended abruptly with the outbreak of the First World War.

The Beyer Building, covered in ivy, on the Old Quadrangle. Close to the Manchester Museum, it originally housed the Geology and Zoology Laboratories and is now home to administrative offices.

philanthropy of prosperous citizens of Manchester and its satellite towns, and on the support of local charities and learned and professional societies. Engineers, manufacturers, merchants, bankers and professional men, many of them Dissenters, some of them immigrants (as was the most munificent donor, Charles Beyer, of the firm of Beyer and Peacock, locomotive builders in Gorton) – these people and their heirs and executors provided the college and the University with land, buildings, professorships, scholarships, fellowships, books, laboratories, sports grounds and centres, the handsome ceremonial hall opened in 1902 and the organ that graced it, several halls of residence for students, and two houses for Vice-Chancellors in the villages of south Manchester, The Firs in Fallowfield and Broomcroft in Didsbury. Generous gifts and some huge bequests were made by individuals, and there were many responses to the appeals for donations and subscriptions which were launched at intervals, some of them by meetings in the town hall.

Leading citizens devoted time to the management of the University's fabric and finances, first as John Owens's trustees and then as members of the College's and later the University's Council. Like the lay advocates of a medieval monastery, they placed at the disposal of the academic community (which some thought intelligent but naive and indecisive) their own extensive knowledge of the world. They took some interest in academic appointments, even junior ones, at least before the First World War, especially where bold moves were in the offing. Hence they debated at length in 1904 the wisdom of appointing a woman to a scientific post as Demonstrator in Botany. Professor Weiss had warned the candidate, young Marie Stopes, that: "The Council has unfortunately some old-fashioned and some timid members, which renders its decision a little uncertain." Miss Stopes, very sound on the subject of coal balls before she won fame as a family planner and the author of *Married Love*, *Radiant Motherhood* and other bestsellers, got the job in the end.

The University of Manchester was not, as were the federations of colleges in Oxford and Cambridge, a self-governing community of scholars, however much liberal academics in the 1960s might have liked it to become one. Lay members of Council, especially the Chairman and Treasurer and in times of expansion the Chairman of the Buildings Committee, exerted immense influence on the shape of the University. Their authority survived undiminished into the second half of the twentieth century, when the University no longer depended on local philanthropy and most of its income – sometimes as much as 75–80 per cent – derived from

Women at Manchester

Margaret Murray (1863–1963)

Margaret Murray spent most of her academic career at University College London and was perhaps best known for her controversial studies into folklore and pre-Christian pagan religion in Europe.

However, in 1908, during a relatively short sojourn at the Manchester Museum, she helped redefine the field of Egyptology by leading a team of medics and scientists in the unwrapping of two Middle Kingdom Egyptian mummies from the Museum's collection. Murray was the disciple and assistant of a great archaeologist, Flinders Petrie, Professor of Egyptology at University College London. In 1907, in return for financial support for his excavations, Petrie allocated to the Manchester Museum the

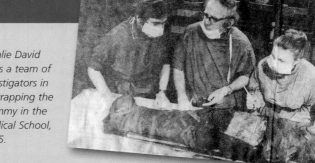

Rosalie David leads a team of investigators in unwrapping the mummy in the Medical School, 1975.

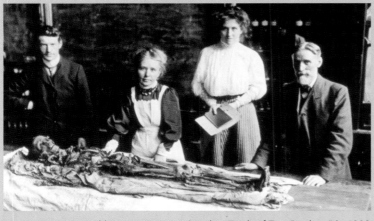

Margaret Murray and her team unwrapping the "Tomb of Two Brothers" in 1908.

contents of a rock tomb of the Twelfth Dynasty, found at Der Rifeh, which he was anxious to keep together. Miss Murray prepared the museum handbook on this discovery, the pride of Manchester's collection, which became known as the "Tomb of Two Brothers".

Herself deciphering and translating the inscriptions, she drew on the expertise of scientists from the University and Tech who reported on the anatomy of the mummies, the chemistry of the remains, the textile fabrics and their colouring matter, while a botanist identified the wood of the body coffins and their pegs, an entomologist the small brown beetles which infested the bandages. Murray's investigations placed the study of mummies solidly on a scientific basis for the first time.

In 1973, Dr Rosalie David's Manchester Mummy Project revived the multidisciplinary approach to the scientific study of Egyptian mummies, when she promoted a new university specialisation – Biomedical Research in Egyptology. Dr David was appointed to a personal chair in 2001, becoming the first woman Professor of Egyptology in the United Kingdom.

government funding. Independent of the academic body, the Chairman of Council took a leading role in selecting the new Vice-Chancellor, and was often the Vice-Chancellor's principal confidant and mainstay in times of stress and trouble.

Manchester was never a "university city". It was a metropolis which in the early twentieth century acquired, in company with Birmingham, Liverpool and Leeds, a university of its own. This was a source of civic pride, a demonstration that Mancunians were no philistines but valued creations of the intellect and the spirit – among which were also the Hallé Orchestra, the *Manchester Guardian*, famous schools for boys and girls, theatres, libraries, art galleries, museums, parks, the imposing town hall, the cathedral and the Literary and Philosophical Society. By the mid-1990s the city had three universities, which bulked very large in the economy and society of south Manchester, for UMIST had become an

independent university, and the Polytechnic, created in 1970 by uniting several city colleges, was now Manchester Metropolitan University. They collaborated with a fourth university in the neighbouring city of Salford.

Fronting on major roads, the universities did not hold themselves apart from the city or pursue a cloistered life. Owens College had opened up in a dirty street with rowdy pubs and a disorderly house for neighbours, with ragged children playing on the steps and before them a "beautiful prospect" consisting of "a very large hole surrounded by broken and dilapidated railings". Lord Bowden, the Principal of UMIST, reflected in 1974 that only twenty years earlier "the old building which we still use ... stood attached to a half-built extension on the edge of some of the worst slums in England". In his day UMIST came to occupy a relatively compact and self-contained site. But even after moving to more imposing premises on Oxford

The University campus, 1957.

Road in 1873, Owens lived at close quarters with "little terraced houses black as ink" and could expand in the 1950s and 1960s only by displacing its neighbours, a crime in the eyes of left-wing students, who accused it thereafter of uprooting local communities and adding to the sum of human unhappiness.

City planners allotted the University and the colleges a large reservation for their development after the Second World War. But architectural journalists remarked that Manchester did not and could not have a campus in the proper sense of the word. It could not be a "university in a garden". What it had was a planned educational precinct, bounded and bisected by main roads. Virtually all efforts to divert through traffic, block cross traffic and create a pleasant enclave like that of the University of Birmingham seemed doomed to failure. Mancunians may seldom have lingered in the University area unless they were visiting the Manchester Museum or Contact Theatre or skateboarding on promising surfaces, but they did pass through it on their way

elsewhere, viewing the scene dispassionately from the tops of buses. Student critics in the 1960s complained that the University now lacked any distinctive architectural style – that its modern buildings were all too reminiscent of warehouses, factories and office blocks, as if the institution had turned into a "knowledge factory" serving the needs of capitalism and become merely an extension of a materialistic, money-making city, indistinguishable from its parent.

Although the University strove between about 1955 and 1980 to expand its own accommodation, it could not house more than 40 per cent of students in its own halls and flats, and most therefore lived in the city, congregating along corridors which led southwards into Rusholme and Fallowfield, and from Hulme to Whalley Range and Chorlton. Some said that students tended to create rooming-house ghettos, that they were throwing up "invisible walls" round Fallowfield and Ladybarn and overwhelming those once-gracious suburbs, forcing upon them their own distinctive style of life. But

The Round House

Some of us were on a rota to help at the University Settlement at the Round House in Every Street, Ancoats. This entailed supervising five- to ten-year-old children painting and drawing, and playing games with them – just to keep them off the streets for an hour or two around tea-time. In the summer these children were brought to Shudehill Market near Victoria Station at an unearthly hour in the morning to buy baskets of strawberries for tea.

Evelyn Duckworth (née Rushton)
BSc Chemistry 1928

Playground at 20 Every Street, Ancoats, c1900.

large city" (among them the practice of playing billiards on licensed premises). In the late twentieth century, amid growing fears of attacks on women in hours of darkness, the city could seem a place of physical danger rather than moral peril. But Manchester's night life was becoming a magnet for students from all over the country, attracted by the city's offerings as much as by the University's courses. The cost of living was lower than in London and the chances of part-time work in bars and restaurants to supplement shrinking grants were far more plentiful than in smaller towns. Students, once drawn to Manchester, created an expanding market for entertainment. A group of urban geographers was told: "When I came to Manchester [in the early 1980s] there was no Cornerhouse, no Green Room, no Hacienda … so much has happened in the last ten years … and so much of that has depended on students." Manchester, said a local journalist, "is a youth culture centre … students come here because of popular culture".

What could the University return to the city that had given it so much? How far could it in conscience ignore the economic misery and stark social contrasts that had made Engels's Manchester "the shock city of the 1840s"? Was it enough to study them with academic detachment?

Inspired by the East London parson Samuel Barnett, the University Settlement movement reached Manchester in 1895–6. Behind it lay the principle that if privileged, educated people were to understand the lives of the workers who produced most of their wealth they must for a time "settle" in deprived areas and live in small communities as the neighbours (not the lodgers) of the poor. University of Manchester settlers moved into Ancoats, otherwise the New Cross Ward, an arid, soot-encrusted and almost treeless "jungle of stone" in which Howard Spring set the opening chapters of his novel *Fame Is The Spur* about the politician, rhetorician and poseur Hamer Shawcross. They found rooms in a corner of Ancoats Hall and took over 20 Every Street, a modest house once owned by the Reverend Doctor Scholefield, a Swedenborgian herbalist and a Chartist sympathiser who had ministered to the bodies and souls of the poor. Attached to the house was a large, circular chapel, now secularised and known as the Round House. The aim was to establish "common ground on which men and women of various classes may meet in goodwill, sympathy and friendship". People helped by the Settlement would themselves become its helpers. The settlers would not administer poor relief or throw money at social problems (the Settlement, struggling with a small budget, had little to throw). Rather, they would do good by having fun and giving pleasure, by organising play-groups, social gatherings, drop-ins and clubs for people of all ages, by taking children and young people on holiday (starting with outings to the cleaner air of Didsbury), by arranging dances (no readmission after

they moved more unobtrusively during the 1980s into the notorious Hulme estate to the west of the University, once a showpiece, now rapidly decaying into an ultra-modern slum. They filled (to the Corporation's relief) places no one else, other than squatters, wished to go. Agile, resilient and unencumbered by push-chairs, students could occupy the upper levels of the great crescent-shaped blocks that had proved unsuitable for families. Though troubled at times by mice, cockroaches, excessively thin walls and asbestos panels, they enjoyed the comforts of central heating and double glazing, to say nothing of low rents.

In the eyes of some vigilant Victorians, the city was a sinister, seductive place from which some students at least ought to be protected by halls of residence exercising a "genial oversight in leisure hours". The committee of Friends' Hall (later Dalton Hall) noted with satisfaction in the 1870s that "these youths have had the opportunity of pursuing their studies at Owens College in comparative safety amidst the many temptations presented by a

Above: A workman bestrides the skeleton of a sperm whale being winched into place at the Manchester Museum, 1898.

Opposite: The Lowry at Salford Quays, as seen from the Imperial War Museum.

nipping out to the pub), and by getting up plays and concerts. Performing in the Round House, refurbished in 1928 under the direction of the Professor of Architecture, the Settlement Players were famous for enterprising productions, and Aileen Barr of the Zoology Department distinguished herself as a female lead.

In 1942–3 a definition of the Settlement's functions alluded to "research into social conditions" (not wholly easy to square with neighbourly relations) and "responsibility for training students in practical social work". Some Wardens held posts in the University's department of social studies and advised certain students to become settlers. From 1928 onwards the mother houses in Ancoats were putting forth branches and beginning to colonise and set up community centres in the new and sometimes bleak Corporation estates to which inner-city dwellers were removed. Eventually, long after the Second World War, the practice of residing in a settlement ceased as the clearance of Ancoats proceeded. From 1977 the organisation concentrated on Beswick in east Manchester, first alighting in a rambling, cavernous rectory and then acquiring, in 1983, its first specially designed, single-storey building. Many people other than Manchester University students, teachers and graduates had always been involved with the Settlement, but it operated under the University's wing, overseen by a council appointed by the University, supported in part by a modest University grant, and was a beneficiary both of Rag Week and of a fête held annually in the grounds of a University hall.

At intervals, from the late 1860s to the early 1970s, Owens College and the University seized opportunities to take over foundations established for the people of Manchester which were beginning to sink into financial mire. They undertook to maintain and expand them in the interests of their own students, of the public, and of the wider scholarly community. Between 1865 and 1872, bearing the needs of teaching and research in mind, Owens cast its eye on two fine collections formed by scientifically minded citizens. Since 1850 these had been housed as uneasy neighbours in a museum on Peter Street in the centre of the city. The Manchester Society for the Promotion of Natural History had originated in 1821, the Geological Society in 1838. Manchester's naturalists had purchased an ample collection of birds and insects and enthusiastic contributors had added to it – the Dean of Manchester in 1846 offered the bones of goats sacrificed 1,400 years earlier in a temple of Zeus on a Greek island, and others had procured from Australia the skull of a dugong, the jaw of a wombat, relics of an extinct species of kangaroo and so forth. The Geological Society consisted (as the first historian of Owens College remarked) "of earnest men who really desired to know more about the strata beneath their feet, and who had a supreme desire to lessen, if possible, the shocking waste of life from explosions and other causes". Mining operations and railway cuttings afforded them excellent opportunities of accumulating specimens and satisfying their scientific curiosity.

Around 1850 the Natural History Society, which had opened its collection to a paying public, took plenty of gate money – over 25,000 visitors passed through its doors. Its annual report noted with satisfaction that a large proportion belonged to the working classes, and observed that "those habits of quiet and rational enjoyment, upon which their own happiness and that of society at large so much depend, are evidently on the increase". But public enthusiasm waned as novelty wore off; by 1863, when only 5,000 people entered, the Society was in debt. In Edinburgh, Oxford and Glasgow museums were attached to universities; should not Manchester adopt the same solution? Both learned bodies were eventually persuaded to hand over their collections to Owens College and to contribute from the sale of their other assets to its new buildings on Oxford Road, to the curator's salary, and to the upkeep and increase of the museum's holdings. On the new site the collections were housed in specially constructed galleries, designed over the years by three generations of the Waterhouse family. The last of several further extensions and programmes of refurbishment was completed in 2003 and financed by a grant of £12.5m from the Heritage Lottery Fund and by grants from other agencies.

With time the interests of the museum, known as the Manchester Museum, extended into several new fields. For

Women at Manchester

Margaret Pilkington (1891–1974)

Margaret Pilkington, along with her sister Dorothy, were members of a wealthy local family. Margaret Pilkington went on to become an art historian and the long-time Deputy Chairman and Honorary Director of the Whitworth Art Gallery at the University of Manchester, between 1935 and 1959. She wrote a history of the museum and bequeathed to it her collection of papers.

Margaret Pilkington was a considerable artist in her own right, notably in the medium of wood-engraving. For many years she was Chairman of the Society of Wood Engravers. She was also one of the pioneers of the Red Rose Guild of Craftsmen, which aimed to promote skilled northern workers in furniture, textiles, pottery and book binding.

The Whitworth Gallery holds a substantial collection of Margaret's works, together with work by her sister Dorothy who was also an artist. Both sisters were generous benefactors of the University.

example, it supported British archaeologists working in Egypt in the late nineteenth and twentieth centuries and received some of the artefacts they found. It gained from the munificence of a keen amateur Egyptologist, the Manchester textile manufacturer Jesse Haworth, who had funded the pioneering excavations of Sir William Flinders Petrie. Haworth financed the extension of the Museum in 1912 and gave it his personal collection of Egyptian antiquities. One of many other features was the Museum's archery collection, the core of which was given in 1946 by Ingo Simon, an expert on the history and development of the bow. Practising as well as studying the art, he had set up a world record in 1914 by firing an arrow 462 yards. He expressed with disarming modesty his hope that the exhibits should be of "some use, however little, to the advancement and retention of knowledge", it being "a great pity when an art – of any sort – gets forgotten". The Museum continues to draw visitors to University premises both by its permanent displays and by its special exhibitions: 26,000 schoolchildren visited in 2005.

In its most affluent days, between the late 1950s and the early 1970s, the University had the means to take over foundations established for the people of Manchester by the heirs and trustees of Victorian entrepreneurs. Roles were reversed: these institutions were now in financial difficulties and the University, supported by parliamentary grants distributed by the UGC, could offer them a degree of security. The Whitworth Art Gallery became part of the University in 1958; the John Rylands Library merged with the University Library in 1972. Both housed collections of almost incalculable value, now threatened because the original endowments were insufficient to meet the rising cost of keeping them in the right conditions and presenting them to the public in the most elegant and effective way.

Founded in 1889, its building completed in 1908, the Art Gallery was the most visible monument of an ambitious (some said a grandiose) scheme of the residuary legatees of the great engineer Joseph Whitworth (1804–88): Lady Whitworth, Robert Darbishire and Richard Copley Christie. These three had set out to establish an Institute for the promotion of the "fine" and the "useful" arts; the Gallery owed most to Darbishire, for Whitworth himself had not been conspicuously interested in painting. With the adjoining park, the Gallery was intended to be "a source of perpetual gratification to the people of Manchester and … a permanent influence of the highest character in the directions of Commercial and Technical Instruction and the cultivation of taste and knowledge of the Fine Arts of Painting, Sculpture and Architecture". The splendid collection of textiles, including tapestries, brocades and ecclesiastical vestments, was designed to give help and inspiration to northern industry. English watercolours, prints, works of modern and contemporary art – all were purchased or given. Arguably, however, the founders and governors had spent too much on the park (formerly called Potter's Field, now drained and provided with bandstand and boating lake), which was handed over to the city in 1904, and had left too small an endowment to the Gallery, which soon had an overdraft. Underfunded, prevented by the terms of its charter from charging entrance fees, its investments flagging, the Gallery

was reduced in the 1930s to selling some of its possessions to pay for the building's upkeep. Its survival owed much to the generosity of Margaret Pilkington, a shareholder in Pilkington Tiles Ltd and a former student at the Slade School of Art. Miss Pilkington acted as unsalaried director for many years, and with her sister Dorothy gave unobtrusive financial assistance to the Gallery.

In the 1950s it was suggested that the University should take over the Whitworth Gallery, which lay conveniently at the southern edge of the University area, and that it should become Manchester's equivalent of the Fitzwilliam Museum in Cambridge. The governors formally approached the University Council in 1954, proposing that the directorship should eventually pass to the Head of the Department of Art History in the University. Two years later, the Pilkington sisters offered to transfer to the University shares to the value of £20,000, to be used to establish a professorial chair and thereby attract a scholar of high calibre to the post. The complicated legal procedures were completed in 1958, and the first Pilkington Professor, John White from the Courtauld Institute in London, took office in 1959. He was succeeded in 1966 by the entrepreneurial Reginald Dodwell, who was determined to resist the power of London as a "big vacuum cleaner" which sucked up everything to do with the arts. He found one ally in Hal Burton, architect, stage designer and impresario, who was bent on leaving his collection of modern art to a gallery outside the capital. In 1967 Wall Paper Manufacturers Ltd offered the Gallery a magnificent collection of historic wallpapers started by one its directors, Alan Sugden, joint author of *A History of English Wallpaper 1509–1914*. The link between art and industry was thus reaffirmed in a manner that would surely have earned the founders' applause.

Mrs Enriqueta Augusta Rylands, born in Havana, the daughter of a Liverpool merchant, became the University's most generous benefactor after John Owens himself and Charles Beyer. Among much else, she endowed in her lifetime the chairs of Biblical Criticism and Exegesis and of Comparative Religion. But the University was not her only concern. A retiring and intensely private but very businesslike woman, with "absolutely no taste for society", she devoted much of her life and much of the huge fortune she inherited to preparing a magnificent memorial to her late husband. John Rylands (1801–88) was the archetypal sober, laborious businessman who scorned worldly honours and applied himself with honesty and integrity to the rational pursuit of profit through the cotton industry. Lancashire's first millionaire and a multi-millionaire at his death, he was called "the Cotton King", and "the old Field-Marshal of the Home Trade". A Nonconformist of broad, indeed ecumenical, sympathies, he was impatient of sectarian wrangling and more interested in morality than dogma, putting the Bible and hymns before all else. A passionate believer in education, he had established libraries and

View from the City

Knowledge-based industry and innovation have always been key drivers for change in Manchester, and our Universities have for many years been at the hub of our knowledge economy. Combined with strong civic leadership, a robust workforce and a nurturing environment, Manchester has a powerful mix of academic economic potential which it is important to maximise.

By joining the strengths of the former centres of education, the new Manchester University is delivering a world-class powerhouse of knowledge, which will unlock academic expertise and associated commercial spin-outs. The knowledge businesses can create local jobs and training opportunities, and their products will improve Manchester's profile as a centre of innovation and creativity.

The University plays a crucial role in development of the City, the main economic engine of both the wider city region and also Northwest England.

Sir Howard Bernstein
Chief Executive, Manchester City Council

Life in the City

I came to Manchester in 1979 to take a degree in Combined Studies at the Victoria University. Looking back, it was the city as much as the degree course which first drew me here. My life has been tied up with Manchester ever since.

I've always been fascinated by this city with such a significant history – political phenomena such as Chartism, the Free Trade movement, women's suffrage movement, and its traditions of radical politics. Manchester has been a crucible of ideas, and a dynamic city as a result, for 200 years. In the late 1970s it was also a place whose cutting edge contemporary youth culture seemed totally in that tradition and that appealed to me personally.

Aside from my studies, the dominant learning experience for me at University was journalism. I cut my teeth working as a roving reporter on *The Mancunion* during my later years as a student, and was fortunate enough to be part of the editorial team which won the prestigious NUS/Guardian Award for Best Student Paper in 1982–3.

Strangely, it was an unsuccessful attempt to be elected to the sabbatical position of Editor which led to my entry into journalism and publishing. Over a Rusholme curry I plotted the launch of an entirely new publication with two fellow student journalists. *City Life*, which launched in December 1983, quickly became a mainstay of and focus for the lively alternative arts scene in the city which had failed to secure coverage in the mainstream media. We ran interviews with leading local artists such as Morrissey of The Smiths, who was an enthusiastic early supporter. Later, when I left *City Life* to become a freelance journalist in 1988, I wrote numerous pieces for national papers on the emergent 'Madchester' music scene whose leading lights were all well known to me through *City Life*.

After a stint as Diary Editor for *The Manchester Evening News*, I set up the public relations agency Spin Media (now Spinoza Kennedy Vesey Public Relations) in 1998. Working for the tourism body Marketing Manchester to promote the positive changes in the city has been a key element of our work, especially around the Commonwealth Games in 2002. In 2004 it was a great privilege to be invited to become first Chair of the Alumni Association at the newly merged University. I hope my strong links with the City can help widen alumni participation in University life and encourage graduates to return here to see for themselves the exciting changes taking place in the City as well as the University.

Andrew Spinoza
Chair of the Alumni Association
BA Hons Combined Studies 1982

schools in his mills, and presented books to impecunious Free Church ministers to keep them up to date with the latest religious thought. His widow determined to establish a library which she at first intended to be a Nonconformist library of theology for the north of England – a sculpture, prominent in the foyer, represented "Theology Directing the Labours of Science and Art" (visitors who mistook Theology for the Virgin Mary would have given Mrs Rylands no pleasure). But Mrs Rylands' interests, influenced by her first librarian, expanded to embrace the humanities and she bought whole collections of books and manuscripts rather than concentrating on a single discipline. She helped to transfer beautiful things from landed estates and country houses, suffering from agricultural depression, to industrial and commercial cities, as if the rising bourgeoisie were gaining on the feudal aristocracy. In 1892 she acquired in its entirety and saved from export the famous library of Althorp, the possession of the Spencer earls, forebears of the late Diana, Princess of Wales, who chose to sell their books rather than their china. In 1901 she purchased the magnificent collection of over 6,000 illuminated and other manuscripts housed at Haigh Hall, seat of the Earls of Crawford and Balcarres, premier earls of Scotland and coal owners in the region of Wigan.

With minute attention to detail, Mrs Rylands supervised the construction of the Gothic library building on Deansgate, designed by the architect Basil Champneys and using the finest available materials. This was an unconsecrated cathedral dedicated to learning, where the side chapels off the nave were readers' alcoves and the saints (reverently if somewhat tamely depicted, in the architect's opinion) were writers, philosophers, artists, theologians and prophets. It rose,

Whitworth Park (formerly Potter's Field) as it was about 1900.

Market Street, Manchester.

by design, in the midst of a slum quarter, as if the majesty of learning were to redeem the misery of ordinary human existence. At the opening of the John Rylands Library in 1899, a speaker proclaimed: "All citizens who desire to see England illumined, reasonable, right, will rejoice that there came into the heart of one who inherited the wealth of this great Manchester merchant the desire to create for him so seemly a monument as this." From the beginning, the Library had a sympathetic relationship with Owens College and the University, the Vice-Chancellor presiding over the Library Council and professors giving on its premises lectures subsequently published in a respected

The Wheel of Manchester in Exchange Square.

learned journal, *The Bulletin of the John Rylands Library.*

The endowments were ample indeed, but they remained virtually unchanged after the death of Mrs Rylands. From 1921 onwards the Librarian was annually alluding to a "disastrously high" rise in costs. Though not driven to the same expedients as the Whitworth, and successful at attracting grants and launching appeals, the Library was standing "insecurely still" in its financial arrangements throughout the 1950s and 1960s, its staff shrinking even as demands upon their time increased. Like most libraries of a certain age, the Rylands was engaged in a perpetual struggle to conserve, protect and catalogue its holdings and to house them in decent conditions, at the correct levels of temperature and humidity, lest they disintegrate through damp and mould or fall victim to fire or theft.

Logic suggested that a permanent solution to the difficulties of the Rylands could only lie in a merger with the University Library on Oxford Road and a division of function between the two sites, with all the rare books and most of the manuscripts and archives concentrated at Deansgate. Effected in 1972, the merger created the John Rylands University Library of Manchester, known in the trade as Jerusalem. Now the fourth great library in England, almost on a par with those of Oxford, Cambridge and the British Museum, it gave impetus to a bold but ultimately unsuccessful campaign to establish a copyright library in Manchester, legally entitled, as were the others, to receive a free copy of every book published in the United Kingdom – a move that would have lifted a great burden from its book-buying budget and released funds for other ends.

Sadly, the merger was far from solving all financial problems, for the University itself faced heavy financial cuts in the 1980s, at a

The John Rylands Library, Deansgate.

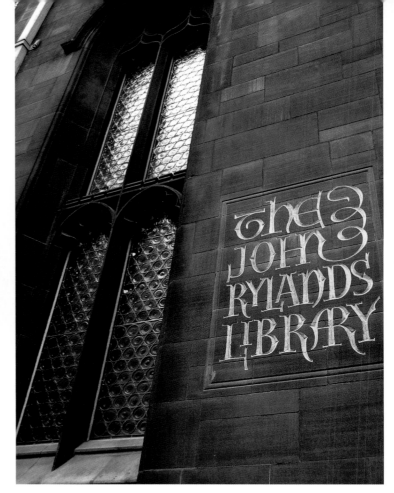

time when the Rylands had made huge acquisitions but fallen behind with the task of cataloguing them. Critics began to insinuate that the library in Deansgate was declining into a mausoleum and that an institution that stored precious items but did not make them available was failing in its duty to the scholarly community. Self-help was called for and plans were devised. Proposals to form a Research Institute and to project a more arresting image of Deansgate's treasures were drawn up in 1986. But one of the methods adopted to finance the new Institute incurred censure and damaged the University's reputation. A small circle of librarians selected for sale by auction about a hundred early printed books, questionably described as "duplicates" of other holdings, taken both from the Spencer library and from another special collection of Renaissance works bequeathed to the University by the lawyer Richard Copley Christie. The University was clearly within the law in selling the books, but its moral right to dispose of such precious goods was publicly and embarrassingly questioned – "Who can imagine the distress which this sale would cause Mrs Rylands?" Was the University breaking faith both with her and with the people of Manchester, and would benefactors ever again trust it to look after their gifts?

Resting on the proceeds (£1.6m) of the sale at Sotheby's in 1988, the John Rylands Research Institute bore a heavy responsibility for redeeming the honour of the University. During the 1990s the Institute, which gave fellowships and bursaries to catalogue archives and manuscripts, helped the Library to know its own possessions and to present itself and them to the world. Resolute efforts were made to dispel the rarefied and slightly sepulchral atmosphere which hung about the Rylands and to present the University's outpost in the city centre as a visitor attraction which would enhance the appeal of Manchester. Appropriately, the new exhibition cases built by Fine Furniture Designs of Evesham first housed an exhibition entitled "Dear Madam", devoted to the tale of Mrs Rylands and the construction of the Library. The Roxburghe Club, a select body of book collectors who had opposed the sale of 1988, forgave the University sufficiently to hold a meeting in Deansgate ten years later.

In the second half of the twentieth century, as well as doing something for the city's intellectual and aesthetic life, the University and UMIST contributed to its material wellbeing. They did so partly by being a presence in south Manchester and, as universities of national and international standing, injecting money from elsewhere into the local economy. They brought money from the UGC and later the Higher Education Funding Council; money from research grants; money from student fees and maintenance grants (later loans). Much of this was spent locally on goods and services, on rents, on popular and highbrow entertainment. The sustained growth of UMIST and the University of Manchester from the late 1950s – curbed only for five or six years in the early 1980s – meant that by 1992–3 the University and UMIST had between them about 20,000 undergraduate and postgraduate students, some 4,000 academic staff, and over 3,000 non-academic staff. About a third of their academic staff and 86 per cent of their students lived within the City of Manchester. As a *Guardian* journalist remarked in 1994, "students, not iron or coal or china clay, are the new natural resource". Education, and providing for the needs of those engaged with it, had become a major Mancunian industry, and the University precinct was said to

Part 2
Academic Achievements and Developments

Arts and Theology

BRIAN PULLAN

Brian Pullan describes the characteristics of two faculties which at first were separate entities but eventually came together in the late 1980s; both have since been absorbed into the present day Faculty of Humanities. His discussion of the Faculty of Arts pays special attention to three outstanding figures: the philosopher Samuel Alexander, the historian Lewis Namier, and the literary scholar Eugène Vinaver.

Between 1903 and 1914 the newly independent University of Manchester divided itself into nine faculties: Arts, Science, Law, Music, Medicine, Commerce, Theology, Technology and Education. The Arts Faculty, sprawling and heterogeneous, containing in the 1950s at least one-fifth of the University's students and two-fifths of the women among them, came to consist in the main of three large building blocks. One comprised languages and literature (ancient, medieval and modern, English, European and Middle though not Far Eastern); another the historical disciplines, including archaeology and the history of art; while a third sector, which housed geography, architecture and town and country planning, studied the built and natural environments. Some departments, such as philosophy, did not fit easily into this general scheme, and others straddled the great segments, as did the interdisciplinary American studies, established after the Second World War and devoted to the study of American history, literature and politics. Intellectually, Arts ranged from the liberal arts to the fringes of the social and natural sciences, both of which found a place in geography, and in the fields of architecture and planning it maintained professional schools. The intellectual foundations of about two-thirds of the faculty had been

laid by the mid-1880s, if not earlier; a chair of Architecture was established in 1903, a chair of Geography in 1930, and a separate department of Town and Country Planning in 1952. During the rationalising late 1980s, the Faculty of Arts absorbed the two much smaller faculties of Music and Theology, and Theology became a department of Religious Studies.

The larger faculties were clusters of cognate departments charged with approving and regulating academic courses. They deliberated through Boards, over which Deans presided. Unlike Senate, these included mere readers and lecturers, but professors, though outnumbered, were still the captains and the kings, and the Boards did not at first represent bold forays into academic democracy. Indeed, the historian A.J.P. Taylor, joining the Arts Board as a lecturer in 1936, was considered uppity for speaking on

The borrowing counter at the Arts Library in 1944.

of doctrine could not be treated objectively or scientifically, and there seemed to be some risk of importing bitter and embarrassing sectarian conflict. Freed from the federal chains, however, the new University launched a Faculty of Theology in 1904, one of only five in the country, and equipped it with Chairs of Semitic Languages, Biblical Exegesis and Comparative Religion. Behind the decision lay some confidence that it would prove possible to divorce facts from faith and to avoid asking examination candidates to state their personal beliefs.

For many years this faculty was, in effect, a professional school for candidates for the ministry, run with the collaboration of the Manchester theological colleges, and particularly of the Nonconformist establishments – Congregationalist, Methodist, Baptist, Unitarian and Moravian. Many of their teachers became part-time university lecturers. Arthur Samuel Peake, the first Rylands Professor of Biblical Exegesis and the author of a famous one-volume commentary on the Bible, was a Primitive Methodist and a layman whose career had been devoted to teaching in a theological college. A devout man of broad sympathies who became the first Dean of Theology, he was called a preserver rather than a maker of peace, because his diplomatic skills never allowed the peace to be shattered. Manchester was the first university to make compulsory for ordinands a course in Comparative Religion (often taught by orientalists, experts in Buddhism and Hinduism). However, the purpose of the move was not to make candidates think twice about their Christian convictions or regard other religions as equally valid: rather, they were to become aware of them as stages in an evolutionary process, moving towards Christianity as the "full, final truth". A genuine acceptance of religious pluralism, a sense of excitement at gaining access to eastern wisdom, belonged more to the late 1960s than to the first half of the twentieth century. In the 1960s and 1970s Theology was offering a general education to most of its students rather than a professional training – between 1954 and 1979, one-third of graduates were eventually ordained, another third became teachers, and the rest took up a variety of occupations, including social work, industry and commerce. The Faculty's most eminent teachers, such as Peake, Manson and Bruce, taught in a non-insistent, non-dogmatic way, presenting students with alternatives rather than telling them what to think. Professor Bruce, a Plymouth Brother and a Fellow of the British Academy, would often conclude with the words, "Ah well! The other fellow may be right after all."

For much of the twentieth century, Arts in Manchester was as distinguished as Science. Many famous names could be mentioned here. Manchester

Above: Sir Lewis Namier, Professor of Modern History, 1931–1953.

Left: A.J.P. Taylor, Assistant Lecturer and Lecturer in History, 1930–1938 (afterwards Fellow of Magdalen College, Oxford).

Below: The bronze bust of Samuel Alexander, by Jacob Epstein, stands in the Arts Building.

behalf of his professor, Lewis Namier, who could not or would not master the tiresome intricacies of everyday business. By the late 1960s, however, the faculty had become notoriously disputatious. An encomium of a former Dean of Arts in that decade called his job "an office which, possibly among all the Deanships, least resembles a sinecure, argumentativeness, clamour and inquietude being almost habitual to the proceedings of the Board of that Faculty".

It had proved politically impossible to organise religious teaching within the federal, transpennine Victoria University of the late nineteenth century. The university colleges in Liverpool and Leeds were more rigidly opposed than Owens to the idea, but everywhere misgivings arose: Owens and the University were not intended to be godless, but were supposed to be "colour-blind to theological and denominational differences". There was no objection to teaching Greek, Hebrew and ecclesiastical history (all things vital to ordinands), but arguably questions

Eugène Vinaver, Professor of French Language and Literature.

scholars are well represented in the *Dictionary of British Classicists* and *The Blackwell Dictionary of Historians,* to say nothing of the British Academy obituaries of their Fellows and the *Dictionary of National Biography,* where their achievements are expertly recounted and analysed. Perhaps invidiously, this chapter will dwell on three figures of great stature and wide learning, whose presence in Manchester for many years brought glory to the University that sheltered them – people whose seminal ideas, disputable perhaps but impossible to ignore, provoked vigorous and prolonged debate in scholarly circles.

Samuel Alexander (1859–1938), born in Sydney, educated at Melbourne and Oxford, the first practising Jew to hold an Oxford Fellowship, was Professor of Philosophy from 1893 to 1924; he was appointed to the Order of Merit by the Labour Prime Minister, Ramsay Macdonald, in 1930. His bust by Epstein, placed in the foyer, has long been the Arts Faculty's icon. Is it revered as an Epstein, or as the image of Alexander? His memory is honoured partly, perhaps, because he realised an ideal often cherished but seldom attained – that the humanities ought to make people civilised, kindly, shrewd and happy as well as able to think and to know. His was "a personality almost unbelievably free from egotism or littleness"; he was nettled only by complaints

that his handwriting was impenetrable, and parsimonious only in his habit of writing on the unused side of old examination scripts. Alexander was the uncrowned king of the mortar-board suburb of Withington whose Wednesday evenings were famous; a left-wing radical unaligned with any political party, and "a sort of godfather of the women's side" in the University. He was very much the endearing, absent-minded professor whose machines for measuring pleasure and vanity (he was drawn to experimental psychology) had about them a touch of Heath Robinson if not of Professor Branestawm. Marie Stopes, dropping in on his classes in search of hints on how to lecture, was distressed to see that he wiped the board with his mackintosh and still more that the students failed to get him a duster. His lectures, at least to advanced honours classes, consisted of thinking aloud, as if in the presence of fellow students. "He poured out to us wisdom so profound and knowledge that was so exciting – and often so disturbing – as to leave us in a state of wonderment as to what we were going to do with it all" (thus the recollections of Frederick Marquis, later Lord Woolton, the future wartime Minister of Food and Chancellor of the University).

Alexander's eccentricities had their practical side: legend reported that if his cycling clothes looked inelegantly bulky, he was probably setting off for a country house weekend and wearing everything he would need underneath, including his dinner jacket and pyjamas. His absent-mindedness could be creative. His question "What are you writing?" prompted the children's author and adult essayist Alison Uttley to take to writing and led to a long Platonic friendship, though he had in fact mistaken her for another former student with the same maiden name. His great metaphysical work, *Space, Time and Deity,* appeared in two volumes in 1920. As A.J.P. Taylor put it: "In his view, God was always round the corner. When you reached the corner, God had slipped round the next one, and on you went." He philosophised, among much else, about what he modestly called "the damned clichés", the eternal questions about goodness, truth, beauty and value. But all knowledge was his province, and he could lecture beautifully about Jane Austen, Molière and Dr Johnson. Refusing the sonorous title of Public Orator, he became the University's first Presenter of Honorary Graduands, and developed the device of the back-handed compliment which has been used until recently. Witness the Alexander tribute to a generous man: "With such pockets it hardly excites wonder that he has the reputation of being the worst-dressed man in Manchester." Pots, as his audience may have reflected, can sometimes call kettles black.

Lewis Namier (1888–1960), born the son of a landowner in Austrian Galicia, commanded less general affection: he was, wrote his second wife in a vivid biography, either loved or detested, seldom merely liked. In 1931 a generous review of Namier's second major book, *England in the Age of the American Revolution*, by the Cambridge professor G.M. Trevelyan, prompted a kindly and impulsive Manchester professor, Ernest Jacob, to telegraph Namier and invite him to meet a Senate Committee with a view to being appointed to the long-vacant chair of Modern History. This Namier was to hold for twenty-two years. He, Trevelyan had said, had found a new way of describing how things happened in the past, "a new method of tasting the intellectual pleasures of history". His approach to the history of politics and the political elite was through the biography of everyone taking part, through knowing as much as could be known about the motives and interests of individuals, however puny, flawed and apparently insignificant they might be. Of the Frankfurt Parliament of 1848, he asked "who the chaps really were and why each was there". Ideas, in his view, had no force in themselves; you must look at the people who held them. A close colleague, John Brooke, wrote that Namier brought to history "the post-Freudian conception of the mind: the belief that the reasons men give for their actions are rationalisations designed to cloak their deeper purposes". He believed not only in psychoanalysis but also in graphology – the journalist Malcolm Muggeridge described his efforts to consult "some necromancer, who specialised in deducing people's characters from their handwriting". Eschewing grand narrative, he and his disciples concentrated on structural analysis of the mechanisms of electoral and governmental processes, rather than on chronicling parliamentary debates or examining the actual exercise of power. His interests lay both in the England of George III and in nineteenth- and twentieth-century Europe, especially in the dire consequences of aggressive German nationalism. A Zionist moved by an abiding hatred of Germany, he was, with his lecturer A.J.P. Taylor, a vigorous anti-appeaser in the late 1930s and a strenuous champion of Jewish refugees.

Namier's critics taxed him with taking the mind out of history, with belittling the role of party in politics. He was called everything from a "towering outsider" to a "Tory Marxist" and a "gigantic, myopic caterpillar", crawling over the letters and diaries of third-rate politicians which he discovered on "paper chases"

In a drawing by C.G. Phillips, an Arts professor loses his notes in Oxford Road.

History in the 1970s

The teaching in the Department of History was uniformly very good and in my experience Drs. Chris Haigh and Ian Kershaw were outstanding as researchers, lecturers and tutors. Despite the background and culture of student radicalism at the time, I remember that my medieval history tutorials with Professor Roskill were very formal affairs. Ladies were invariably addressed as "Miss" (whether married or not) and male students always by their surnames.

I have abiding memories of sharing the lift in the Arts building on several mornings with Professor Gaston Gadoffre, Professor of French, and with the evil miasma of his smelly, rasping Gaulloises. You emerged on the second floor impregnated with the *Entente Cordiale* on your clothes for the rest of the day. It was many years later that I learned that our own Head of Department (Professor M.R.D. Foot) had been an MI9/SOE liaison officer with Gaston Gadoffre's *Resistante* group in France in 1944. I have often wondered what were the odds that both would find themselves working as academic colleagues in an English Northern University some twenty-five years later. But then Manchester in the early 1970s was just that sort of place.

My idyll came to an end in the summer of 1973 when I graduated at the age of 20. I never really realised how well we were taught until five years later when I took a History PGCE at a leading university in the southwest of England. The students of course came from over thirty different universities and polytechnics but I discovered that few indeed had ever read *Beowulf* in Anglo Saxon, Dante's *Inferno* in Italian or the *Gesta Henrici Quinti* in medieval Latin. I am profoundly grateful to Manchester for all those experiences, undergone ambivalently at the time but in retrospect so enriching.

Kevin Tuhey
BA Hons History, 1973

through English country houses. But since, as he observed, "What I really like is to train the young in research," he fitted well into the history school founded by T.F. Tout, which demanded that even undergraduate finalists should practise the trade, sift evidence for themselves and write modest dissertations under the supervision of established scholars. Namier loved to show promising pupils the best way to use the Manuscripts Room in the British Museum. He struck home, too, at first-year level: a favourite pupil, Ninetta Jucker, remembered him setting an essay on "what is and should be in a newspaper; it determined my future career".

The entrance to the newly refurbished Arts Building on Oxford Road.

Some found Namier's prose as fine as Conrad's. Memorable judgements punctuate the masses of intricate detail in his pages – as when he writes of the House of Commons under George III: "Men went there to 'make a figure' and no more dreamed of a seat in the House in order to benefit humanity than a child dreams of a birthday cake that others may eat it; which is perfectly normal and in no way reprehensible." Loved or loathed, he himself made a figure in Manchester and the academic world beyond. In the words of the historian John Kenyon:

> Witness after witness testifies (as I can myself) to the overwhelming impact of his person and his personality. His physique itself was impressive to a degree: the guttural, rather toneless voice, intense and implacable; the broad shoulders, the beaked nose, the fathomless eyes, above all, his absolute stillness, the stillness, one felt, of a flywheel revolving too fast for the human eye.

This calls to mind an undergraduate description of Macaulay in Cambridge in the 1820s, as "a presence with gigantic power instinct". Namier, who had no use for Whigs, heroes, idealists or tales of unfolding liberty, was in that sense Manchester's Macaulay.

No less cosmopolitan, Eugène Vinaver (1899–1979) was the Professor of French Language and Literature who shone new light on the first great English prose epic. His masterpiece, first published in 1947, was an edition of the works of Sir Thomas Malory, the disreputable (or much maligned) Warwickshire knight who composed in prison his own distinctive version of eight romances extracted from the French Arthurian cycle of the thirteenth century. The son of a Russian lawyer and politician who had emigrated with his family to France after the Revolution of 1917, Vinaver was drawn to Manchester in 1933 by the presence in the Rylands Library of one of the two extant copies of the version of Malory's *Morte d'Arthur* published by William Caxton in 1485. Vinaver had almost completed his work, and was beginning to turn to Racine, when the Librarian of Winchester College discovered a manuscript of Malory's writings, ampler and more authentic than Caxton's printed book. This made it possible, in the editor's words, to see Malory's work in the making, as "a series of separate romances each representing a different stage in the author's development". Vinaver argued that Malory's achievement lay partly in devising a new literary form – in combing out into separate strands and forming into self-contained units stories in the Arthurian cycle which had once been interlaced in a manner so complex as to make immense demands on any reader's memory and concentration. He provoked much scholarly dispute by denying the unity of Malory's work, which he deliberately published under the title *Works*. But he would not have it that all literature should be judged by unchanging, absolute standards which put a premium on unity and demanded that every literary venture should have a beginning, a middle and an end; aesthetic judgements must take account of changes in taste and fashion, and Malory's "modern" simplicity was not necessarily better or more advanced than the "medieval" maze of the French romances. He wrote:

> To become absorbed in the less obvious features of Flaubert's novels, in the strange labyrinth of James Joyce, in that of Marcel Proust and the apparent incoherences of T.S. Eliot is to become receptive to medieval verse and prose and to accept them on their own terms as they are and for what they are.

Kindly, civilised, wise, and wearing his learning lightly (it was never confined to the Middle Ages or to France), Vinaver was an inspiring teacher who never regarded first-year language classes as a chore unworthy of a professor: it was on the youngest students that the deepest impressions might be made. An outspoken academic liberal, Vinaver delivered to the staff forum in 1961 a forceful attack on the hierarchical principles that governed most British universities outside Oxford and Cambridge; universities, for him, were institutions designed for free inquiry, and he rejected analogies with entities such as business corporations, whose purposes and functions were altogether different. He was an entrepreneur himself, however, not only founding learned journals (Arthuriana developed into Medium Aevum), but also suggesting Arthurian subjects to a Swiss ceramics firm which made collectors' plates and securing a royalty that funded the publications of the Vinaver Trust. He was something of a university politician, although his elegant style was not always well received in an institution given to bluntness. One glimpse of him sharing his wisdom comes from Not

Today and Tomorrow

The 'arts and theology' students of today will, according to their discipline, find their home in the School of Languages, Linguistics and Cultures, or the School of Arts, Histories and Cultures.

Behind the structural re-organisation lies a fundamental commitment at the University to pursue research and educate students at a multi-disciplinary level. In consequence, many areas of emerging strength in the humanities at Manchester draw in academics from a wide range of schools and disciplines.

The School of Arts, Histories and Cultures embraces some eight disciplinary areas creating many opportunities for synergy in research. Areas in which the School has strong interests include the cultural and historical study of war and politics, popular culture, collective and personal memory, sexuality and gender, and belief systems. The launch by the Archbishop of Canterbury in November 2006 of the new Institute for Religion and Civil Society is a particularly exciting development. The Institute is dedicated to advanced research into the relationships between religion and civil society, seeking to better understand, for example, the changing role played by religion within the public sphere.

Much work in the Humanities manifests a strong global outreach. In the School of Languages, Linguistics and Cultures, this is demonstrated by the investment of nearly £1m to establish a Centre for Chinese Studies in 2004. The Centre provides a focus for

Martin Amis, novelist and Professor of Creative Writing at Manchester.

the University's research and teaching programmes designed to understand and engage with the emergence of China as a world power. The presence of over 1,600 students from China at the University, as well as the prestigious award of the UK's second Confucius Institute to the City of Manchester, underlines the significance of the University's efforts to develop expertise in the World's next superpower.

An exciting development for 2007 is the establishment of a Centre for New Writing at Manchester, designed to develop and refine students' creative and critical work, and to explore and research collaboration between creative and critical writing. This move is accompanied by the appointment of leading British novelist, Martin Amis, as a Professor of Creative Writing at the University, in his first teaching post. He joins the University as the latest in a series of iconic appointments of world-renowned scholars, including Nobel Prize winner Professor Joseph E. Stiglitz and leading social scientist Professor Robert Putnam.

Entitled, the autobiography of the critic Frank Kermode, a Professor of English towards 1960 who was outsmarted in a contest for the allocation of junior posts by Bernard Lovell, the radio astronomer of Jodrell Bank. Retreating in confusion, Kermode accepted Vinaver's invitation to share a cigarette. "He meant this literally, for he took a cigarette out of his case, produced a small pair of scissors, and cut it in half. As we smoked the fragrant fragments, he explained to me the hopelessness of going into meetings of the kind we'd just left without preparation, without, that is, hours of persistent and crafty lobbying …"

In Arts as in other regions of the University, complete academics of the stature of Alexander and Vinaver, and formidable, eccentric innovators of the calibre of Namier became progressively rarer from the 1960s onwards. Arts was vulnerable to suggestions that the glory had departed, that great traditions were beginning to ossify: as the academic profession expanded, the lure of new universities was added to the insidious attractions of Oxford, Cambridge and London. In the 1980s Arts suffered particularly

heavily from government disfavour and a shortage of funding for research in the humanities, a situation partially remedied in the following decades. But certain parts of the faculty, including Middle Eastern studies and some language departments, benefited from the policy of concentrating highly specialised minority subjects in favoured universities. And the faculty continued to provide the University with poetry, scepticism, novels, satires, and a measure of self-mockery. As a highly articulate body of academics, inclined to suspect higher authority of being up to no good and to believe that the price of liberty was constant vigilance, Arts was the despair of more than one Vice-Chancellor. But it was shrewd enough to respond to demands that, in return for aid and encouragement, departments should coalesce into larger units called schools and practise economies of scale, in the hope of saving administrative time and concentrating on scholarly work. With the advent of the new University in 2004 the faculty itself was caught up into the larger paradise of the Faculty of Humanities, joining forces with the social sciences on which it had once impinged.

Physics and Radio-Astronomy

BRIAN PULLAN

In his Anatomy of Britain *the late Anthony Sampson observed that "the outward appearance of universities is no clue to their scholarship: Manchester, one of the bleakest, produced three Nobel prizewinners in a row and for twenty years contained the most distinguished historian, Sir Lewis Namier, while several pleasant places are classed as 'academic Siberia'." This chapter is not a comprehensive scholarly dissertation on one of Manchester's most famous schools, but a lay person's tale of the impact on Manchester and the scientific community of three Nobel prizewinners who in succession held the Langworthy Chair of Physics: Ernest Rutherford, who reigned from 1907 to 1919; William Lawrence Bragg, professor from 1919 to 1937, and Patrick Blackett, who held the post from 1937 to 1953.*

The Schuster Building, by H.M. Fairhurst (one of the group of science buildings east of Oxford Road erected between 1957 and 1967). It replaced the Physics Buildings of 1900 and 1932 in Coupland Street.

In the autumn of 1906 Arthur Schuster, eighteen years Langworthy Professor, the scientific son of an immigrant German merchant family, was fondly disposing of his chair as if it were a cherished private estate, with little intervention from university administrators:

> I am so strongly attached to the place that I could not bear to leave my position here except to someone who will keep up its reputation and increase it. There is no one to whom I will leave it with greater freedom from anxiety than yourself. I hope to find a seat on the Council here and you may be sure that I shall always stand up for the interests of the Physical Department.

He was rich enough to contemplate early retirement and generous enough to finance from his own pocket for a few years a new Readership in Mathematical Physics. The rising star in his sights was a research professor at McGill University in Montreal, correctly rumoured to be eager to return to the intellectual mainstream in Europe and secure prompt publication for the results of his experiments.

Ernest Rutherford (1871–1937) was a New Zealander schooled, as Schuster himself had been, at the Cavendish laboratory in Cambridge, and a protégé of J.J. Thomson, the discoverer of the electron, who had been a student of Owens College before proceeding to Cambridge. Rutherford's field was radioactivity, the new natural alchemy: certain rare elements, it seemed, were transforming themselves over time into other things, and doing so by firing off minute particles at great speed; their atoms were disintegrating spontaneously and "emanating"

The radio telescope at Jodrell Bank, Cheshire.

Academy) as a tool for exploring the ultimate mystery of the physical universe – the constitution of the atom and the secrets of its nucleus.

The new professor was a large, boisterous, unceremonious man of bucolic appearance often compared with a colonial farmer or (less literally) with a force of nature, no respecter of rank and a foe to the pretentious. He was an inspirer, an optimist, none the less prone to outbursts of fury, a tribal chieftain known as "Papa" who "gingered up", occasionally railed at and frequently entertained his team of researchers without undue aggression. Generously, he allowed full credit to junior colleagues for researches that he had suggested and they pursued, and was no lover of public wrangling or jealous contests for public recognition. "To be with Rutherford is like spending a weekend at the seaside," wrote a fellow New Zealander, David Florance. "His mind was like the bow of a battleship," said James Chadwick, the discoverer of the neutron, who worked with him at Manchester and Cambridge. "There was so much weight behind it, it had no need to be sharp as a razor."

Rutherford's department soon became both classless and truly international. His reputation brought to England Hans Geiger from Erlangen, who devised with Rutherford and years later perfected a famous instrument for counting alpha-particles. Schuster's readership supported Niels Bohr from Copenhagen, who helped Rutherford improve his model of the atom. The team included Harry Moseley, whose outstanding work on atomic numbers, setting out elements in numerical order from hydrogen to uranium according to the number of protons in the nucleus, would surely have won him the highest distinction had he not been killed in the Dardanelles.

Chaim Weizmann, then a lecturer in chemistry at Manchester, saw Rutherford as the antithesis of Einstein. "As scientists the two men were contrasting types, Einstein all calculation, Rutherford all experiment ... He worked by intuition and whatever he touched turned to gold." His mind's eye, not given to abstraction but to exact visions of the invisible, to pungent metaphors and to striking analogies, saw the minute world of his investigations in lively terms: ions, famously, were "jolly little beggars ... I can

new substances or gases endowed with different properties from their parent bodies. This prospect had opened before him in the late 1890s with the discovery by other pioneers of the radioactive properties of uranium and thorium and the extraction by the Curies of polonium and radium from pitchblende. Rutherford had distinguished between alpha-, beta- and gamma-radiation and worked on the borderlands between physics and chemistry with a bright and astringent collaborator, Frederick Soddy; his authoritative book, *Radioactivity*, was in its second edition. Within a year of arriving in Manchester, Rutherford (then engaged in territorial disputes with the local professor of Chemistry) was awarded the Nobel Prize for Chemistry, an event that prompted jokes about his own "instantaneous transformation". His Nobel address in Stockholm was on the chemical nature of the alpha-particles proceeding from radioactive substances, describing them as projected helium atoms releasing some of their electrons as they plunged through matter. During his twelve years in Manchester he was to use radioactivity (with radium borrowed from the Austrian

Above: Students at work in an old Chemistry laboratory, 1940.

Right: Hans Geiger (left) and Ernest Rutherford in Basement Room 1 of the Coupland Building, 1909.

almost see them". In the Cavendish tradition he favoured relatively simple, inexpensive apparatus, preferably constructed by the investigator himself, though a skilled glassblower was needed to make the tubes of exquisite thinness required to demonstrate that the alpha-particle was a helium nucleus. "Papa says you'll do," said kindly William Kay, the laboratory steward, to a new recruit, Edward Andrade, in the session of 1913–14. "He saw you making that plateholder out of cardboard and thought you made a good job of it." Rutherford's dictum, "Gentlemen, there is no money, we shall have to use our brains," has resurfaced in various forms. Curiosity alone drove him; he had little thought of any military applications or medical or commercial potential for his work, save that his wartime researches on the detection of submarines by sound waves were of direct practical importance and he had some claim to be one of the inventors of sonar. Speaking in Manchester in 1961, the elderly Professor Andrade recalled the halcyon days of the craft physics workshop which preceded the modern degree-and-discovery factory, a vanished idyll with "the professor in closest touch with all his research men, who, with little thought for their future living, were eagerly engaging themselves in obtaining results that seemed remote from any possible application'.

Rutherford's department was not the best place for students to acquire a solid grounding in classical physics, but they were themselves on the edge of discoveries. The startling results of an experiment in the scattering of alpha-particles assigned to a third-year undergraduate, Ernest Marsden, enabled Rutherford, after pondering for more than a year, to say that he now knew what the atom looked like; he propounded the theory depicting the atom as something like a planetary system, with electrons orbiting in empty space round a tiny, densely charged nucleus, no larger proportionately than a fly in a cathedral. Of Marsden's result which, on a screen viewed through his microscope in a darkened room, showed particles rebounding from a sheet of gold foil, he said, "It was almost as incredible as if you had fired a 15-inch shell at a piece of tissue paper and it came back and hit you."

To study the nucleus you must break into it and, through disintegration, transform an element – man-made alchemy, an artificial transmutation, must join the natural alchemy of radioactive substances. In 1917–19, assisted only by William Kay as observer, Rutherford snatched time from war work to conduct the experiments in which he used alpha-particles from a form of radium to disrupt a nitrogen nucleus and knock hydrogen nuclei out of it. He was not precisely splitting atoms but certainly

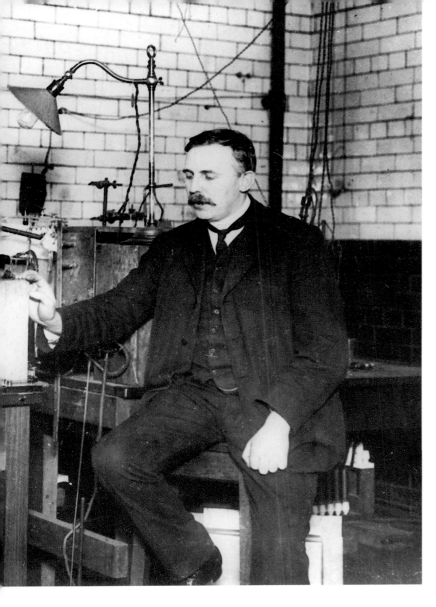

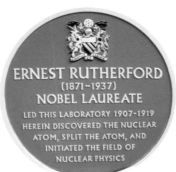

Memorial plaque to Rutherford, Coupland Street.

chipping one, and turning nitrogen into a form of oxygen. The "ultimate importance" of this discovery, he was reported to have said, was "far greater than that of the war".

Rutherford's company of researchers had scattered when war broke out. He himself left for Cambridge in 1919 to succeed J.J. Thomson (by now Master of Trinity) as Professor of Physics and Director of the Cavendish Laboratory. "They were happy days in Manchester and we wrought better than we knew," he wrote to Hans Geiger, years after his departure. Though revolutionary, the methods employed at Manchester, using particle-projectiles moving at their natural velocity, could inflict the desired damage only on a few light elements – including, as well as nitrogen, boron, sodium, aluminium and phosphorus. In the mid-1920s, however, a former Manchester student joined Rutherford's laboratory in Cambridge. This was John Cockcroft, from Todmorden in the Calder Valley. He had read mathematics at Owens (and heard Rutherford lecture) before joining up, and electrical engineering at Tech under Professor Miles Walker after his release from the Royal Artillery in 1919. Cockcroft had been a

"college apprentice" in the Research and Education Department of the Manchester firm of Metropolitan Vickers; acting as "spare-time honorary electrical engineer to the Laboratory", he provided liaison between Metro-Vick and the Cavendish. With their assistance, he helped to develop high-voltage apparatus designed to accelerate charged particles to very high speeds (his mathematical skills enabled him to calculate that the voltage would not have to be astronomical – 300,000 might do, whereas 8–10 million had been talked of). By trial and error, in an enterprise lasting over three years, Cockcroft and his colleague Ernest Walton built the machinery that enabled them to split the nucleus of an atom in Cambridge in April 1932, by firing protons (hydrogen nuclei) at lithium, giving rise to the equation "Lithium + Hydrogen = two atoms of Helium + some energy".

At Manchester, Rutherford was succeeded by a very young Nobel prizewinner, William Lawrence Bragg. He would win the Physics Department great eminence in a field that some scientists regarded as scarcely a branch of physics, if only because it impinged on several other disciplines. This was the use of X-rays to reveal the structures of increasingly complicated crystalline substances. As Bragg's Royal Society biographer, Sir David Phillips, explained:

> Walking along the Backs in Cambridge one day in the autumn of 1912, William Lawrence Bragg had an idea that led immediately to a dramatic advance in physics and has since transformed chemistry, mineralogy, metallurgy and, most recently, biology. He realised that the observations of X-ray diffraction by a crystal, which had been reported by von Laue and his associates earlier in that year, can be interpreted very simply as arising from reflection of the X-rays by planes of atoms in the crystal and hence that the X-ray observations provide evidence from which the arrangement of atoms in the crystal may be determined.

William Lawrence Bragg (1890–1971) was the son of William Henry Bragg (1862–1942), an English-born professor who had embarked on research at the age of forty when holding a chair at

William Lawrence (later Sir Lawrence) Bragg, Professor of Physics 1919–37; Nobel Laureate 1915.

Adelaide; in 1904 he had embarked on lengthy correspondence with Rutherford, then in Montreal, about the range and flight path of radioactive particles. Now adjusting to the grimness of Leeds and sustained by Rutherford's friendship, Bragg senior worked closely with his son and developed the spectrometer on which the life work of both depended: the son had the revelation and formulated "Bragg's law", the father devised the instrument for pursuing the idea. Together they analysed the structure of the diamond and in 1915 they were jointly awarded the Nobel Prize for Physics. But their relationship became uneasy; Bragg senior, a gentleman and no heavy father, was kindly and generous, bursting with pride in his boy's achievements, but it was often supposed too readily that as an established scientist he must have been the guiding figure in their partnership, and the son's longing for direct recognition affected his own self-confidence.

Faced with the well-nigh impossible task of succeeding Rutherford, Lawrence Bragg enjoyed the wholehearted support of the Vice-Chancellor, Sir Henry Miers, formerly Professor of Mineralogy at Oxford, who held a special chair of Crystallography at Manchester. Miers would have liked a department of "pure crystallographic research", free of "elementary teaching and immediate applications". But Bragg and the researchers who came with him, R. W. James and E.C.S. Dickson, had to learn in the most painful way the lecturer's trade, of which they had scant experience. Their considerable military records earned them no instant respect. Bragg and James, serving with the Royal Artillery, had developed the science of sound-ranging, the technique of identifying the positions of enemy guns by means of a series of listening posts or microphones that noted the different arrival times of gun reports; Bragg was an ex-major and held a Military Cross. But post-war undergraduates were restless, wild, irreverent; medical students were especially rumbustious, and used to kick the panels of benches into matchwood when the new arrivals gave lectures. The Vice-Chancellor began to get anonymous letters accusing the novices of incompetence; luckily these outpourings eventually found other targets and ceased, as the Vice-Chancellor noted in 1924, "with the disappearance of one of the junior staff to another post (with his wife)".

Though increasingly self-confident, Bragg was not always a hit with the more literal-minded, run-of-the-mill undergraduates, on account of his anxiety to explain broad issues rather than supply every possible detail. In 1927 he noted: "The air of detachment when one is explaining a general principle and the eager scribbling in notebooks when one comes out with a fact are well known to every lecturer." His research took off again. He and his father divided the labour between them, the elder Bragg concentrating on organic structures and the younger on inorganic compounds and the physic of crystals and diffraction; a particular concern after 1925 was the structure of silicate minerals, and Bragg *fils* and his team later turned to metals and alloys. Corresponding with Rutherford in 1929 about a possible post in Cambridge, he sang the praises of Manchester, with its advantages of running a "big physics laboratory" with twenty or twenty-five research workers, and of working in a mainstream physics department rather than wearing the restrictive label of a crystallographer. A man of almost military appearance but artistic temperament (once compared in that respect to Elgar, though music was not his forte), Bragg reproached himself for lacking prosaic virtues such as the ability to remember names and cope with committees. Depression overtook him more than once in Manchester, though one bout was partly alleviated by a move from Didsbury to Alderley Edge in 1933. "You and I find *things* easier than people," he once said to his sister Gwendy.

In 1937 Bragg left Manchester with two fellow-researchers, J.A. Bradley (who had been his first research student) and Henry Lipson, at first for the National Physics Laboratory at Teddington and then, soon after Rutherford's death, for the directorship of the Cavendish. This move took nuclear physicists aback, but Bragg came to justify the tribute in the journal *Nature* to his "tact and gift of leadership", decentralising the laboratory and dividing it (by 1948) into groups working on "nuclear, radio and low-temperature physics, crystallography, metal physics and mathematical physics, with some minor groupings". One of his disciples, Lipson, returned to Tech after the war as head of Physics and also of Ophthalmic Optics; he built up crystallography in Sackville Street, persuaded Tech to start degree courses in both his subjects – Applied Physics in 1954 and Ophthalmic Optics (on the grounds that eyes were surely as important as teeth) in 1966. He became a professor in 1954, and a Fellow of the Royal Society in 1957. Mildly depressed in 1975 by an academic trade unionist's desire to involve everyone in a series of tedious and indecisive committees, Lipson warned the University against a time-wasting cult of "uninspired mediocrity" in which "the days of the Rutherfords, Alexanders and Osborne Reynoldses will never be able to recur".

Research in the physics department changed direction dramatically with the arrival in 1937 of Patrick Blackett (1897–1974), much to the pleasure of a young assistant lecturer, Bernard Lovell, who was given the task of transporting a small automatic cloud chamber from Blackett's previous quarters at Birkbeck College, London, and getting it up and running. This was an all-absorbing job which quite distracted him from routine teaching duties and earned a reprimand. His inspiring new boss was a former naval officer who had served in the Battle of Jutland. He had read mathematics and physics at Cambridge and become one of Rutherford's most promising young men in the Cavendish, charged in the wake of the great Manchester experiment with photographing the disintegration of nitrogen nuclei. He had succeeded in automating the cloud chamber invented by C.T.R. Wilson (another Manchester–Cavendish man) and in taking within a few months thousands of photographs tracking alpha-particles; a tiny number of forked paths, less than ten out of some 400,000, represented the process of atomic disintegration which Rutherford had prompted. Blackett seemed as proficient in theoretical as in experimental physics. Finding Rutherford too dictatorial, threatened with too much lecturing in Cambridge and eager to run his own show, he had changed his interests in 1932 (the Cavendish's miracle year) and begun to use his cloud chamber to explore the nature of cosmic rays – streams of minute electrically charged particles arriving from the sun and the stars, perhaps even from other galaxies, and constantly bombarding Earth and its atmosphere. He and a colleague,

Giuseppe Occhialini, using a cloud chamber controlled by Geiger counters, provided crucial evidence for the existence of the positive electron. After four years at Birkbeck he brought his interests to Manchester, turning towards astronomy and astrophysics, and also towards the study of Earth's magnetic field. Here his researches involved, among much else, taking measurements of magnetism in deep mines – he once caused a colleague in post-war Manchester to descend 1,240 metres down a Lancashire coal mine to collect essential data. At Manchester, too, he set out to plot the history of Earth's magnetic field through the study of rocks, using his magnetometer on rocks hitherto regarded as too weakly magnetised to serve this purpose – for example, red sandstones from Cheshire, which afforded one of his groups a triumph in 1953–54 when Blackett was in transit with some of his followers from Manchester to Imperial College, London. He was awarded the Nobel Prize for Physics in 1948 and delivered his Nobel lecture on "Cloud chamber researches in nuclear physics and cosmic radiation".

Arriving in Manchester, Blackett had refurbished existing territory and annexed new premises; the boldest move of all, symbolic of a new regime, was to move Rutherford's time-honoured steward, William Kay, from the top floor to a room by the entrance of the laboratory. A man of strong left-wing principles (at least, a Fabian socialist) and a champion of university expansion, Blackett was a formidable scientific politician who nevertheless discredited himself with the government for many years between 1948 and 1964 for his criticism of Anglo-American atomic policy and his seemingly pro-Russian stance. The public orator pronounced in 1962, when the University awarded Blackett an honorary Doctorate of Science:

> When he left us, with an Honours School enlarged six-fold, new Chairs of Theoretical Physics and Astronomy and Radio Astronomy established, outstations pitched on the Jungfraujoch and the Pic du Midi and a device in the making at Jodrell Bank, the Bursar must have heaved a sigh of relief that we were still solvent; but he has richly recompensed us by his company, his scientific leadership and his far-seeing ideas about the development of the University.

Since 1935 Blackett had been involved with the development of radar and of coastal stations designed to defend the country against enemy aircraft. One of his ex-assistant lecturers, Bernard Lovell, spent the war developing airborne radar devices for night fighters and bombers, and for the detection of U-boats in the Bay of Biscay; he served for some time as a principal scientific officer at the Telecommunications Research Establishment at Malvern. At the end of the war, Blackett saw the possibility of using radar to investigate radio echoes from high-energy cosmic ray showers; his colleague, who had returned as a lecturer, was well placed to

Left: Patrick Blackett (later Lord Blackett), Professor of Physics 1937–53; Nobel Laureate 1948.

Above: Sir Bernard Lovell at a press conference, 1971.

acquire at minimal cost in 1945–6 much surplus equipment, which would otherwise doubtless have disappeared down some disused mineshaft. At first inelegantly parked outside the physics department, the equipment reacted badly to passing trams; at the suggestion of the deputy bursar (supposedly as a temporary measure), it was removed to the University's outlying botanical gardens at Jodrell Bank, near Lower Withington in Cheshire. For similar reasons, Blackett found at Jodrell Bank a good place to house his magnetometer, which he installed in a copper-nailed wooden hut.

Lovell and his colleagues set up great aerials, including a "giant wire saucer" or transit telescope which began to receive radio emissions from outside the solar system and, by 1950, from the M31 spiral galaxy in Andromeda. If only the telescope beam could be directed to any point in the sky, a new map of the heavens could be drawn without relying on light waves alone. About 1950, with Blackett's approval and under Lovell's direction, a consultant engineer, H.C. Husband, began to prepare detailed designs for a "fully steerable paraboloid", a vast steel saucer with a pointer at its centre like a modest pylon, powered by motors and gear-racks salvaged from the obsolete battleships *Royal Sovereign* and *Revenge*. From this point on, Lovell found himself drawn

inexorably into the problems of planning, designing and obtaining (none too smoothly) finance for "big science", for one of those monumental pieces of grand equipment which had troubled Rutherford so little. The project sank into deep water, costs more than doubled between 1952 and 1957, the tonnage of steel required was underestimated, and high winds seemed to threaten the structure; there was even the grim prospect for Lovell of being personally sued for an impossibly large sum of money.

Fortunately, in 1957 the telescope was able to prove its relevance, not only to fundamental science, but also to national defence, for it succeeded in tracking the carrier rockets that had launched the Russian satellites Sputnik I and Sputnik II into orbit (both were intercontinental ballistic missiles in the making). The telescope was not designed for military purposes, but its contributions to national defence in the space age appealed to public opinion, and Lovell exploited this asset with great skill. Lord Nuffield paid off the last of the heavy debts in 1960, half from his personal fortune and half from the resources of his foundation, saying: "I find it quite humiliating that this great research tool, which has done so much to raise the prestige of our country in this particular field, should be in such an invidious position." Jodrell Bank was now on the brink of great discoveries in the physics of the stars. In the early 1960s, a research group headed by Henry Palmer succeeded in compiling a catalogue of about a hundred small objects in the radio sky. These proved to be the most powerful entities in the universe and were known as "quasi-stellar objects" or "quasars", thus opening the way to an extra-galactic astronomy prepared to range far beyond the Milky Way. Soon recognised as the University's most spectacular piece of apparatus, combining

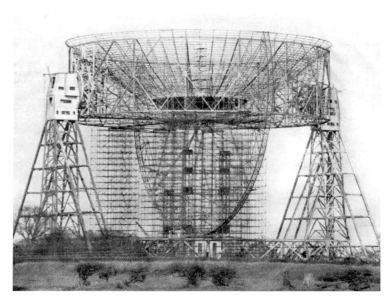

Nearing completion: the radio telescope at Jodrell Bank, April 1957.

Canada, Bragg in Cambridge and with his father in Leeds. But much of Rutherford's most significant work, on the structure of the nucleus, was done after winning the prize for chemistry, and it was in an almost deserted laboratory in Manchester that he first changed one element into an isotope of another. Two of the three were immensely confident, inspiring, humane, resolute but not domineering. Rutherford was the "happy warrior", tunelessly chanting "Onward Christian Soldiers" round the laboratory when things were going well; Bragg, surprisingly approachable and free of pomposity, was perhaps the most prone to self-doubt; Blackett may have been the most versatile, less obsessive than Rutherford, brilliantly combining the experimenter and the theorist, the boldest in changing direction, and the most politically aware. Jodrell Bank was his indirect legacy, Bernard Lovell his protégé. All of them, attracting distinguished visitors, importing with them researchers of promise, fellow veterans and wartime colleagues, changed the face of the department and steered it in new directions, making it a centre for researches of international reputation. The establishment on the Cheshire plain of a scientific icon that eventually became a symbol of the BBC's regional news North West, gave the University and some of its science an impressive local presence outside Manchester. The Lovell Telescope also marked, as few things did so strikingly, a transition from the sealing-wax science of Rutherford and Blackett (nothing was quite so good for closing vacuums as Bank of England red wax!) to the expensive and complex engineering of the post-war decade.

bulk, grace and mystery with a touch of H.G. Wells, Jodrell Bank, surrounded in time with an arboretum, a planetarium and many engaging displays and exhibitions, cast its spell on innumerable visitors who may never have connected it with the University.

None of these three Nobel prizewinners ended his career in Manchester: two were lured away by the prestige of the Cavendish which had nurtured them, one by Imperial College. At least two won their awards for work done before their arrival – Rutherford in

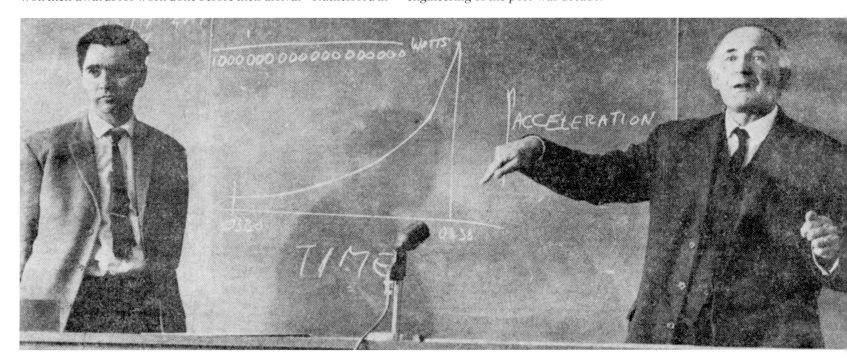

Sir Bernard Lovell lecturing at Jodrell Bank on the Russian space craft Venus 4, October 1967.

Today and Tomorrow

At the formation of the new University of Manchester in 2004, a School of Physics and Astronomy was instituted within the new Faculty of Engineering and Physical Sciences. The School not only absorbed the rich tradition of teaching and research in the fields of Physics and Astronomy at the Victoria University, but also drew in expertise from UMIST. Astronomers, cosmo-chemists and astro-physicists from UMIST are contributing directly to research being undertaken at the University's Jodrell Bank Observatory.

Professor Andre Geim from the School of Physics and Astronomy is one of the Faculty's most prolific scientists. In 2005 he discovered a new class of material called graphene, just one atom thick, which is set to change the face of physics. The discovery has the potential to lead to a whole new generation of computers made from a single molecule. Similarly, Professor

Andrew Lyne at the Jodrell Bank Observatory has led the way to the discovery of new planets, stars and most recently a double pulsar 2000 lights years away. The Lovell telescope has undergone a major upgrade which will keep it at the leading edge of astronomical research. Now astronomers are on the verge of a new era of discovery with the development of the World's most powerful radio telescope, MERLIN, which the Observatory operates as a national facility for the whole of the UK. Building on the existing MERLIN radio-telescope array, an ambitious £8m upgrade is underway called e-MERLIN, which will use fibre-optic technology to connect the networks of telescopes across Britain to the Lovell Telescope.

In 2007, the Faculty will complete its latest development with the opening of a new £55m building (the AMPPS Building).

The Astronomy, Maths, Physics and Photon Science (AMPPS) building incorporates a canopy bridging between buildings, which features a 'rack' mounted louvre photovoltaic system to provide shading, as well as creating a sustainable energy output which can be used to offset the site's power demand.

Computing in the University

HILARY KAHN

Manchester became famous in and after 1948 for the design and construction of the world's first stored-programme computer by Professor F.C. Williams and his assistants Tom Kilburn and Geoff Tootill. The University has since maintained a leading position in the field. Hilary Kahn, Professor in the School of Computer Science, describes the principal developments in research, teaching and the provision of computer services both at the University and UMIST.

The earliest computing in Manchester did not, as one might have expected, involve the kind of digital computer with which we are all now so familiar, although that came along soon afterwards. The first computer at the University was a differential analyser, an mechanical analogue computer designed specifically to help in the solution of differential equations. Douglas Hartree, Beyer Professor of Applied Mathematics, had seen a similar machine at MIT in the USA and in 1935, with the help of a postgraduate student, Arthur Porter, created a small version of his own using Meccano. Information about this was even published in the Meccano hobbyists' magazine. The simple Meccano model was soon followed by a more substantial version built with the help of Metropolitan-Vickers, a major company in the heavy engineering industry, who used it to help in their design projects. The machine, relatively primitive as it was, was an important step on the way to getting serious help for mathematicians, scientists and engineers who were finding it increasingly hard to do the complex calculations their work demanded using only hand calculators.

The Second World War then intervened and there was an inevitable gap at the University in progress towards ways of helping to do calculations. But, from 1945 onwards, men who

Tom Kilburn in 1965.

had gained knowledge and experience in helping towards the war effort, were returning to academic life. One of the first to come to Manchester was Max Newman, who after working at Bletchley Park became the Fielden Professor of Mathematics. He had seen the power of electronic calculating engines through his work on Colossus, a specialised code-breaking computer used to crack the Lorenz codes, and when he came to Manchester he wanted to pursue the idea of using them. At the time there was no stored programme computer anywhere in the world, so he obtained a Royal Society grant to set up a "calculating machine laboratory at

Manchester University". There was a capital sum of £20,000 and an annual sum of £3,000 for staff salaries. However, there was no machine available for him to buy, so he planned to build a computer. He decided to base the design on a computer being planned at Princeton University; the Selectron was intended to provide the memory for this machine. When the Selectron failed to work, Newman's plans were severely delayed.

Top: Kilburn (left) and Williams at the console of the Manchester Mark 1 in 1949.

Above: Alan Turing (right) with two colleagues and the Ferranti Mark 1.

The World's First Stored-programme Computer

Meanwhile, another person returned to academia after distinguished service in radar and other fields at the Telecommunications Research Establishment (TRE) at Malvern. This was F.C. (Freddie) Williams, who had been at Manchester before the war and who returned in December 1946 to take up a Chair in the Electro-Technics (later the Electrical Engineering) Department. From his contacts and experience during the war, Williams was aware of the potential of computers and knew that the major stumbling block was the lack of a way of storing data so it could be processed at electronic speeds.

When he returned to Manchester, Williams brought with him Tom Kilburn, a mathematician from Dewsbury, who had joined Williams at TRE in 1942 on graduating from Cambridge. In Manchester Kilburn concentrated on addressing the problem of how to store information for a computer. The idea was to use a cathode ray tube (CRT), a technology with which they were familiar from their radar work at TRE. Progress was good and by December 1947 Kilburn and Williams could demonstrate the ability to store a certain amount of data on a CRT. What remained was to show that the CRT store would actually work reliably at the speeds required to support electronic computation. And what better way to prove this than to build a small computer with a very limited set of instructions as a test bed? So this is what Kilburn did, with the assistance of Geoff Tootill – also seconded from TRE.

On June 21 1948 this Small Scale Experimental Machine – better known as the Manchester Baby – successfully ran its first program. The program, which calculated the highest factor of a number, was designed to use all the instructions and to be able to iterate so as to test out the reliability of the CRT store over a longer computation. From that point on, computing has never looked back.

The work was rapidly recognised by the UK Government and by scientists. Alan Turing – who was to come to Manchester as a Reader in Mathematics in October 1948 – began to write programs for this computer and, even before coming to Manchester, sent programs up for someone to run on the machine on his behalf. Newman realised that the computer he wanted had been developed within the same university – he and his colleagues began to use the Baby and, importantly, acted as consultants on programming and mathematical issues. The CRT storage was adopted by computer developers worldwide, including IBM.

The Baby was physically large – about 16ft long and weighing half a ton. It contained 650 valves, consumed 3Kw of power, had a random access memory equivalent to just 128kb and had a computing speed of 1.2 milliseconds per instruction. By way of comparison, a typical personal computer available in 2006 might have 512mb of memory and a computing speed of 1 nanosecond per instruction. However, when the Baby worked in 1948 it offered the promise that calculations that had previously taken weeks or months could be done in a matter of minutes.

Computer Developments

The Baby was essentially seen as a research prototype; Kilburn and Williams, and the team that grew around them, immediately started enhancing the machine. It therefore evolved over the next year into a larger and more sophisticated machine that became known as the Manchester Mark 1. By mid 1949, the design of the Mark 1 was being transferred to Ferranti who developed it into the world's first commercial computer. By early 1951, the Manchester Mark 1 was replaced by the Ferranti Mark 1, a machine that continued to serve the University until 1958. As the Senate papers of the time show, it was soon acknowledged that the capabilities of the machine were far in excess of the University's demands for computing. So time on Mark 1 was sold to outside users from, for example, industry and Government departments. This was clearly felt to be a sound procedure since it disseminated knowledge of computer possibilities over the widest possible range at a time when only one or two other computers existed in the country. In addition, the income so derived was used to pay for the operation and maintenance of the machine, to pay the mathematicians associated with the exploitation of its potential and to support further research in machine design. The first programming manual for this machine was written by Alan

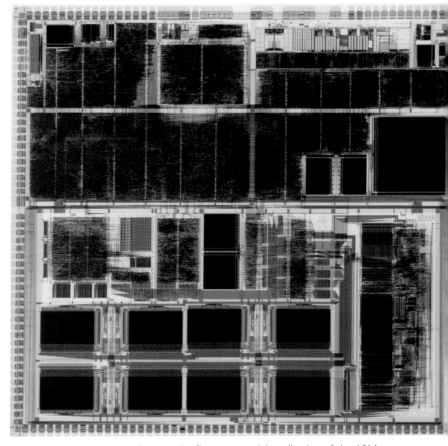

Steve Furber's DRACO SoC design – the first commercial application of the ARM 32-bit asynchronous RISC microprocessor.

Turing. Once the Ferranti Mark 1 was in place, Turing had no further direct involvement in the computer developments.

In 1954 a Mark 1 programming language, known as an "Autocode", was created by Tony Brooker. It was an "easy to learn scientific programming language" that most programmers used in preference to programming in the basic machine code even though it slowed the machine down. 1954 was also the year in which Electrical Engineering moved to a new building in Dover Street. This included a room specifically designed to house the Mark 1. Between 1951 and 1957 Ferranti sold at least nine machines – though it is thought that one or two other machines were sent secretly to government agencies.

From the early 1950s, Williams began to take more of a back seat as far as computing at Manchester was concerned. His commitments as head of department and his wide range of research interests inevitably drew his attention to other matters. Kilburn, however, remained passionate about the challenges of computing and continued the drive towards more powerful (and so more useful) computers, innovating in the field of computer

Below: Kilburn (standing on right) at the console of Atlas c1962.

Right: Dai Edwards (seated) and Gareth Edwards working on the Manchester Mark 1 in 1949.

University computing service until 1963 and had sufficient additional capacity to support outside users as well. Ferranti sold nineteen machines and the Mercury became a mainstay of scientific computing in the UK.

Kilburn's focus on larger, faster and more effective machines remained as sharp as ever. Soon he and his team were tackling an even larger project. The machine they planned was initially called MUSE, and it was to be one of the world's first supercomputers. It contained a large number of new ideas involving challenging software and hardware innovations and introduced ideas that are now taken for granted in every computer. After some delay, Ferranti once again decided to get involved and that machine too had its name changed; it was supplied by Ferranti (later ICT) as the Atlas computer. The team working on Atlas included Dave Howarth who designed the Supervisor, the sophisticated operating system for Atlas, and Tony Brooker who led the work on compilers and developed the Atlas Autocode programming language. Other key members of the team were David (Dai) Edwards and Frank Sumner, who each played major parts in the future development of computing at Manchester. The new ideas in Atlas and their practical implementation had a significant influence on computer thinking worldwide, with Virtual Memory and the Compiler among the most important examples of ideas originating specifically from Manchester. Atlas was inaugurated

architecture and, with the ever-growing team around him, in the area of software development too. He also used technological advances, such as the arrival of the transistor as a viable component, to great advantage.

Once the Ferranti Mark 1 was installed and working, Kilburn started work on the design of two further computers. One, which was probably the world's first transistor computer, was designed and built explicitly to allow the team to experiment with the new-fangled transistors of the time. An early prototype of this machine was working in 1953. In the end, a number of these transistor machines were built and used by Metropolitan-Vickers as the MV950. In parallel with the Transistor Machine, Kilburn started the development of a new machine initially called MEG. The goal was to provide improved performance and extra support for users, in particular the provision of floating point hardware, which allows accurate calculations to be done very efficiently. Once again Ferranti took the prototype design and commercialised the machine as the Mercury. The University took delivery of a Mercury in 1958; that machine provided the

Multi-access teletypes on-line to the Mod One computer.

time it was ICL (the successor to Ferranti and ICT) who used the design as the basis for their 2900 range of computers.

As computing worldwide became ever more sophisticated in terms of machine architecture, hardware technology and the range of system and user software required, it eventually became impossible for a single department in any University to compete with industry and its levels of funding and manpower. Instead, the focus needed to turn to new architectures and to experimental prototypes in software and hardware. There were therefore experiments with a smaller machine (known as MU6) and with dataflow architectures, as well as software developments in various application areas including databases, compiler and language developments, graphics and computer aided design. The subject area – and the University's commitment to it – grew apace.

Developing Computer Science as a Discipline

The digital computer developments at the University of Manchester started in late 1946 in the Department of Electro-technics (later Electrical Engineering) and soon resulted in the formation of a Computer Group, led by Tom Kilburn. He became the University's first Professor of Computer Engineering in 1960. As interest in the area grew, it became clear that the new-fangled subject of Computer Science was worth pursuing in its own right and in 1964 Kilburn, with the support of Williams, established the Department of Computer Science. The new department was founded with the twelve staff from the Computer Group, but grew rapidly. The staff appointed in those days, of course, had an odd assortment of backgrounds, including mathematics, electrical engineering, chemistry and even classics, because the subject was so new.

Kilburn established the UK's first undergraduate degree course in Computer Science in 1965; the first cohort consisted of just twenty-eight students. Within fifteen years, the annual intake had grown to over one hundred and by the 1990s to about two hundred. The department from the beginning had a thriving postgraduate school offering a one-year taught Master's degree in Computer Science as well as PhD courses. The department's focus was on a range of computing topics, principally computer engineering and fundamental software systems, with applications involving databases and other topics of wider interest emerging strongly as well. The firm basis in computer engineering and systems software was natural given that the Department of Computer Science emerged from Electrical Engineering; this distinguished (and still distinguishes) it from most subsequent Computer Science departments in other universities, as those typically emerged from Mathematics. Not surprisingly graduates of these courses are much sought after.

in December 1962. The full working machine, which was about 2500 times more powerful than the Mark 1, was installed at the University and provided the University's main computing power as well as computing facilities for other universities, research organisations and commercial users around the country. This triggered another important development, the creation of a formal computing service which was one of the forerunners of the large computing services centre currently at the University.

However, before moving onto other aspects of computing in Manchester, there are one or two other major developments to be noted. Kilburn together with a large group of researchers, including engineers from ICL, led by Dai Edwards, Frank Sumner, Jeff Rohl and Derrick Morris, worked on yet another major computer development, MU5. This machine, which first operated in 1972, was specifically intended to provide support to improve the efficiency of system software and user applications written in high-level languages. Like all the preceding machines designed by Kilburn, it too was developed in conjunction with industry. This

Experimental board including a chip designed by Furber's Advanced Processor Technology Group.

A student experimenting in the School's Robotics Laboratory.

The University of Manchester was not of course alone in recognising the importance of computing to the scientific community. At the Manchester College of Science and Technology, for example, staff and students in the Statistics Section of the Mathematics Department were regular users of mechanical calculators and moving on to using computers was a natural step. Thanks largely to the vision of Lord Bowden, a move was made to acquire expertise in the field of computing and under the guidance of Stan Gill, who was appointed as Professor of Automatic Data Processing, a taught Master's degree on computing subjects was established within the Mathematics Department in the mid-1960s. Students on this course wrote programs which were sent on papertape to the Atlas computer at the University to be run; the mode of transport was either a bicycle or a local bus. Gill left soon afterwards to be replaced by Gordon Black who, with support from Bernard Richards, established an undergraduate degree course in Computation (by which they meant "the use of computers"). This course took its first students in 1968, still under the auspices of the Mathematics Department. The strength and importance of the subject was soon recognised and in 1970 the computing group left the Mathematics Department and established the Computation Department, which flourished for many years. The BSc in Computation grew from small beginnings in 1968 to a course admitting some two hundred students whose abilities were welcomed by employers in industry.

Establishing a Computer Service

It was clear from the earliest days of Mark 1 that the existence of a computer at the University of Manchester would attract scientists, engineers and researchers from industry, research institutes and Government. These were people who had serious calculations to do and were struggling to make any headway using mechanical and electro-mechanical calculators. So an embryonic computer service was in existence from the very beginning. As the machines Kilburn developed became ever more powerful, so the service that they were able to offer improved – and the range and geographical locations of users expanded. But by the mid-1960s it was clear that it would not be enough to offer a computer service based on Atlas alone. A 1964 University of Manchester Senate paper noted that the demand at Tech (UMIST) for computer time on the University facility would clearly continue to increase and a shared computer service would be desirable to enable the best use to be made of finance, buildings and staff.

In 1965, the idea was further endorsed by the Flowers Report which stated that three major computing services should be established – in Manchester, Edinburgh and London. The ideas were accepted and the basic University of Manchester Regional Computer Centre (UMRCC) was established in 1969 combining a machine at UMIST with the service provided by Atlas. When the purpose built Computer Building (now renamed the Kilburn Building) was completed in 1972, UMRCC moved into the ground floor and the Department of Computer Science moved into the rest of the building. UMRCC continued to grow installing ever more powerful machines.

Today and Tomorrow

All the aspects of computing in Manchester continue to grow from strength to strength. The School of Computer Science (which is the new name for the Department of Computer Science founded by Tom Kilburn) has always received the top rating possible for research and teaching. By 2005 it had over sixty academic teaching members of staff and very large numbers of researchers. Through the work of Steve Furber it continues to play a world-leading role in hardware design and exploitation, concentrating on low-power chip design as one of its key areas. Exciting new research in areas such as formal specification and analysis methods, e-Science, bioinformatics, robotics, graphics and visualisation continue to attract enormous interest and support.

The Department of Computation maintained a focus on applications of computing, and with the merger between UMIST and the Victoria University of Manchester initially concentrated on issues relating to the social impact of computing in its new role as the School of Informatics within the Faculty of Humanities. However, by late 2006 the importance of the synergy that exists between parts of the School of Informatics and the School of Computer Science allowed the groups to evolve a closer relationship. As a result, numbers of members of the School of Informatics are now being absorbed directly into the School of Computer Science; others with a more management systems inclination have joined the Manchester Business School. And the computing service has been restructured into Manchester Computing (MC) and IT Services (ITS) with leading-edge computing facilities. MC provides research computing services and in-depth support to The University of Manchester as well as a wide range of external services to the UK and international research and learning communities. ITS provides the campus IT services for staff and students of the University.

Researcher in the clean room of the School's Centre for Mesoscience and Nanotechnology.

Engineering and Industry

HAROLD HANKINS AND TIM YATES

Professor Hankins and Mr Yates explore a theme of great importance, in the practical contributions made by the academic research of Tech and Owens to industrial development in the Northwest, in the fields of electrical, mechanical, civil and aeronautical engineering.

A journalist visiting UMIST in 1970 wrote: "There is a very curious thing about UMIST. If you go to almost any member of staff and ask what purpose is served by its existence, they will almost certainly reply 'to benefit industry'." This birthright, handed down from Tech's founders, has been carried forward by its various principals, particularly John Henry Reynolds who set out in 1879 "to provide courses relevant to the region's industries", and by Vivian Bowden, who in 1956 declared: "We must become Industry's university."

But it would be wrong to suggest that Tech was alone in this task. In 1867 a committee was established in Owens to find its first engineering professor, backed by Sir Joseph Whitworth, William Fairbairn and Charles Beyer who saw the need to supplement part-time education for mechanics and artisans at the Mechanics' Institution with engineering studies at Owens. The eventual emergence of full-time engineering teaching and research at both Tech and Owens led to the inevitable question of what their respective roles should be. A self-denying ordinance suggested that Tech should concentrate on technical science and Owens on engineering science. But this was an unreal distinction; with time, both were to work across the whole spectrum of engineering and to cooperate where necessary to mutual advantage.

The early days of engineering in Manchester were characterised by men of exceptional ability. In March 1868 Osborne Reynolds

was appointed to the first Chair of Engineering at Owens, retiring in 1905, the year that the first two engineering professors at Tech were recognised under the concordat. By this time, Reynolds had established a worldwide reputation and placed engineering at Owens on the map. His achievement was all the more remarkable because he had no access to well-equipped engineering laboratories until 1873, when Owens moved from Quay Street to its present site. Initially he worked on electricity and magnetism and later on hydrodynamics and hydraulics. He developed a fundamental

Left: The UMIST Centrifuge (Civil Engineering) and without the lid (below) showing the 4.3 metre diameter rotor.

The Royce Laborarory
(Manufacturing Division).

Osborne Reynolds.

George Edward Davis.

model for turbulent flow which became the standard work used everywhere in the study of hydrodynamics and aerodynamics. He was elected a Fellow of the Royal Society in 1877.

At Tech in 1887 George Edward Davis gave a series of twelve lectures in the Department of Applied Chemistry, which were later considered to be of historical importance in establishing chemical engineering as an independent subject ranking with electrical, mechanical and civil engineering. Today he is remembered as the father of chemical engineering and his classic *Handbook of Chemical Engineering* is widely recognised as the first definitive treatise on the subject. In 1934, at Tech, Professor James Kenner FRS belatedly introduced the first UK undergraduate course in chemical engineering.

The organisation of engineering at both institutions developed differently in the second half of the twentieth century. It could be argued that, apart from well-educated engineering graduates, industry's essential needs were for access, on one hand, to academic skill in analysis, simulation and experimentation and, on the other, to inventiveness. At Tech the extension to the Main Building was eventually completed in 1957, providing vital space for Vivian Bowden's planned expansion to meet the national need for engineers and scientists. Adequate space was now available for an ample library and offices for administration, as well as to provide a temporary home for those academic departments waiting for their buildings to be completed. The plan for the twenty-five-acre site was clear. The River Medlock would be culverted under the campus, and slum housing and redundant factories would be cleared. A centrally located building equipped for lectures, the Renold Building, would be erected with peripheral individual buildings for engineering within easy walking distance. These buildings would have teaching and research laboratories, with some equipped to operate on an industrial scale. Civil Engineering would be housed in the Pariser Building; Mechanical Engineering in the George Begg Building, with its Applied Mechanics and Thermodynamics Divisions, and an industrial-scale machine tools laboratory in the Manufacturing Division, the Royce Laboratory, located in the Main Building; Electrical Engineering in the Ferranti Building, together with a high-voltage industrial-scale laboratory, and Chemical Engineering in Jackson's Mill, together with a full-scale chemical engineering plant known today as the Morton

The Bristol Olympus turbojet engine, used in Concorde.

Laboratory. Although the total student population at Tech was much less than that of a full-service university, its engineering departments were as large as any, with Electrical Engineering at one stage home to about eight hundred students. As a consequence, part of the accommodation for the Electrical and Mechanical Engineering departments remained in the Main Building.

A different approach was undertaken at Owens. Although Electrical Engineering had its own separate building in Dover Street, the Civil and Mechanical Engineering departments shared the Simon Engineering Building, affording better opportunities for cross-disciplinary co-operation than at Tech.

After the war, advances in science and technology profoundly affected work in engineering departments. At Owens, Professors Frederick Williams and Tom Kilburn returned from wartime research and, in the department of Electrical Engineering, designed and built the world's first stored-program computer (see pages 101–3). They established a unique working relationship with the Ferranti Company for the construction of a production version. Professor Williams stayed on to lead a high-quality department in which fundamental research flourished, particularly in the areas of control engineering and variable speed alternating current motors. At Tech, Professor Colin Adamson, later to become Rector of the Polytechnic of Central London, became head of the department of Electrical Engineering in 1961. He was an inspirational leader and went on to convert a small but distinguished Electrical Engineering department into the largest of its type in the country, covering every aspect of electrical and electronic engineering and electronics. The department was organised into research groups with interests ranging from

electrical power systems to solid state electronics, and from digital processes to communication engineering. Each was led by a professor and each ran a Master's course, ensuring that teaching kept abreast of the latest advances as well as providing a stream of doctoral research students. The origins of the Master's course lay in the development of an advanced engineering course, by Norman Hancock at Tech and Lester Taylor from Metro-Vickers' research department. This built on the close relationship that Tech and Metro-Vickers had developed through Professor Miles Walker. The course was designed to give postgraduate-level education to selected graduate apprentices from the company by means of advanced lectures, tutorials and laboratory work. Sadly, it came to an abrupt end when the company was taken over by GEC in 1967. As with Owens and the Ferranti Company, there was an easy interchange of staff between academe and industry.

In later years, the availability of interactive and powerful off-line computers run by the University Computing Service provided new opportunities for engineering research and teaching. The use of computers for engineering analysis, simulation and modelling became an alternative to building expensive equipment for experimentation. To take a few examples: in the early 1970s a postgraduate Control Systems Centre was established at Tech where powerful digital and analogue computers were used to develop control theories that had application to all engineering departments and disciplines, from the control of chemical plant to the control of jet engines. In Mechanical Engineering, software packages were developed to model the flow of gases in internal combustion engines, and these packages were subsequently licensed to the world's engine manufacturers. In Civil Engineering, a large software package was developed to analyse stresses and strains in bridges that was used to help in the design of the Forth and Severn suspension bridges. In Mechanical Engineering, design techniques were developed for computer-aided manufacture. But not all simulation and modelling research could be carried out using computers. In Civil Engineering, large mechanical centrifuges were developed and built to study soil mechanics and hydrodynamics, with experimental facilities for modelling coastal areas and estuaries. Many research centres were also established, to bring a critical mass of researchers together in well-equipped laboratories to solve real engineering problems. At Owens a centre for aerospace systems was established in the 1990s, recognised by BAE Systems as a primary academic partner, with a wind tunnel facility at Barton Aerodrome. In Chemical Engineering at Tech, the Satake Company financed the establishment of a grain-processing research centre in 1994, studying the application of chemical engineering techniques to the grain-processing industry. In Electrical Engineering, the industrial

The School of Materials

Manchester has enjoyed a long association, both academically and industrially, with all the materials most vital to economic and social development: biomaterials, polymers, ceramics and glasses, metals and light alloys, textiles and paper and composites. The development of academic activities in materials at Manchester has mirrored that of local and UK industry from its foundations in engineering, steel and textiles in the nineteenth and twentieth centuries, to modern and expanding industries of the twenty-first century. These include aerospace, automotive, nuclear power generation, electronics and telecommunications, plastics and rubbers, corrosion control, healthcare and biomedical applications.

Textiles and paper have long been studied at Manchester. In 1903 the Textiles Department of the Municipal School of Technology housed machinery for the manufacture of paper that led to the development of undergraduate and postgraduate studies in Paper Science. UMIST became the only place in the UK where this subject was studied at university level. Studies in textiles within the Textile Technology department at UMIST continued to expand in the 1960s and 1970s with new degree courses that now encompass Textile Design, Marketing and Management, Science and Technology, and Fashion Retailing.

In the 1960s, Manchester boasted two Metallurgy departments, one at VUM in the Faculty of Science, and the other at UMIST. However, in 1975, the decision was taken to create the Joint Departments of Metallurgy and Materials Science within a new purpose-built building, in a prescient move to bring together and enhance the academic excellence at both universities. A single undergraduate programme for all students from both universities was created with final year specialisations that included an embryonic Materials Science and Engineering course combining the study of metals, ceramics, glasses and polymers.

Studies of corrosion and its prevention also have a long tradition in Manchester. In the 1960s they were amply developed in the Corrosion Science Division of the Department of Chemical Engineering at UMIST. The Government's Department of Trade and Industry gave impetus to co-ordinated efforts to solve industrial corrosion problems, and the Corrosion Science Division became independent. In 1972 it was reconstituted as the Corrosion and Protection Centre, the first such postgraduate department to be created in a UK university. The success and growing importance to industry of the corrosion activities led in 1973 to the creation of a spin-off company, CAPCIS Ltd, an independent organisation providing an industrial focus for the knowledge and technology emerging from UMIST. Significant technology transfer between CAPCIS Ltd and the Corrosion and Protection Centre has facilitated the development of corrosion science and engineering, so crucial for the conservation of materials and the development of new materials, and innovative production processes and protection strategies for use in industry.

A new Department of Polymer and Fibre Science, established at the College of Science and Technology (soon to become UMIST) in 1962, was the first of its kind in a UK university. It absorbed existing research groups in Textile Chemistry and Paper Science and included a new group concerned with Polymer Science and Technology. Following a major reorganisation in 1981 forced by governmental funding cutbacks, Textile Chemistry staff were moved into the Textile Technology department and separate departments of Paper Science and Polymer Science and Technology were formed from their respective groups. Further re-structuring followed with the merger in 1988 between the UMIST Department of Polymer Science and Technology and the Joint Departments of Metallurgy and Materials Science to form the Manchester Materials Science Centre. The Centre rapidly developed to become the largest academic materials activity in the UK offering comprehensive undergraduate and postgraduate teaching and research functions across the core areas of metals, ceramics, polymers, biomedical and composite materials. Most significantly, the close academic collaboration between materials science and corrosion activities in Manchester produced important synergy that has been recognised by the highest ratings in the past two UK research assessment exercises, a key indication of international research quality and impact.

The creation of the new University of Manchester following the unification of UMIST and VUM in 2004, has enabled the Corrosion and Protection Centre (UMIST), the Manchester Materials Science Centre (UMIST/VUM) and the Department of Textiles and Paper (UMIST) that operated previously as independent departments, to join forces and become the new School of Materials in the Faculty of Engineering and Physical Sciences, thus forming the largest single materials grouping in any European university.

In 1936, work was in progress in the Coupland II building on a model of the Severn Estuary, complete with water.

The National Grid Transco High Voltage Research Centre.

scale high-voltage laboratory in 2003 became the National Grid Transco High Voltage Research Centre. Owens established a Maintenance Engineering and Asset Management Research Centre, the largest of its type in the world. Industrial units staffed by project officers were also set up to generate income by providing advice to industry, for example the Corrosion and Protection Consultancy Industrial Service (CAPCIS), established by the Corrosion and Protection Centre at Tech.

In recent years, the teaching of engineering courses has been influenced by the registration requirements of the Engineering Council leading to chartered engineer status; engineering departments and their courses have been accredited by visits from their respective professional institutions. As part of the recognition process, four-year undergraduate degree courses have been introduced, leading to the award of an MEng degree. Graduates can then aspire to become chartered professional engineers with appropriate professional development and industrial experience. An interesting course was the four-year course in Engineering, Manufacturing and Management, designed to produce technocrats with skills in management, run jointly by the two departments of Mechanical Engineering with lectures provided by the School of Management at Tech, and the Faculty of Law at Owens. Only four such courses were established in the UK, each with an intake of high-quality students. Although

Tech ran more MSc courses than almost any other university, special programmes for doctoral students were also introduced in the 1990s. These included the Total Technology PhD, where research is supplemented by lectures in management; the four-year engineering doctorate, EngD, where students work on industrial problems with substantial financial support from a company interested in their solution, and post-graduate training partnerships, where PhD students are placed in a company to work on industrial projects – some fifteen research students from

From the New Scientist *22 March 1984. Cartoon by Richard Willson of the recently appointed Principal of the Tech, Harold Hankins, transferring 'Know-how' from Academe to the Market Place.*

Today and Tomorrow

In an increasingly interdisciplinary research environment, research activity in engineering is developing in varied and interesting directions in a series of new Schools within the Faculty of Engineering and Physical Sciences. The merger brought together a number of distinguished former departments from both Victoria University of Manchester and UMIST.

A long history of collaboration between departments of Materials Science at both institutions helped them to amalgamate into the new School of Materials. It led to the award of £2.1m to the University to host the Northwest Composites Centre (NWCC) for research into aerospace composite design and manufacture.

Artist's impression of the Manchester Bobber.

The main thrust of this research is to devise low cost, low energy routes for making polymer composite materials, which are fast becoming the materials of choice for constructing lighter, more fuel efficient aircraft.

There are increasing demands for energy-led researchers to work with industry and Government to develop improved supplies from a variety of sources. Grasping the importance of this, the University is leading the UK in the development of nuclear science and engineering, through the Dalton Nuclear Institute. But seeing the importance of a wide range of options, the University is equally supporting traditional and renewable forms of energy. In 2006, the Joule Centre for Energy Research was launched as the Northwest's first centre for the development of sustainable energy technologies. Focusing on low-carbon technologies, engineers are investigating new wave, tidal and micro-hydro technologies.

The Manchester Bobber, a unique wave energy device, is the latest example of the Faculty's pioneering research and development in this field. Backed by the Carbon Trust and a wide range of industrial partners including Royal Haskoning, the device is designed to generate electricity by bobbing up and down in the sea. The aim is to provide a series of devices using disused oil rigs to provide an abundant and cost-efficient energy source.

Working closely with industry is part of the philosophy of the Faculty, which has long-standing relationships with many companies, including Rolls-Royce, British Energy, IBM and AstraZeneca.

Tech were placed in E.A. Technology Ltd at Capenhurst, under joint industrial and academic supervisors.

During the 1980s, as the manufacturing base in the UK continued to decline, universities were encouraged by government to exploit their intellectual property and to transfer technology arising from engineering and science research programmes into new companies, financed by venture capital. Owens and Tech had both established services for research and consultancy; indeed, Tech was the first in a UK university to do so. In 1986, Tech started UMIST Ventures Ltd to identify, protect and exploit intellectual property; it set up 75 licensing arrangements with a diverse range of industries, as well as facilitating the start-up of 40 new companies, three of which are now quoted on the Stock Exchange. Owens established VUMAN to finance new companies arising from the results of the university's research. By 2003, University of Manchester Intellectual Property Ltd, together with UMIST Ventures Ltd, had set up some one hundred licences and sixty new companies. In 1984, Owens established the Manchester Science Park to provide accommodation and services, including academic contacts, for selected high-technology companies with a capacity for growth and innovation. Today it is located on two sites accommodating some eighty companies. A landmark of the advancing enterprise culture in universities is the Manchester Science Enterprise Centre. One of twelve established by government, it works with staff and students to help release the commercial potential of their knowledge. This is certainly a far cry from the 1960s, when a senior industrial manager complained that Manchester's engineering graduates "were over-educated for industry".

Medicine and Life Sciences, 1903–2000

JOHN V. PICKSTONE

Student nurses practicing on the wards in Manchester.

Following on from his previous chapter on the early medical school, John Pickstone surveys the principal academic developments and organisational changes in pre-clinical and clinical work in the departments, schools and teaching hospitals of the University. He considers the changes for better or worse in the reputation of Manchester's biology, botany and zoology and of its clinical research. Professor Pickstone explores with emphasis pioneering developments such as the promotion of nursing as a graduate profession from the 1970s and the creation of a school of biomedical sciences from the 1980s onwards.

Edwardian Manchester was a rich city on the world stage. It was an international centre for music and for physical sciences – for both of which it owed much to Germany, as it did for its philosophical and historical studies. The University boasted a range of excellent facilities, including a new teaching hospital when the Manchester Royal Infirmary (MRI) moved to Oxford Road, and a new dental school and hospital next to the Museum.

It also benefited from Empire, and before the First World War three of its best-known academics were from the antipodes. Grafton Elliot Smith came from Sydney, Cambridge and Cairo universities; Rutherford, the colossus of atomic physics, came from New Zealand, via Cambridge and McGill. They joined the philosopher Samuel Alexander, who had studied in Melbourne and Oxford and worked on experimental psychology in Germany. All three were members of a Manchester University reading group which at one time included the chemist and Zionist Chaim Weizmann, the medieval historian T.F. Tout and the Danish theoretical physicist Niels Bohr.

Smith and Alexander collaborated to develop psychology courses and were central to the intellectual community of Manchester medicine. Three of the local medical graduates who worked under Smith in the anatomy department were to help shape the medical school through to the 1950s. They were John (Sebastian Bach) Stopford, Harry Platt and Geoffrey Jefferson.

But for models of academic medicine, young men looked increasingly to the new American universities, built on German patterns with strong pre-clinical sciences; and to the new or reformed teaching hospitals which were driven by full-time professors in the main clinical disciplines. In 1908, around the opening of the new Royal Infirmary, the University brought in a

new professor of medicine, well known for experimental treatments of thyroid disorders. Such moves disturbed the local consultant hierarchy, but while George Murray was soon recognised as the successor to Dreschfeld in private practice, he did not produce much research.

That the new MRI was not especially attuned to the German–American research pattern is also suggested by the lack of specific provision for X-ray diagnosis and treatment. After the discovery of X-rays in 1895, the MRI had been served by Mottershead's, the commercial chemists who took the X-ray photographs. But in 1908, the hospital appointed Alfred Barclay as radiologist, a Manchester man who had trained in Cambridge and London and then made his reputation at Ancoats Hospital and in private practice. This specialism, which was eminently practical and also related to Rutherford's physical science, did well in Manchester.

The First World War brought immediate and drastic change, and fundamentally altered the nature of the city. For four years, teaching was improvised; as younger men went to war or to war work, hospitals recalled veteran clinicians. Colleges, asylums and private homes were turned into hospitals for the train-loads of casualties brought back from France. The war advanced surgical specialisms, and Stopford and Platt worked together on nerve injuries at a special centre improvised near Platt Fields. Medical intellectuals, such as Elliot Smith, served in asylums for the mentally wounded. Anti-German feeling ran high, and the city would never regain the richness of its pre-war German culture.

Most of all, as was clear by 1920, the years of war effectively undermined the international position of the Lancashire cotton trade. Manchester was no longer clearly a world city but the leading centre of the northern English provinces, all of which suffered industrial depression for most of the 1920s and 1930s. Unlike the American universities, Manchester no longer had access to large new endowments; the major postwar private investment was for the new dental school and hospital, funded by William Turner of the asbestos company. But most new industries developed in the Midlands and around London and, as industries were cartelised, their corporate research labs tended to be

Top: Professor Delépine and colleagues in the Public Health Laboratories.

Above: Grafton Elliot Smith and friends in camp in New South Wales, on a hunt for platypus.

established in the south. Manchester had to run to keep its place in the world of learning.

In the universities and medical schools, the immediate post-war years saw a national round of promotions. Young men were getting their chances. Henry Dean had become Professor of Pathology in 1915; in 1919 Elliot Smith went to University College, London, and was replaced as Professor of Anatomy by the young John Stopford. Stirling at last retired from physiology and the University appointed A.V. Hill, a young Cambridge graduate, whose work on muscle heat was to earn a Nobel Prize. The medical faculty considered creating full-time chairs of medicine, surgery and obstetrics, but the proposal was deferred. Manchester tried to get Edward Mellanby as a clinical researcher, but failed – he saw the MRI as unreformed and went instead to the small but research-minded faculty at Sheffield. In 1922 Dean moved to Cambridge and the following year Hill went to

University College, London. Their successors as medical scientists were the physiological chemist Henry Raper in physiology, and the bacteriologists W.W.C. Topley and then H.B. Maitland. These were distinguished national figures, but they did not draw international talent as Physics did under Lawrence Bragg or Chemistry under Robert Robinson and Michael Polanyi.

Clinical research showed a similar pattern of ambition, frustration and limited progress. The Department of Pharmacy grew strongly in terms of student numbers once the university became recognised as the only professional school in Manchester; its head, R.B. Wild, was one of the local enthusiasts for cancer research. A clinical research laboratory was established at the MRI, and a young physician with a background in physiology was encouraged to take charge. Crighton Bramwell was a cardiologist, a specialism developing through physiological investigation, notably the ECG. But he preferred to be a physician first and a researcher second. The lab was thereafter run by a Manchester PhD chemist turned doctor, John F. Wilkinson, who became the regional expert on anaemia and worked closely with Boots the Chemist. But Wilkinson was not a favourite of the national Medical Research Council which had been established just before the war, nor was he in the inner circle of the medical school.

Perhaps the best-known of the young clinicians were the surgeons John Morley, Harry Platt and Geoffrey Jefferson. The latter two were contemporaries and friends of Stopford, who soon became Dean of Medicine. Platt specialised in orthopaedics, Jefferson in neuro-surgery; both worked first in minor hospitals and were then promoted to the MRI; both had strong American connections. The other specialist to attract attention, though not a member of the inner circle, was Ralston Paterson, appointed in 1930 to direct the Christie Cancer Hospital and the Holt Radium Institute when they together moved from the MRI site to a new building in Withington; by the late 1930s, Manchester was an international centre of radiotherapy.

Through the First World War and the 1920s, botany and zoology remained small and classical – focused on comparative anatomy, taxonomy and evolution. For a few years before the war, the civic universities had been persuaded to support biological studies that were relevant to the economy, especially entomology, which briefly thrived in Manchester. But after the war, in biology as in industrial research, state funding shifted south, towards London, Oxford and Cambridge. In the 1930s, local funding was again provided to encourage horticulture under

Commandant Herford of the Voluntary Aid Detachment in the Old Quadrangle during the First World War.

Professor Drummond, an expert in plant breeding and educated at Glasgow like several other Manchester botanists. He developed the botany experimental grounds at Jodrell Bank (which later became famous for the University's radio-telescope). This broadening of scope was less obvious in zoology, headed from 1931 by Graham Cannon, a young man with his FRS for studies of feeding mechanisms in arthropods. After the Second World War he became a controversialist in opposing the neo-Darwinians and objecting to the teaching of genetics.

The Second World War brought disruption, but not on the scale of the first war; and partly from the lessons then learned there was much more planning, both for the war itself and for a post-war Britain. Higher education and the health services benefited hugely from the ways in which war-time promises were carried through by the Attlee government, and Manchester benefited more than most universities. In the physical sciences and engineering, war work on the atomic bomb, radar and computing led directly to civilian projects. In the biological sciences, penicillin seemed to open new avenues for "economic botany". Experience on the penicillin project was one of the reasons why ICI created a pharmaceutical division at Alderley Park; one of its first projects was to develop a replacement for chloroform, and University staff were involved in the testing of halothane.

Sir Robert Platt, Bt. (later Lord Platt), Professor of Medicine 1945–65, renal specialist and President of the Royal College of Physicians 1957–62.

But the major boost came from state funds for universities and the NHS, including special funding for teaching hospitals. Between 1945 and 1950, undergraduate numbers doubled. Even medical students could now expect a grant for all their years of study, unless their parents were rich. From the 1950s, departments substantially increased their staff; and since hospital consultants were now salaried and the elite were given merit awards, universities could appoint full-time professors to head the clinical departments. In this respect, as in several others, the plans dating from the first war were realised after the second.

Manchester appointed Robert Platt (no relation to Harry) to a full-time Chair of Medicine. He had studied and practised in Sheffield, specialising in renal medicine, and had then developed his private practice, but he took the chance to lead a department partly because of his wartime experiences. His second-in-command was Douglas Black. Both came to be national figures and presidents of the Royal College of Physicians, and Manchester became known for nephrology. Paediatrics, too, got a major boost, including a link with the dental school for a department of Preventative Dentistry and Research, sponsored by the Nuffield Foundation: from the opening of the century, if not before, bad teeth had been recognised as a public health problem.

Manchester, as an industrial city, was naturally associated with occupational health and rheumatology, marginal specialisms that could now be developed. That was part of the background to the work in orthopaedics by John Charnley, a protégé of Harry Platt who was appointed to the MRI in the 1950s and then left to develop total hip replacements in a former tuberculosis hospital at Wrightington near Wigan. By the mid-1960s, it was clear that Charnley's devices were more effective than the competition – hip replacement came to be a common operation and the basis of a global industry in artificial joints.

During the Second World War, Stopford had been a key member of the National Committee on Medical Education. This had stressed the role of science, and over the post-war decades good A-Levels in science became essential for most entrants – the days of family connections, sport and a conversion course in biology, physics and chemistry were fading. The committee also advocated more education in social medicine, but that proved far harder to implement. It was well recognised that medical education was geared to would-be specialists, and that there was little exposure to general practice, or even to the work of normal district hospitals. But training in general practice was not effective until the 1960s. When, from 1970, the University needed more training places in hospitals, the main response was to develop two more teaching hospitals – in South Manchester, using Withington and the new hospital at Wythenshawe, and then in Salford at

Memories of Dentistry

Wesley Johnson was the Senior Lecturer in the Prosthetics Department. With Finals approaching, he reminded us that we had to construct a set of dentures for a patient without any help from the tutors. One of the stages in the construction of such appliances involves the "trying in" of the selected teeth, set in wax, in the patient's mouth. My friend Gordon, having completed this stage, dismissed his patient and turning to his workbench realised that the incomplete dentures were gone.

"He's probably gone off with them in his mouth," I said on hearing about the problem. "What if he has a cup of tea? They'll melt." We looked at the patient's records. He lived in a particularly insalubrious part of Moss Side. "You'd better get on your bike", I suggested.

An hour later, Gordon reappeared with the try-ins in his hand. "I rang the bell and he answered the front door, pointing to his mouth," he reported. "My word lad, them teeth are a good fit."

"They may be," replied Gordon, "but for Heaven's Sake, can I have them back. They're not finished yet".

W.A. Hale
BDS Dentistry 1968

Hope Hospital. Hope soon became known for internal medicine, especially gastroenterology under Leslie Turnberg, and for surgery, perhaps especially neurosurgery. Withington was known for psychiatry under Neil Kessel and David Goldberg, and Wythenshawe for cardiovascular surgery under John Dark.

Nursing education had been practical rather than academic; the MRI had a residential nursing school, Sparshott House, developed in the 1920s, which under the NHS came to serve all the central hospitals. Academic education for nurses had been considered nationally after the Second World War, but matrons feared losing the work of trainees on the wards. It was through Community Nursing that university training for nurses was established in Manchester. The Professor of Social and Preventative Medicine, Fraser Brockington, fought for it – not least against the Vice-Chancellor's (medically trained) wife, who was chair of the Education Committee of the MRI.

A diploma was established from 1959, with a degree from 1969. More generally, from about 1970, the profession was moving up the scale, shedding some of the domestic work and gaining new roles in management. In 1973 Manchester University established a separate

Department of Nursing and the following year Jean McFarlane became England's first Professor of Nursing. The department was centrally involved with the transformation of nursing in the 1980s in its focus on the Nursing Process, using elaborate records for individual patients, and in Project 2000, which planned for all nursing training to be attached to institutions of higher education.

Increased accommodation for the pre-clinical medical students was provided in the Stopford Building, planned by Bill Beswick, physiologist turned executive Dean of Medicine, and opened in 1973. This was the last of the big new buildings for the sciences opened since the 1950s to the east of Oxford Road; from 1976, the new Williamson Building contained all of geology, botany and zoology. The old science spaces, west of Oxford Road, were taken over for pharmacy, nursing, psychology, social sciences and administration. The Stopford departments were mostly pre-clinical, though Ian Isherwood developed there a new department of radiology, including the first CT scanner in clinical service, and Alwyn Smith led an interesting department of Community Medicine.

The pre-clinical sciences now had solid reputations, especially in kidney physiology, but none was nationally outstanding. In 1982, a biochemistry department was created by combining the biological section of chemistry with the medical biochemistry department which had split from physiology. But in the 1970s, many of the pre-clinical and life science departments were more concerned with teaching than research, hence they valued breadth more than specialisation. The undergraduate medical course remained the major commitment, though all the departments now had honours degrees of their own.

Life Sciences

After the war, a new Professor of Botany was brought back from Australia where he was already involved with the international politics of higher education. Eric Ashby expanded the staff, and several of his appointees went on to chairs elsewhere, but he left in 1950 to be a vice-chancellor. His successor Sidney Harland was a cotton geneticist, a subject that fitted the University rather better than Harland did himself; he did not get on with Graham Cannon in zoology, and Manchester was slow to develop subjects such as genetics and cell biology in ways that were truly integrated across botany and zoology. Rather more continuity and creativity was evidenced by Claude Wardlaw in botany, first in the study of plant diseases and then in morphogenesis, both of which became Manchester strengths. Indeed, it was the botanists working on lower plants who contributed most to economic botany. Kathleen Drew Baker studied the red seaweeds; in 1949 her discovery of a stage in the life cycle of *Porphyra* saved the Japanese *nori* industry.

Top: Cartoon of Sir Douglas Black, Professor of Medicine 1959–77, who worked on body fluids (Chief Scientist to the Department of Health and Social Security 1973–77, and President of the Royal College of Physicians, 1977–83).

Above: The old Zoology Laboratory.

She had been an assistant lecturer, but after marriage to Henry Wright Baker, Professor of Mechanical Engineering at UMIST (who designed her culture tanks), she worked without pay, since the University would not then employ a married couple.

Cannon continued until 1963 and is commemorated by the vivarium in the Museum. His replacement as Head of Zoology was Ralph Dennell, who for some years had held the second chair, doing what he could to update Manchester zoology. The relationship between zoology and botany improved, several talented staff were recruited, and an electron microscope unit was created. But by the 1970s, Manchester's biology degree programmes looked rather dated. Elizabeth Cutter had come back from the USA to continue work on morphogenesis, but found it far harder to fund research students in Britain. Under John Colhoun, there remained a strong programme in plant diseases, but in

A Gardener's View

My ground breaking doctoral research into the production of antibiotics by soil fungi failed to produce even a tiny ripple in the Ocean of Science. Nor did it become involved in the future course of my life. Clearly the laboratory was not for me.

Despite this, my stay at Owens College between 1951 and 1953 did play a fundamental role in my fifty year career as a gardener writer. To begin with, I learned the craft of desk research – the need to spend countless hours getting to know the subject before putting pen to paper. And then there was my road to Damascus in 1953. I held up a bound book with my work inside and my name on the outside. I knew then that producing books was going to be the only life for me.

And the final spin off. Manchester University gave me the right to put 'Dr' in front of my name. So I became 'the Doc' to the horticultural world and its media – so much nicer than my flowery Armenian name!

Dr D.G. Hessayon
PhD Soil Science 1954

Turning Form, by Denis Mitchell: a memorial to Kathleen Drew Baker in Ashburne Hall.

general Manchester was losing out to the new universities, several of which were strong in biology. They integrated plant and animal studies, so that cell biology and genetics were central, whereas in Manchester they still tended to be add-ons.

When Mark Richmond became Vice-Chancellor in 1981, he was the first scientist in that role since Stopford's retirement in 1956. After the national cuts in university grants in the 1980s, it was clear that future funding would be more competitive, both for teaching and research. Large buildings, created as symbols of high scientific status, now had to be paid for from earnings; accounting, management and planning came to the fore. Richmond was a medical microbiologist, impressed with the possibilities of life sciences for medicine, and especially with molecular biology. He was not impressed by life and medical sciences in Manchester, and nor were a number of young professors recently appointed or promoted in botany, physiology, biochemistry and to the new department of basic dental sciences. Richmond wanted reform, and the new professors had a plan. Their mechanism was a committee under John Wilmott, Head of Physics. In 1986, all the staff of botany, zoology, anatomy, physiology and biochemistry etc. were asked to join a new School of Biological Sciences (SBS), officially located in both the Faculty of Science and the Faculty of Medicine, but with considerable autonomy. They could choose

between four departments – Biochemistry and Molecular Biology, Cell and Structural Biology, Physiological Sciences and Environmental Sciences. They were all to be accommodated in the Stopford Building, a move not fully completed until 1994 after a further reorganisation in 1993 into a structure that had been more or less envisaged in the mid-1980s but that was not then politically feasible. The new School of Biological Sciences had no departments as such, only loose research groups and a variety of teaching programmes, and it would be essentially a faculty. It was agreed that UMIST would develop in biotechnology.

By most standards the new arrangements were successful, and they served as a model for other universities. There was strong central direction from the key group – Professors Michael Grant, Tony Trinci, Maynard Case and Mark Ferguson, and later Keith Gull, a former student of Trinci who came as Professor of Molecular Biology and led the development of postgraduate programmes. When staff retired, replacements were appointed for their research potential; teaching was reorganised to facilitate research; and some parts of biology were not supported so that resources could be focused on the strengths. Ecological sciences declined or emigrated, as programmes were built around cell biology, biochemistry and molecular biology. The Wellcome Trust Centre for Cell Matrix Research proved very successful under Michael Grant and then Martin Humphries. Bright young staff were recruited and supported, including Nancy Rothwell, and they provided much of the leadership when the originators of the school retired and Gull moved to Oxford.

Several subsequent changes in Manchester biomedicine might be seen, in part, as knock-on effects of the 1986 reorganisation. For example, the abolition of the old pre-clinical departments meant that the medical curriculum could be redesigned as a single

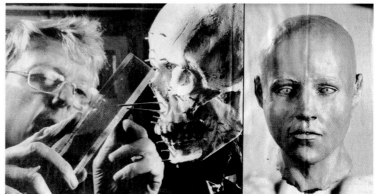

Richard Neave, medical artist, rebuilds the skull of a murder victim, 1989.

Hospital art: 'Giving Sight to the Blind', terracotta panel on the Oxford Road façade of the Royal Eye Hospital (1886).

programme rather than as a package of lectures from each of the departments. Complaints against British medical curricula had been common for decades, though the only major innovations had been in new schools such as Nottingham; but from 1991 Manchester devised a radical new programme based on problem-based learning. The Faculty of Medicine was also reorganised, mainly to improve research performance after a poor showing in the national Research Assessment Exercise of 1996.

Historically, the pre-clinical sciences had been subordinated to clinicians in the Faculty of Medicine, just as the biological sciences and psychology had played second fiddle to physics and chemistry in the Faculty of Science. By the 1990s, the weaker ends had joined and become strong – so there were now three major groupings on the science side of the University. If the rise of biomedical sciences in Manchester is a particularly clear example of a worldwide phenomenon, so too are closer links with industry – not just for chemical drugs (which was so evident in the early twentieth century), or for hormones and antibiotics, but for new remedies based on knowledge of growth factors, stem cells or the genetics of disease. Alongside the new building for academic bio-medicine and clinical research are buildings for "spin-offs", especially the Renovo Project for scar-free healing. And at the Christie Hospital's Paterson labs, Mike Dexter discovered how to grow stem cells *in vitro* for use in treatments of leukaemia.

Project Unity

By the new millennium, the School of Biological Sciences (SBS) was seen by many as a success story and a model of organisation that the rest of the University might follow. This gave strength to

arguments that the SBS should remain an independent faculty in the new merged structure, even though it was much smaller than the others. It could claim to be the fastest-growing area of the University, and one of those most likely to bring renown.

Bio-medical sciences were not one of the problems that Project Unity was intended to cure, but UMIST had a Department of Biochemistry which could be integrated with mutual benefits. That department had originated between the wars as a department of brewing, and its expertise had proved useful in antibiotic manufacture after the Second World War. By the 1960s, it taught biochemistry more broadly and was headed by a young professor, Alan Eddy. Much of the research was still on yeast, which might have seemed rather old-fashioned – but fashions change and, by the 1980s, biotechnology was touted as a subject of the future. The UMIST department developed strengths in medical biochemistry and its links with chemical engineering were promoted; so, too, was UMIST's investment in analytical sciences. In the late 1990s, when Mike Dexter became Director of the Paterson Lab at the Christie, he developed a scheme for research chairs at UMIST. And when Project Unity was under discussion, UMIST was planning a new bio-medical building, funded by the Wellcome Trust, of which Dexter was now Director.

This considerable asset is now part of the Faculty of Life Sciences. So, too, is the programme in Ophthalmic Optics, developed at Tech for the training of opticians but noted from the 1960s for research on vision, especially under John Cronly-Dillon. Other extras in the new faculty include Egyptology and the Centre for the History of Science, Technology and Medicine (CHSTM) which derived from the History of Science and Technology Department at UMIST and was created at Owens in 1986.

Except for these incorporations, the structure of the new faculty was little changed. A new Dean, Alan North, came from Sheffield along with a large research group working on pores in cell membranes. Much of the work in molecular bio-medicine is

Today and Tomorrow

Within the new University of Manchester the biosciences are organised for teaching and research purposes into the Faculty of Medical and Human Sciences and the Faculty of Life Sciences. However, the two faculties are led by a single Dean, Vice-President Professor Alan North, in a unique arrangement which is intended to improve opportunities for collaboration between clinical research in the medical field and cognate fundamental research in other parts of the University.

The Faculty of Medical and Human Sciences enjoys a research income of £51m, almost a third of the University's total research income. More students graduate in the School of Medicine than in any other UK medical school. The School's Medical Genetics group has founded the North West Genetic Knowledge Park (Nowgen), housing in purpose-built facilities a team of clinicians, scientists and communicators, who are dedicated to applying research in medical genetics and the social sciences to the benefit of patients and society.

In November 2005 the University assumed responsibility for the activities of the Paterson Cancer Research Institute and established the Manchester Cancer Research Institute (MCRC). The MCRC is working in close partnership with Christie Hospital and Cancer Research UK to consolidate the largest cancer research centre in Europe. Its overall aim is to expand research efforts and to foster translation of the knowledge gained into the development of better and more specific therapies for cancer patients.

The £25m Core Technology Facility (CTF) provides a next stage in terms of developing actual treatments for cancer and other diseases such as HIV. This 'hothouse' facility provides specialist accommodation for biotech companies, as well as laboratories for academic staff from both faculties. An example of the type of research unit to find a home in the CTF is the North West Embryonic Stem Cell Centre opened in 2006. The Centre boasts some of the most high-tech facilities in the UK, and will be a major contributor to stem cell research aimed at developing new treatments for diseases such as cancer and diabetes.

The Faculty of Life Sciences has moved into a purpose-built new home in the Michael Smith Building. As one of the largest unified research and teaching organisations of its kind in Europe, the Faculty operates on the principle that all barriers to collaboration between disciplines should be removed. The Faculty's research encompasses the entire spread of the life sciences from the molecule to the cell to the organism, spanning all fields of biology from environmental studies to cancer biology, from neuroscience to post genomics, and from structural biology to organ transplantation.

Scientists from both faculties are also collaborating in the Manchester Interdisciplinary Biocentre. This pioneering £35m facility was opened in 2006 to provide a base for more than five hundred scientists and up to eighty-five research groups.

The Michael Smith Building, named after the Manchester graduate who shared the Nobel Prize for Chemistry in 1993, houses research groups in molecular cell biology.

now housed in the Smith Building, named after Michael Smith, a Manchester chemistry graduate whose work on DNA replication won the Nobel Prize.

The Faculty of Medicine had already incorporated the departments of Nursing and Dentistry. Pharmacy had arranged to move from Science to Medicine, and after much debate Psychology made the same move. Both had benefited from the new patterns of student intake from the 1980s, which favoured professional courses and those that spanned arts and sciences.

The extra resources and ambitions associated with Project Unity open new vistas for both Science and Medicine, separately and in collaboration. Between the traditional Manchester strengths in physical sciences and clinical medicine is a newly strong faculty for the rapidly evolving sciences of life.

Law at Manchester

MAUREEN MULHOLLAND

Maureen Mulholland, a Manchester graduate who has taught in the Faculty of Law since 1964, is well equipped to describe the organisation of law teaching in Manchester since the early days of Owens College, its services to the legal profession, and some of the outstanding graduates and teachers that it has produced and sheltered.

The first Professor of Law and Jurisprudence at Owens College, appointed in 1855, was Richard Copley Christie. A scholar and antiquarian, he was also Chancellor of the Diocese of Manchester and had a successful practice at the Chancery Bar in Manchester. After his retirement in 1869 he gave to the University his collection of 7,500 books as well as the Christie Library, now converted to other uses, where he is commemorated by a portrait in stained glass and a bronze plaque.

The systematic teaching of law dates from 1872, when James Bryce instigated a syllabus that contained the basic subjects necessary for the practice of law and also included Roman law and jurisprudence. Bryce, an eminent Victorian radical and Liberal, held the Chair of Jurisprudence and Law until 1874 and he too practised at the Bar in Manchester. He was also responsible for engaging A.V. Dicey, author of *The Law and the Constitution,* and Thomas Erskine Holland, author of *Elements of Jurisprudence,* as lecturers at Owens College, albeit for only a short period. Both men later held Oxford chairs. Bryce himself left Manchester in 1880 to take up the Regius Chair of Law at Oxford. He published several works of distinction, became an MP, held office in Gladstone's last administration and later entered the House of Lords.

In 1875 Alfred Hopkinson was appointed to the Chair of Law and Jurisprudence which he held part-time until 1889. After a

The lawyer as bibliophile: stained-glass portrait on a staircase in the Christie Building.

Women at Manchester

Irene Zubaida Khan (1956–)

Irene Zubaida Khan has been the Secretary General of Amnesty International since 2001, the first woman, the first Asian and the first Muslim to lead the World's largest human rights organization. Her appointment just prior to the attacks of 11 September propelled her into the role at a critical juncture when increasingly grave violations of human rights were occurring in several parts of the world.

Khan grew up in Bangladesh, influenced in her thinking by the poverty and human rights abuses she witnessed in her nation's fight for independence from Pakistan. Eventually she was forced to flee as a refugee to the UK where she attended school in Northern Ireland, before coming to the Victoria University of Manchester to study law. Later she went on to the Harvard Law School, specializing in public international law and human rights.

Looking back, Irene remembers Manchester as the place in which her activism really started. She served as Overseas Officer in the Student Union and recalls protesting against the Portuguese Military Dictatorship and against South Africa in the 1970s. 'I boycotted Barclays and refused to eat Outspan oranges,' she reminisced on receiving the John Owens Award from the University in 2003.

Interested in working directly with people to change their lives, Irene Khan helped to found the development organization Concern Universal in 1977, and began her work as a human rights activist with the International Commission of Jurists in 1979. She joined the United Nations High Commission for Refugees (UNHCR) in 1980 and was appointed UNHCR Chief of Mission in India in 1995, the youngest UNHCR country representative at that time. She also led the UNHCR team in the Former Yugoslav Republic of Macedonia during the Kosovo crisis in 1999 and was appointed Deputy Director of International Protection later that year.

During her time at Amnesty International, Khan has been particularly identified with calls for better protection of women's human rights.

---

brief parliamentary career, he returned in 1898 as the first full-time law professor, remaining in office until 1913. He became the Principal of Owens College in 1898 and was later the last Vice-Chancellor of the Victoria University and the first of the independent Victoria University of Manchester. He was a graduate of Owens College, whence he had proceeded to Oxford, and the first Manchester-educated lawyer to become one of its professors. He, like Christie, practised at the Chancery Bar and became a Bencher and Treasurer of Lincoln's Inn. Other early law students of Owens College were Richard Pankhurst, a founder of the Independent Labour Party, barrister, husband of Emmeline and father of Sylvia and Christabel of suffragette fame; and George Henry Emmott, Associate Professor at Johns Hopkins University, Baltimore, who lectured in Washington D.C., and eventually became Professor of Law at Liverpool.

The early law students of Owens College were usually articled clerks and, until University status was acquired, those who wished to obtain a degree sat for the London University external LL.B.

Law was one of three faculties set up in the Victoria University, and one of five in the independent University in 1903. In that year, Christabel Pankhurst entered the faculty, the first woman to study law at Manchester University. In 1905 she was called before a disciplinary committee of Senate after she and Annie Kenny had been arrested and briefly imprisoned for disrupting a political meeting at the Free Trade Hall. Having given the University an undertaking to be of good behaviour in the future and concentrate on her studies, she graduated in 1906 with a first-class degree. Women were not yet admitted to the legal profession, but she demonstrated her legal skills and earned the epithet "the Suffragette Portia" when she defended herself and other suffragettes in a magistrates' court in London.

In establishing law teaching in Manchester, Bryce and his successors were encouraged and supported financially by the Manchester Law Association, established by Manchester solicitors and attorneys in 1821 as part of a move to improve the education and status of their profession. In 1905 the Faculty

Advisory Committee was set up, consisting of members of the Manchester Law Association (later the Manchester Law Society) and faculty staff, as well as representatives of the Bar and of the Law Society. This committee continued to support legal education in Manchester until the 1960s.

The First World War affected the University and its students as drastically as it affected the rest of society. Lectures were suspended on two afternoons a week for OTC training in the main quadrangle. There were forty-nine undergraduate students in the faculty in 1913–14, but numbers dwindled sharply as patriotic fervour led young men of all classes to volunteer. The Faculty of Law introduced a two-year LL.B. course to accommodate the needs of wartime, and special provision was made for those ex-servicemen who returned to obtain a degree. Reginald A. ('Ray') Eastwood graduated with a first-class degree in the first year of the war and joined the staff in 1915; apart from his war absence until 1919, he spent his whole career in Manchester University, becoming Professor in 1923.

The number of law students rose steadily between the wars, years that also saw the admission of the first women law students since Christabel Pankhurst. In 1922, Edith Hesling and Isabel Ritchie both graduated with first-class degrees. Edith Hesling went on to become the first woman to be called to the Bar in Gray's Inn and the first woman lecturer in the Faculty of Law.

Many Manchester students studied for the LL.B. degree at the same time as their articles, but it was possible to qualify as a solicitor without a degree. When, in the 1920s, the Law Society instituted an Intermediate and a Final Examination, J.L. Brierley, professor from 1920 to 1923, arranged for articled clerks who were not undergraduates to attend weekly lectures in basic law subjects for the Intermediate exam. These classes for the "statutory year", at first combined with classes for undergraduates, were later held separately and continued into the 1960s. A further development occurred in May 1938, when the faculty instituted a system of personal tutors; each LL.B. student would now have a member of staff as mentor and adviser throughout his or her course. This system was one of the characteristics of the Law Faculty, and has continued to the present day.

When war was declared in 1939, the University again made provision for degrees to be awarded in special circumstances to serving members of the armed forces. The war years were again marked by a drastic fall in the number of students; non-scientific courses, such as law, conferred no exemption from military or alternative service, and members of staff as well as students enlisted or were conscripted. Other members of staff undertook duties on the home front, including fire watching in the University. After the war, the numbers of law students increased; some were

Sir Alfred Hopkinson, K.C., law professor, Principal of Owens College 1898–1903 and Vice-Chancellor of the Victoria University of Manchester 1903–13.

straight from school and some ex-services, most of the latter not war veterans but young men who had completed their compulsory two years of national service.

Law students of the 1950s were conservative in dress and habits. Typical dress for men were flannel or corduroy trousers, ties – especially faculty or Law Students' Association ties – and jackets. Faculty scarves were worn by most students and the few women law students wore skirts, not trousers, for lectures or seminars. Students were addressed formally as "Miss X" or "Mr Y". Lectures were few, and exam standards rigorous. There were virtually no re-sits and failure in a summer exam would often be accompanied by exclusion or transfer to the Ordinary LL.B. course.

The 1950s were an era of stability in the faculty. Professor Eastwood, eccentric, deaf and fierce of eye, gave deceptively simple lectures and set savage exams; Professor Wortley, elegant in black

Peter Bromley (left), Professor of Law, later of English Law, 1965–86 with Rodney Brazier, Professor of Constitutional Law.

coat and striped trousers, lent an air of distinction. He took a kindly paternal interest in his students but, despite his expertise in international law, his lectures, said to be of the "shuffle and cut" method, were eclectic and opaque. In 1956, Harry Street, an outstanding Manchester graduate, returned to his *alma mater* as professor, having been professor at Nottingham University. He was visiting professor at Harvard during the session 1957–8 and on his return to Manchester he introduced the case method of teaching tort, in which students participated in the class; this became a feature of law teaching in Manchester. Professor Street combined a mild, kindly and unassuming manner with a strong insistence on high academic standards: many a student entered the lecture room at 9.30am with a feeling of cold fear that he or she would be called upon. In addition to his innovative work on tort, Street championed the "new" subject of Administrative Law on which, with John Griffith, he published an influential academic textbook. Peter (later Professor) Bromley specialised in Family Law, contributing, not least with the publication of *Family Law,* to the academic development of the subject.

The Law Students' Association (LSA) organised lectures, debates, moots and social events – including the annual dinner and parties (at the Christmas party, Peter Bromley recently reminded us, Professor Eastwood always had to win at musical chairs). For several years, the LSA also produced its own magazine. There was a football team and a mixed-faculty hockey team, and hikes in the Peak District led by Professor Eastwood and Mr Elliott. The LSA was later succeeded by the Manchester University Law Society. Perhaps because of a larger and mixed law student body, perhaps because, after the 1970s, students were formally members of the Board and committees, its emphasis was mainly social.

Professor Eastwood retired in 1960, after being Dean of the Faculty for thirty-seven years. From now on, the dean would be elected every two years, perhaps a symbol of the many changes in the University and the faculty. The new spirit of the 1960s hit the University as it did the whole of society. The decline of deference led students and junior members of staff to question the concept of government from the top by professors. Among law students actively involved in student activities were Dan Brennan (now Lord Brennan QC), President of the Union in 1965, and Margot Jacobs (now Professor Margot Brazier), who joined the great student sit-in of 1970. Sir William Mansfield Cooper, the Vice-Chancellor of the day, was a lawyer and a member of the Faculty Board. His retirement was a sad occasion for former colleagues or students who knew and respected him and mourned the dispute that eventually estranged him from the student body.

The expansion of higher education, following the Robbins Report of 1963, brought an increase in student numbers, and annual admissions to the law faculty in the 1960s increased to over one hundred.

The Faculty of Law has had a number of homes. The first, at Owens College, was Cobden House in Quay Street, described in contemporary reports as insalubrious and dangerous for the young gentlemen who attended lectures there. Later, the University moved to the present site in Oxford Road. From 1880 to 1926, however, law lectures were held in the Manchester Law Society's Law Library in Kennedy Street in the city centre until, because of increased numbers, they were moved to the main building in Oxford Road. In 1929 the faculty moved to 248 Oxford Road; then, in 1947, to Dover Street. During the 1950s its home was the so-called T Building, a large, single-storey Nissen hut and a miracle of post-war austerity, situated next to the Arts building. In 1965 it moved to the Humanities building, also using extra rooms in the Joint Matriculation Board and the German Church; in 1977 to the Mansfield Cooper Building and, in 1997, to the Williamson building.

One of the greatest changes in the faculty has been the steady increase in the number of women law students. From a mere handful each year in the 1950s, approximately half the intake each year is now female and the proportion of women members of staff has also increased. Gillian White was the first woman professor in the faculty, followed by Brenda Hoggett (Hale), Margot Brazier and others.

There have been many changes in the syllabus. The requirement to pass an Arts subject was abolished in 1961, and soon afterwards Roman law ceased to be a compulsory subject. Jurisprudence, true to the ideals of the founding fathers, has remained compulsory in the LL.B. course, which still provides most of the basic subjects for professional examinations. The range of law options, however, has been widened to include new subjects, such as Law, Medicine and

Ethics; Law and Economics; Media Law; and Intellectual Property Law. In the early 1990s, the University replaced three terms with a two-semester year, with modular courses often lasting for one semester only. The School of Law still retains the ideal of teaching in small seminars, one of the proud boasts of Manchester law teaching.

The LL.B. degree was the only undergraduate Manchester law degree until, in the early 1980s, Law combined with the departments of Economics and Mathematics to offer a joint four-year degree, the BA in Law and Accounting. Since then, the University has cooperated with the University of Burgundy at Dijon in an LL.B. in English and French Law and, with the Department of Government, in a BA in Law and Government. More recently, the School of Law has instituted a degree in Intellectual Property.

From its beginning, the law faculty was concerned with legal research, and postgraduate studies have become an increasingly important part of its work. Until 1979 the LL.M. was a research degree, but when the first taught LL.M. course (in International Business Law) was introduced, the first postgraduate research law degree became the M.Phil. Other taught Master's courses have

Professor R.A. Eastwood, Dean of Law, 1923–60.

Above: Law students gaining mooting experience.

Right: Ben Wortley, Q.C., Professor of Jurisprudence and International Law 1946–75.

followed. The MA in Medicine, Law and Ethics was introduced with the formation of the Centre for Social Ethics and Policy by Margot Brazier, John Harris and Mary Lobjoit, and the LL.M. in Law and Economics, involving partnership with two European continental universities, attracts an international following. There is now a strong emphasis on postgraduate work, with students from many countries, as well as home students, pursuing doctoral studies, though funding for such research is not easily available.

In 1991 a number of graduates and staff members formed the Manchester University Law Graduates' Association (MULGA) to further contacts between law graduates and the faculty. It has organised reunions and social events and contributed to funding to assist research students, especially through the Desmond Heap Fund.

Many Manchester law graduates and former members of staff have gone on to chairs at other universities. The majority of graduates still enter the legal profession, in which many have served with great distinction, including Lord Justice Russell, in the Court of Appeal; several High Court judges, including Douglas Brown, Joseph Cantley, Charles Mantell, Roger Buckley and Joyanne Bracewell, one of a small number of women; and Michael

Sachs, the first solicitor to be appointed to the High Court bench. Sir Rhys Davies was Recorder of the Manchester Crown Court and many Manchester graduates sit on the Circuit bench or chair tribunals. Lord Brennan QC and Lord Borrie are members of the House of Lords. Former members of staff have also achieved distinction, notably Baroness Brenda Hale, the first woman to be appointed to the Law Commission and the House of Lords, the highest court in the English legal system; Sir Maurice Kay in the Court of Appeal, and Sir Peter Smith in the High Court. Dr Julian Farrand was a Law Commissioner, then Insurance Ombudsman and Pensions Ombudsman.

The establishment, in the 1990s, of the *pro bono* Legal Advice Centre, where students encounter members of the public and learn under supervision to deal with legal problems, has strengthened traditional links with local solicitors and with the Manchester Bar.

The Faculty of Law ceased to exist in 2000 when it was succeeded by the School of Law within the Faculty of Economic and Social Studies and Law. A further change occurred with the establishment of the new University of Manchester in 2004, when the school became part of the Faculty of Humanities, but the tradition of sound teaching of law and good relationships with the profession continues in the twenty-first century.

Today and Tomorrow

Since law was not taught at UMIST, the School at VUM did not have to merge with any other body when the new University was created in 2004. Law retains its identity as one of eight schools within the new Faculty of Humanities at the University.

Tradition and modernity live side-by-side – for example, emphasis is being placed on theoretical and policy aspects of the discipline, on the many links which exist between law and society, and on the related disciplines of criminology and bio-ethics.

The Centre for Criminology and Socio-Legal Studies was created following the merger in 2004, and brings together staff from the former School of Law with staff from the former Department of Applied Social Sciences. These academics use a range of social science methods to study crime, the justice system and the way law works in society.

Another major research facility is the Centre for Social Ethics and Policy (CSEP), which is one of Europe's leading institutions undertaking research and teaching in bio-ethics and bio-law. Rapid and radical developments in medical and biosciences raise fundamental questions about society's understanding of life and death. Themes for research arise from the utilisation of human tissues from the living and the dead, the ethical implications of human genetics upon reproductive medicine and reproductive choice, genetics and health management, stem cell research and cloning, the creation of artificial life and the ethical implications of ageing and of life extending therapies.

Since 2000 the School of Law has run a free Legal Advice Centre, which is managed by School staff in association with the College of Law of England and Wales. Its work is supported by local solicitors and barristers as well as by the Manchester Law Society. The Centre aims to offer a reliable service to those with

Cherie Blair and Dinah Crystal (Director of Clinical Education and Practice) at the Legal Advice Centre.

legal and associated difficulties, and to provide practical experience for the Law School's students who are supervised by practitioners.

The School's newest research centre is the Institute for Law, Economics and Global Governance. The Institute brings together staff with an interest in law and economics, and staff whose work has an international dimension. With the foundation of the Brooks World Poverty Institute in 2006, it is likely that the role of law in developing countries will become an important element of future research activity within the School.

Economic and Social Sciences Since 1903

SAM MOORE

This chapter concisely describes the development in Manchester of a range of related academic disciplines, from economics and politics to sociology and social anthropology, from statistical studies to accounting and business finance. Sam Moore, a statistician who has applied his skills to solving the problems of high-level university policy and administration, has exhaustive knowledge and experience of the University at all levels – from undergraduate and research assistant to Acting Vice-Chancellor in 1990–92 and Robert Ottley Professor of Quantitive Studies.

Economic and Social Studies in the City prior to 1903

It is one of those unusual coincidences of history that Manchester in the 1840s was home to Friedrich Engels who, with his great friend Karl Marx, was the author of the *Communist Manifesto*, and also to Richard Cobden and John Bright, leaders of the Anti-Corn Law League and followers of the Manchester School of Economics. Cobden and Bright were believers in free trade and the efficacy of markets.

But one should not make too much of such coincidences. Manchester – the first industrial city – was growing at an incredible rate, and this growth generated many awful social problems. These were ably documented by Engels in his pioneering work of social investigation, *The Condition of the English Working Class*. Engels wanted to get those conditions improved – but so did Cobden and Bright. Abolition of the Corn Laws benefited the working and middle classes and in recognition they, in numbers, contributed to a memorial

fund for Cobden, which still pays for a Cobden Prize and a Cobden Lectureship at the University. In 1833, a number of local businessmen came together to found the Manchester Statistical Society. It had the objective of investigating and reporting on matters affecting the wellbeing and moral character of the labouring poor, and was very influential.

As the century progressed, and as the worst working and social conditions were alleviated, the attention of Manchester's business and professional community turned to other matters. One of these was education. The establishment of Owens College in 1851 was a signal of self-confidence. Soon after its foundation, the subject of political economy was being taught. The Cobden Lectureship was intended to bring political economy to the intelligent layman through the medium of evening lectures. In 1866, W.S. Jevons was appointed Professor of Logic and Political Economy. Jevons was a remarkable man who had had a colourful early career in Australia before returning to England to become an academic. He also died a brave death, drowning after rescuing another.

Jevons was among the first to use mathematics to attempt a rigorous foundation for economic analysis. But he was also curious about many practical matters: for example, he was controversial in his day for propounding a positive link between increased sun-spot activity and harvest yields. Jevons realised that teaching political economy as a branch of logic – while good training for the mind – did not link it to the

W.S. Jevons.

needs of practical businessmen. With the creation of the Victoria University of Manchester in 1903, a more practical approach was envisaged by the establishment of the Faculty of Commerce.

The Faculty of Commerce 1903–27

The Faculty of Commerce was created to meet the specific needs of young men who intended a career in private enterprise. With a general curriculum consisting of political economy, some law, accountancy and optional subjects, the new faculty in fact began to recruit both men and women (the latter slowly at first). One of the first to graduate with the degree of B.Com was Leonard Behrens, who went on to take M.Com (by thesis), and had a notable career as a Manchester businessman. Behrens made a huge contribution to the University, partly through personal benefaction and also because his daughter, Mary, married Lord Flowers who was to become Chancellor – a family connection lasting almost a hundred years.

Through the first fifteen years of its existence, the establishment and support of the faculty fell on just a few shoulders, notably Professor Sydney Chapman, Professor of Political Economy, who had steered it into existence. It grew slowly, but there was strong support among the business community. To tap into that support, evening classes were offered for young men who were working during the day. The First World War profoundly affected recruitment as young men rallied to the colours. But, as the war ended, returning servicemen wishing to resume or start their careers looked to the University – and every part of the University, including the faculty, did its bit to help them. Recruitment boomed.

During the early 1920s, the curriculum was extended, most notably by the addition of options in foreign languages for those wishing to conduct business abroad. The basic curriculum was strengthened – with, for example, more options in political economy. During this period the faculty produced one of its most distinguished graduates: John Jewkes. He graduated B.Com with a distinction in political economy, and later M.Com (by thesis). He became a professor in the faculty, and at Oxford, and an economic adviser to the war cabinet.

At the faculty's foundation, there had been a desire, but insufficient resources, for a curriculum to provide preparation for a business career but also for a career in public administration. Now, in 1927, as the faculty approached its twenty-fifth anniversary it was renamed the Faculty of Commerce and Administration. With the agreement of the Faculty of Arts, it was allowed to award BA and corresponding MA degrees in Commerce and Administration. And so, as the 1920s drew to a close, the new faculty entered a period that would be exciting and vigorous, intellectually and in other ways.

The Economics Building in Dover Street, formerly the High School for Girls, by Mills and Murgatroyd (1881–6).

The Faculty of Commerce and Administration 1927–46

As the new faculty came into existence, the world economy entered the slump known as the Great Depression. The manufacturing and exporting industries of the Northwest were badly affected, and the faculty realised that academic research was required to understand the impact of these changes, both on the industries themselves and also on the wider local economy. Thus was born the Economic Research Section. This pioneering unit brought together economists, administrators, statisticians and lawyers and was financed by benefactions, grants and fees. John Jewkes was soon appointed Professor of Social Economics and director of the section, supported by other home-grown talent. D.N. Chester, who had graduated through the evening classes, brought expertise in public administration; Harry Campion, who had been a day student, brought expertise in statistics, and Henry Hardman, a graduate in political economy, brought expertise in economics. It is remarkable to think that these three young men, working together in Manchester, were to achieve high public office in later years – Sir Norman Chester as Warden of Nuffield College; Sir Harry Campion as Director of the Central Statistical Office, and Sir Henry Hardman as Permanent Secretary to the Ministry of Defence.

The Economics Research Section was new in two important ways: first, it was interdisciplinary in its approach and, secondly, it brought new rigour to the collection, analysis and interpretation of data. Although not unique, the facility it provided for young scholars to spend time on research, with minimal teaching duties, was also unusual. It soon began to produce research reports, papers and books. It established its own research journal, *The Manchester School*, which still exists. It attracted worldwide interest, particularly from the USA. With the support of the Rockefeller Foundation, a number of members of the section visited North American universities to explain the work they were doing, and to learn from work being done in those institutions.

This was important and exciting work, but the more routine aspects of academic life had to continue. Students had to be recruited and taught. At this period the post-war growth peak in students had ended, and all universities had stable student populations, comprising about 5 per cent of the age group. The faculty had additional flexibility (and difficulty) because of its evening programme. Strong support for evening study came from the town hall, where young employees of promise were encouraged to undertake the evening degree. Many did so, and later went on to senior positions in local government.

The routine of faculty business fell on the shoulders of two people in particular: T.S. Ashton, Reader in Currency and Finance, and an economic historian of note; and Frances Collier, Secretary to Faculty Board, a formidable lady who commanded respect and awe in equal amounts. Throughout the 1930s, the faculty consolidated its reputation both in academic work and in teaching. Towards the end of the decade, as war threatened, the faculty appointed J.R. Hicks as Professor of Economics. Later (as Sir John Hicks) he was to win the Nobel Prize for Economics.

The period of the Second World War was to have more profound effects on the faculty than the first war. Initially, the concern was how to make arrangements for the students. Evening classes would be impracticable during the blackout, so they were rearranged and provided on Saturdays and Sundays. Full-time male students could, under certain circumstances, defer military service until after the

Professor J.R. Hicks who was made a Nobel Laureate in Economic Sciences in 1972.

completion of a degree. In common with other universities, shortened degrees were provided by Manchester, which allowed a student to graduate in two years rather than three, and the faculty rearranged courses so this was feasible. But the wartime government realised its need for special expertise in economics, statistics and administration, because it saw that the war had to be conducted on many fronts. As a consequence, Jewkes and his colleagues were soon called away from the faculty into government service. After the war, they did not return or, if they did, soon moved on to other things. As the war ended, the faculty faced a future that was to prove as exciting as any period in the past.

The Faculty of Economic and Social Studies 1946–60

In 1946, as it moved to Dover Street, the faculty was renamed the Faculty of Economic and Social Studies and, for the first time, had its own honours degree, the BA(Econ), although for the next twenty-five years students taking the BA(Com) and BA(Admin) would still be in the majority. Intellectually, the change recognised that economics was only one way of looking at the workings of society.

Far left: Professor Arthur Lewis who taught at Manchester from 1947 to 1958 and was made a Nobel Laureate in Economic Sciences in 1979.

Left: Sir Frank Worrall's plaque on the front of the Dover Street Building. The famous West Indian cricketer was a student at the University in 1950s.

Political science, social administration, social anthropology and, a little later, sociology all had a valid role to play. New appointments were made: Bill Mackenzie created a new Department of Politics; Max Gluckman established Social Anthropology, and Teddy Chester established Social Administration. An outstanding appointment in economics was that of Arthur Lewis (later Sir Arthur Lewis and a Nobel Prize winner) who, it is said, was the first West Indian to be appointed to a chair in a British university. A very unusual appointment was that of Michael Polanyi as Professor of Social Studies. He, in effect, transferred from being Professor of Chemistry (in Manchester) to the new post created for him; he had previously been a professor of medicine in Europe.

These scholars saw social sciences as a group of interrelated disciplines with mutual benefit from each other. The Wednesday afternoon seminar where they gathered became famous for its rigour and the breadth of the papers given and views expressed. Dorothy Emmett, Professor of Philosophy, was a frequent attender. Ely Devons, newly appointed Professor of Economics, became respected for the way he could find the weak points in any argument, and the trenchant way in which he exposed those weaknesses.

The curriculum of the BA(Econ), while allowing specialisation in the third year, ensured that students would be exposed to a variety of social sciences in the first two years of the degree. During this time higher education in economic and social studies came to be seen less as a direct preparation for employment and more as an education in its own right. The research interests of the new appointees were national or international in scope, rather than local or regional. These developments were assisted by two generous benefactions, both made in the 1940s. The first was by H.M. Hallsworth, who wished to support political economy (broadly defined), and the second by Lord Simon who wished to support social sciences.

The Faculty of Economic and Social Studies 1960–2004

In 1960, Jack Johnston arrived from Wisconsin to take the first Chair of Econometrics in a British university. He brought with him ideas for a graduate school that would provide taught Master's degrees. That development also brought a new BA(Econ), in which a two-year social science general programme led to a much more specialised third year. The old ordinary egrees in commerce and administration were abolished. The new Master's programmes were soon a success and recruited well, but the tension at the heart of the BA(Econ) continued. Nevertheless, it provided an excellent education: among its many graduates were Anna Ford, the broadcaster and future Chancellor of the University; Lord Levene, who became Lord Mayor of the City of London, and Lord Burns, who became Permanent Secretary to the Treasury.

The range of the social sciences continued to expand. Peter Worsley was appointed as the first Professor of Sociology, and Wat Thomas the first Professor of Agricultural Economics. Agricultural economics had a background that extended back to farm management investigations in the 1930s; it had been given established status with the Farm Management Survey after the war. There were close links with economic history.

The establishment of a Chair of Accounting – and the appointment of Bryan Carsberg to it – completed the range of the social sciences provided by the faculty. But now a new tension appeared – between subjects that were less quantitative in approach, and those that were more so. A further revision of the BA(Econ) was undertaken, which led to a degree with only one year of general social science (including some quantitative training), and two years of specialisation. This structure proved stable, and has formed the basis of undergraduate education for more than thirty years. Although some specialist degrees have been established, the core undergraduate curriculum is still, today, delivered through the BA(Econ) programme.

The implementation of the Robbins Report saw undergraduate numbers double during the 1960s. Over the same period, the graduate programme proved an attraction for overseas students whose numbers also increased dramatically. One such student was Erskine Sandiford, later to become Prime Minister of Barbados.

Today and Tomorrow

The School of Social Sciences (SoSS) in the new University of Manchester comprises five distinct groups: Economics, Government (including Philosophy), Social Anthropology, Sociology and the Cathie Marsh Centre for Census and Survey Research.

Academics in the social sciences at Manchester have long worked with colleagues from other disciplines and institutions. The School generates substantial external research income and is involved in a number of prestigious Economic and Social Research Council Centres, notably the Centre for Research on Socio-Cultural Change (CRESC) and the National Centre for e-Social Science (NCeSS).

The CRESC, launched in October 2004 in partnership with the Open University, is the first major research centre in Britain to develop a broad, empirically focused account of cultural change and its economic, social and political implications. Meanwhile, the NCeSS, formed in partnership with the University of Essex, seeks to raise awareness of, and expertise in, e-science within the social science research community.

Looking ahead, a key development for the School has been entry into a partnership with Harvard University in 2006. The two institutions are joining forces to help Britain and America better understand the challenges of contemporary society. Researchers from the two universities will conduct a series of transatlantic comparative studies on topics such as inequality, immigration, religion, the changing workplace and civic engagement. They will investigate what drives social change, how it relates to the well being of members of society and the implications for policy makers – issues which confront political leaders on both sides of the Atlantic.

Professor Robert Puttnam.

This joint project is to be directed by Professor Robert Putnam, Peter and Isabel Malkin Professor of Public Policy at Harvard's Kennedy School of Government. Professor Putnam, who takes up a Visiting Professorship at Manchester, is renowned for his influential research into community ties. His book *Bowling Alone*, published in 2000, charts the thirty-year decline of social connectivity in the US and has been the subject of heated debate among politicians and commentators – including Tony Blair, Bill Clinton, and George Bush.

As the 1970s came to an end, it would be fair to say that the faculty had become comfortable and perhaps a little complacent. The announcement in the summer of 1981 that it had to face budget cuts of 18 per cent ended that complacency, but it proved very skilful at delivering the cuts with minimum damage. The skills of the economist and social scientist were brought to bear on the problem – and what the faculty had been teaching for so many years now proved valuable. It emerged from this period stronger than before.

The major intellectual revolution of the next twenty years was (as in so many other areas of modern life) the growth in the use of computers. From the early 1960s, computing had been used for econometric studies and survey analysis. By 1970, the faculty had decided to create its own support unit to assist with computing problems. At that time, all computing was done on large mainframe computers, and expert help was needed to use them. Political scientists, sociologists and accountants all began using computers extensively. By the end of the 1990s, the personal computer had become the essential teaching and research tool for every social scientist.

Although the faculty remained a cohesive group of economic and social scientists, there were important links to other groups. The Health Services Management Unit had grown out of initiatives by Teddy Chester and Gordon Forsyth. And PREST (Policy Research in Engineering, Science and Technology), while an independent research unit, had close links to the faculty, particularly to economics and to politics.

Perhaps the most important development relating to the work of the faculty over this period was the creation of the Manchester Business School. Professors Bruce Williams, Charles Carter and Douglas Hague all made significant contributions to its establishment and initial success. As the faculty achieved its centenary, it looked forward to vanishing, then reappearing, as part of the Faculty of Humanities of the new University of Manchester – and to another hundred years of teaching and research.

Business and Management

JOHN ARNOLD, KEN GREEN AND CHRIS HUMPHREY

The Faculty of Economic and Social Studies was originally called the Faculty of Commerce and was at first designed to help students already engaged in business, many of whom took part-time degrees by attending evening classes. In the 1960s, Lord Franks recommended the establishment of business schools "to increase competence in managers or those who will be managers" and to provide them with "framework knowledge". Three leading figures in the new Manchester Business School of 2004, John Arnold, Ken Green and Chris Humphrey, describe the development in four separate places in the University and Tech of business studies as an academic discipline, and show how these schools, departments and institutes eventually congregated under a single umbrella.

On 1 October 2004 four partners came together to form a new school of business and management (the new Manchester Business School) in the new University of Manchester. In this chapter we provide a brief history of each of the partners and outline the strategy for the new school.

Manchester School of Management

Manchester School of Management can claim one of the longest pedigrees of any management or business school in Europe, tracing its history back to the Department of Industrial Administration that was set up in 1918.

While Industrial Administration continued into the 1950s, with a small number of staff teaching part-time post-experience students, it was not until the 1960s that management education really took off in UMIST. In 1965, UMIST set up a Department of Management Sciences, based on a large undergraduate degree,

with one hundred students by 1970. Such a degree was a novelty, the focus in other universities being on postgraduate business and management education.

With the active contributions of Professors Roland Smith, Ronald Beresford Dew, George Bain (later to become head of the London Business School), Cary Cooper, John Goodman and John Pickering – who between them covered a wide range of management and business functions in their teaching and research – the Department of Management Sciences went from strength to strength in the 1970s and 1980s. The strength was based initially on the department being the largest recruiter of undergraduate students in UMIST. However, there was a much stronger focus on research and the recruitment of doctoral students, which was rewarded when the department's research was recognised as outstanding by the 1985 Research Assessment Exercise (RAE), a

Entrance of the Manchester Business School East, by ORMS, 1997.

The Manchester Business School West, designed c.1972, by Cruickshank and Seward.

The Manchester Business School East.

distinction shared with only one other department of business and management, Warwick Business School.

In 1988, there was a change of name to Manchester School of Management (MSM). New, internationally-focused undergraduate degrees were launched, but the biggest innovation was the development of one-year specialist Master's degrees covering all the subjects in which the school was actively engaged in research. By 1991, the school had 600 undergraduates, 200 postgraduates and 70 teaching staff, with a growing research reputation. It obtained the top research ratings from the RAE in 1992 (5) and 1996 (5A*). This success was also recognised by employers: throughout the 1990s, MSM was in the employers' top five schools in the UK for recruiting business studies students. In 1998, the school moved to a new building close to its partners in the Federal School of Business and Management, established in 1994 to facilitate collaboration between those schools and centres actively engaged in business and management teaching in both UMIST and the Victoria University.

By the end of the twentieth century, MSM had become a major international player in management and education research, with over one thousand students and 100 teaching and research staff.

Manchester School of Accounting and Finance

Having been taught as an optional subject initially within the BCom, and subsequently the BA(Econ), Accounting and Finance was visibly established within the Faculty of Economic and Social Studies in 1969, when Bryan Carsberg was appointed as the first

Professor of Accounting at the Victoria University. The then-named Department of Accounting and Business Finance had just six academic staff, with around twenty students enrolled. It expanded steadily during the 1970s, with Professors John Arnold, Robert Scapens and Tony Hope leading the development of the subject area at Manchester. Having served as Dean of the Faculty of Economic and Social Studies, Bryan Carsberg left to become professor in accounting at the London School of Economics and has subsequently held a number of high-profile public offices.

The title of the department was changed to Accounting and Finance in 1986 and to the Manchester School of Accounting and Finance (MSAF) in 1997. It expanded and developed rapidly in the 1980s and 1990s, eventually under the headships of professors Martin Walker, Trevor Hopper and Stuart Turley, resulting in the establishment of a strong international research reputation across a broad range of accounting and finance disciplines, with provision of a wide range of quality programmes at undergraduate, master's and doctoral level. MSAF's top-class research status was notably evidenced by all the RAEs undertaken to date, culminating in the granting of its 6* status as a result of its high ratings in both 1996 and 2001.

The influence of Manchester on the academic accounting and finance community can be readily seen by the numerous former staff holding senior professorial positions in other universities in the UK and overseas. It is also reflected in a key element of the accounting and finance tradition at Manchester, the maintenance of strong professional links. Manchester has not only provided the accounting and finance professions with many graduates who have gone on to pursue highly successful careers – one of the most notable being Robert Herz, the current chair of the Financial Accounting Standards Board in the USA – but its staff also play important roles in the operating and governance committees of national professional bodies.

Manchester Business School

Manchester Business School was formed in 1965 following a period of intense debate during the early 1960s about the need for US-style business schools in the UK. A report and subsequent deliberations by Lord Franks recommended the establishment of two graduate business schools – one (inevitably) in London and the other in Manchester.

The school's first Director was Grigor McClelland. As both a businessman and an academic, McClelland was the ideal choice; the new school was to be business-led and characterised by continuous innovation, with academics who were multi-disciplinary.

The first phase of the school's life was characterised by a series of successful post-experience programmes and the launch of a full-time MBA in 1967 – the first of its kind in the UK. Both types of programme involved project-based learning (now often called experiential learning) using live projects. Both were also aimed at mature students with some work experience. This approach became known as the Manchester Method and variants are now widely adopted in the business school community worldwide.

The 1970s saw the second phase of the school's development. While post-experience programmes continued with some success, the MBA failed to grow at the rate originally predicted, stabilising at an annual intake of some sixty to seventy students. This led to two concerns – an imbalance between post-experience and degree-bearing programmes, and a lack of adequate finances. In 1977 Professor Tom Lupton took over as director.

The 1980s saw two further changes in director (Dr Rab Telfer, a businessman, in 1984 and Professor Tom Cannon in 1989). The decade, which might be termed the third phase, also saw significant changes in direction. The first was a move away from general open management programmes to client-specific programmes, tailored to the needs of particular organisations working in partnership with the school. The second was the launch of part-time executive and degree programmes. The third, and perhaps the most significant, was the increasing recognition of the importance of conventional academic research to a university-based business school – especially in the face of disappointing results in the RAEs of 1986 and 1989. RAE results steadily improved until, in 2001, the School came close to achieving the highest grade on the scale.

A major watershed was reached in 1991 when the University rejected a proposal that the school should become an independent company in favour of the establishment of a Federal School of Business and Management comprising the four partners that were eventually to come together to form the new Manchester Business School.

The final phase of development, from 1991 to 2004, saw the appointment of Professor Tony Cockerill as acting Head from 1991 to 1994 and the appointment of Professor John Arnold as Director from 1994 until the merger. The full-time MBA programme, with an annual intake of over one hundred, was by now competing with over a hundred schools in the UK and many hundreds in the USA, continental Europe and elsewhere. The part-time MBA was launched, as was a suite of distance-learning MBAs. The part-time programme was a joint venture with UMIST's Manchester School of Management. Executive programmes were almost all tailored to the needs of individual organisations.

In spite of all the changes, much of the philosophy espoused by the school's founding fathers remained. It continued to recognise the importance of business requirements in both the private and public sectors; it pursued a policy of continuous innovation; it encouraged interdisciplinary approaches to both teaching and research; and it made extensive use of experiential learning.

Institute of Innovation Research

The Institute of Innovation Research was established in 2000 as a joint research and graduate teaching centre between UMIST and the Victoria University. By 2003 it had been re-housed in a refurbished building, financed by a £6m UK government grant to support the development of research in all aspects of innovation policy and management.

The Institute brought together three existing highly-rated research centres: PREST (Policy Research in Engineering, Science and Technology), CROMTEC (Centre for Research on Organisations, Management and Technical Change) and CRIC (Centre for Research on Innovation and Competition).

PREST was the oldest of these centres, dating from 1977, when it was established as the research wing of the University's Department of Liberal Studies in Science, one of the first European university departments to run undergraduate, master's and doctoral

Bronze bust of Lord Haslam of Bolton, Chairman of the MBS from 1986–90.

Today and Tomorrow

The New Manchester Business School

The vision for the new school is perhaps best captured in the phrase "Creating the Ideas and Business Leaders of Tomorrow". MBS seeks to become one of the world's leading and most innovative business schools by making its provision relevant to leading organisations in the private, public and voluntary sectors and by being the first business school truly to achieve a virtuous cycle linking the practice of leadership in such organisations with the advancement of knowledge about how such organisations succeed.

In parallel with other schools within the Faculty of Humanities, the Business School is actively engaged in a number of interdisciplinary research activities. The Institute of Innovation Research (IoIR), established in 2003, is one of the key sites in Europe for postgraduate training provision in the fields of science policy, technology management, economics of technological change and innovation studies. The Institute houses a number of major research groups, including the Economic and Social Research Council Centre for Research in Innovation and Competition (CRIC).

The CRIC undertakes fundamental research into institutional, economic, organisational and cultural aspects of the 'Emerging Innovative Economy'. Its research is organized into three overlapping programmes of work: innovation in services; the relationship between innovation and consumption; and the evolving bio- and medical economies. The Centre enjoys close connections with government and leading firms in the UK and global economy. It also participates in several major international research networks, adding an important comparative dimension to the research.

An exciting new initiative is the establishment of the Herbert Simon Institute which aims to become the pre-eminent centre of public policy and management in Britain and a leading international centre of excellence. Across the developed and developing worlds, governments are struggling with issues of how to provide efficient and effective public services which can earn the trust of the public and increase social well-being and cohesion. The global debate has moved beyond public versus private – the recognition of the importance of the public domain is now widespread, including its role in facilitating effective markets. As a result, debates about policy and management of the public domain have never been so prominent.

In January 2007 Professor Michael Luger joined the Manchester Business School as its new Director. Professor Lugar was formerly Professor of Entrepreneurship and Director of the Center for Competitive Economies at Kenan-Flagler Business School, one of the leading business schools in the United States.

Professor Michael Luger.

programmes in science and technology policy and management. The department and PREST proved an excellent place for the training of researchers and policy-makers in the management of innovation.

CROMTEC was established in 1987 in UMIST's School of Management, with a focus on research on the role of technological change in management practice and in the functioning of organisations. Its first work concentrated on information and communication technologies, but this soon expanded to work on biotechnology and environmental technologies. CROMTEC's founder, Rod Coombs (now Vice-President for Innovation and Economic Development in the new University), established a knowledge transfer arm when he established the Technology Strategy Forum in 1995, bringing together senior technology and research and development managers of leading UK companies.

CRIC was a joint venture between UMIST and the University, established in 1997 and funded by the UK's Economic and Social Research Council to work on the relationship between innovation and competition. It has quickly established itself as an internationally renowned research centre in areas such as innovation and consumption and innovation and services. CRIC continues in the new University as a joint venture between the Business School and the School of Social Sciences.

The bringing together of these three entities into the Institute of Innovation Research was made easier by the long-term collaboration between the centres. The opening of the Institute marked the beginning of a new phase in the development of studies in innovation, a phase marked by new challenges posed to technological development by globalisation, the growth of the knowledge economy and new imperatives of environmental protection and sustainability.

Education

ALEX B. ROBERTSON AND COLIN LEES

Alex Robertson and Colin Lees describe the prehistory and history of the Faculty of Education, which the University established in 1914. They show how the theory and practice of education became (despite some scepticism) a university subject; explore the University's relationship with teacher training colleges (later called colleges of education); and describe some of the specialities that made Manchester famous – including the training of teachers of the deaf.

In 1890 government took steps to strengthen the pupil teacher system by encouraging universities to set up training colleges. After considerable heart-searching the University agreed, and a college for male students opened that year. This low-key endeavour, with no guarantee of permanence, survived to become one of four new faculties that followed independent status in 1903, and its success was due to such stalwart supporters of the academic study of education as Professors Alexander, Tout, Lamb and Dixon, who were convinced of its appropriateness as a university study. In 1892 a college for women was added and brought to Manchester the woman who did so much to raise the profile of the subject in the early years, the creative and flamboyant Catherine Dodd. Steeped in the philosophies of Froebel, Herbart and Rein, she brought a new approach to the teaching of young children. This challenged the passive and memory-based learning that was still dominant, and was researched in an experimental school founded by her in Brunswick Street.

Because the University had set the first two years of the degree course as a benchmark for new and untried students, standards were high, and soon training for secondary education was included. The education work was to bring the University into greater contact with regional local government than any other of its responsibilities. So successful were these early years that the idea of a Chair of Education, then a rarity, gained credibility, and in 1899 Harry L. Withers, principal of the prestigious Borough Road College, was appointed to what became in 1901, after a major endowment, the Sarah Fielden Chair. In 1903 Joseph Findlay was appointed to the Fielden Chair following the death of Withers, and the distinguished civil servant, Michael Sadler, to the personal Chair of History and Administration of Education.

Findlay was one of the country's most influential educationists and made his department one of the best known at home and abroad. His determination to raise the research profile of an

The Centre for Deaf Education, 1965.

activity that many academics still believed incapable of being studied seriously led to the granting of faculty status in 1914, the first in the country – a measure of how far Education had come since its tentative beginnings. Due to Findlay, Manchester became the first university to appoint a woman as dean. His prolific writing, speaking and experimental work, particularly exploring the work of Dewey and Montessori in the internationally influential Fielden Demonstration School, drew his staff and large numbers of students into what was the beginning of modern training methods and the serious study of the constituent disciplines of education. A Master's degree in Education was soon established, and before Findlay's retirement in 1925 the first doctorates were awarded. One development that enhanced the reputation of department and University was the foundation in 1919 of a lectureship in the education and teaching of the deaf, made possible by the generosity of Sir James Jones in memory of his son, and enhanced in 1921 by the endowment of Ellis Llwyd Jones Hall at Old Trafford. This made possible the appointment of Irene Goldsack, who was soon to marry Alexander Ewing and create the internationally prestigious Ewing partnership.

The increasing involvement of Whitehall in national education brought University and faculty under the oversight of the Board of Education, a situation disliked by the department for its bureaucracy and by the University as an infringement of its autonomy. However, it ensured that the University was cognisant of new trends, which had implications for its own recruitment. For a period after Findlay's retirement, the faculty lost its reputation for experimental work, partly due to the University's continuing scepticism that education was a university subject, and partly to the financial stringency of the time. It was respected, however, under professors Smith and Duff, for the excellence of its teacher training and its continuing significance in emerging primary education.

There were two significant innovations in the inter-war years. The first was the University's response to the introduction in 1917 of the School Certificate examination, which was to become not only a leaving certificate but also a major element in the selection of undergraduates. Inevitably, the faculty was called upon to guide University policy by providing senior representation on the Matriculation Board. The second was cooperation with government's attempt to improve standards in the traditional training colleges by creating clusters of colleges or Joint Boards, validated by a university, to influence their work and raise standards. Despite some University hesitancy, this initiative survived to become, a generation later, of major importance in the region.

The years before the Second World War saw some attempt to modernise the education system in response to the Hadow

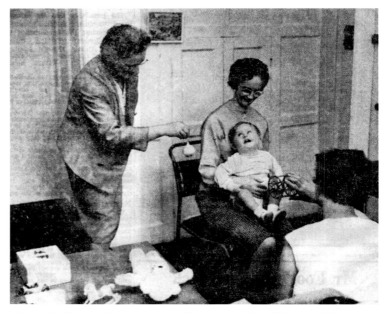

Above: Hearing test for a baby at the Department of Audiology and Education of the Deaf, 1961.

Reports, while legislation in 1944 introduced a radical new system. The man responsible for leading the department through this and guiding the University in its responses was Richard Oliver, appointed to the Sarah Fielden Chair in 1938 and remaining, despite a huge increase in the faculty's responsibilities and size, the main policy-maker until 1970. Oliver's preoccupations were academic excellence and high-quality research. Despite the austerity of the post-war years, he appointed specialists in research methods, statistics and experimental education, and an upsurge in the reputation of the department began. This was aided by a convergence of departmental expertise and the national interest of the time. Oliver was a psychologist specialising in psychometrics, which was about to become a vital, if controversial, aspect of the new three-tiered education system. His department rapidly became a leader in this field and its research contributed to the national strategy for assigning children to appropriate schools. Stephen Wiseman headed the advanced work and put the teaching of doctoral and master's research on a sound administrative footing for the first time, although his main interest was in the social aspects of education and how a child's background affected the ability to study and succeed. From this developed research on the curriculum implications of raising the school-leaving age.

Departmental reputations were highly regarded, consultancy work flowed in, and the faculty became a powerhouse of staff moving to chairs elsewhere. Oliver was influential nationally and sat on the Secondary Schools Examination Council and the

National Foundation for Educational Research. In particular, his reputation persuaded the University to adopt the most radical recommendations of the McNair Report of 1944. This greatly extended the role of the old Joint Boards by firmly integrating the training colleges in the University through an Area Training Organisation (ATO). The ATO was governed by a complex network of representative committees coordinated by a School of Education in the Faculty of Education. In addition to being a validating body, Oliver's aim was to create a two-way process of interaction and research which would unite all the regional training work; for over thirty years the influence and character of the faculty was enriched by this responsibility. It included in-service training for experienced teachers through short lecture courses, and the introduction of specialist diplomas that reflected the basic disciplines of education; by Oliver's retirement, these had been extended to include youth work, educational guidance, the education of those with disabilities and community education. It was carried a stage further after the Robbins Report of 1963 when teacher training institutions were permitted to award Bachelor in Education (B.Ed) degrees, and the faculty took on even more extensive validating and monitoring responsibilities.

Audiology work had grown in reputation, achieving department status; the physicist Dr T.S. Littler was recruited, adding greatly to the Ewings' work in developing aids to improve residual hearing. In 1949 Oliver succeeded in establishing a Chair of Audiology and Education of the Deaf. This was paralleled in the same year by the establishment of a Chair of Adult Education for Ross Waller from the extra-mural work in the University. This became one of the pioneering departments of adult studies, and one of its most important initiatives was to extend its services to overseas students. Out of this grew a diploma, the Teaching of English Overseas, destined to be a long continuing area of the faculty's work. Another department of Oliver's years was Physical Education, which had responsibilities throughout the University but was integral to teacher training programmes.

Before the 1960s all the departments and the School of Education were scattered across the campus. A move to the former Manchester High School for Girls in Dover Street improved this, before a move to the new Humanities Building brought the faculty together, except for Physical Education which was housed in the McDougall Sports Centre. Oliver's last initiative was to increase the prominence of a caring aspect of education by negotiations that led to the Hester Adrian Research Centre in 1967, focusing on the education of children with mental disabilities. In 1973 its director, Peter Mittler, became Professor of

Programme of lunch-time lectures organised by the Extra-Mural Department, 1968–69.

Special Education, the first such chair in the UK. Oliver's retirement in 1970 created an inevitable watershed – he and Findlay had controlled the first fifty-four years of the department's existence. Politically, education was soon to enter a new phase of government intervention, which greatly affected how the department was structured and worked.

Because the last thirty years of the twentieth century witnessed almost continuous modification of the education system, the Faculty of Education found itself in need of major and frequent adaptation to reflect the national situation. There was some continuity with the past as existing practice was adapted to meet current thinking. Work in audiology, for example, continued, although with changes in respect of the teacher training dimension. The trend in the long run was for the department to move closer to Medicine, with which it recently integrated. Special needs flourished due to a national emphasis on children with learning difficulties, and the work gained international prominence. The policy for comprehensive schools and the abolition of selection for secondary education did not decrease the major role of psychology, which was vital in mainstream, special needs training and in-service work. The other traditional disciplines – history, philosophy, sociology and comparative studies – enjoyed a golden age, upgrading the skills of lecturers in colleges of education to meet B.Ed criteria, but it was short-lived, and by the new millennium all had vanished.

The multicultural nature of British society led to the creation of a chair for the internationally respected Professor G.K. Verma.

Today and Tomorrow

The new School of Education within the University of Manchester hosts one of the largest graduate education and research communities in the UK and has numerous links with external agencies. It offers twenty-five taught programmes ranging from certificate through to doctoral studies, including an MSc in Educational Research recognised by the Economic and Social Research Council. The School maintains a national reputation for research excellence in the fields of Inclusive and Special Needs, Pedagogy and Teacher Development, Leadership and Management in Educational Contexts, and in Urban Education and Research Methods.

The School hosts the Centre for Educational Leadership (CEL) which was established in 1997. It is recognised increasingly as a world-class leadership centre and is one of the largest providers of public sector leadership programmes and qualifications with over 8,000 clients working regionally and nationally.

CEL's Research and Development Directorate was formed to bring together the work being undertaken across the fields of consultancy, educational leadership and design and development, and the research projects and initiatives which naturally flow from these areas. The Design and Development Unit has grown from within the Research and Development Directorate to develop programmes and materials for both national and international clients. The first national programme was Leading from the Middle, an innovative blended learning programme combining face-to-face, online and school-based activities. International work now includes working alongside partners in Kenya and the Czech Republic to produce leadership materials for schools.

Participants gather in the atrium of the Centre for Educational Leadership's main centre, based in The University of Manchester's School of Education, prior to a leadership training event.

The Centre for Equity in Education involves practitioners, policy makers and researchers in collaborative development and research projects. It aims to develop a better understanding of the nature of the challenges facing the education service particularly in the education of vulnerable groups.

The faculty itself took on an international aspect, with many postgraduates from abroad and the development of consultancies in developing countries.

Dramatic changes occurred in response to the national curriculum and its testing procedures. The department already had an established reputation for curriculum development and evaluation and, due to the reputation of Professor Christie, much advisory and research work was undertaken in this field. M.Ed and doctoral courses were redesigned to be flexible and relevant for the needs of students. Devolution of initial training to schools changed course and work patterns dramatically. Emphasis on improving senior teacher effectiveness led to chairs in educational leadership and management, and the faculty became responsible for a major initiative in head teacher training. An attempt by the University in the 1980s to extend community access led to a long-lasting part-time BA in education. Government emphasis on research encouraged dramatic changes in the profile of the faculty as departments were dismantled and research centres constructed around related themes to enhance research relevance and quality. Committee and other structures were reconfigured to emphasise research, and high-level training courses were introduced for postgraduates. At the time of writing, these trends and uncertainties continue as, more than most areas of university work, the study of education is susceptible to outside factors. In the changes following the foundation of the new University in 2004, Education ceased to be a faculty in its own right and became a school within the Faculty of Humanities.

Part 3

Student Life

Residences and Lodgings

ARTHUR MAWBY AND GERARD MCKENNA

Manchester students lived at home, in lodgings supervised by landladies, in flats or houses owned by the University or by private landlords, or in specially designed halls of residence which were not just hostels but could rival the unions as centres of social life. Arthur Mawby and Gerard McKenna describe the wide range and great diversity of accommodation. Dr Mawby taught in the History Department and was until recently Warden of St Anselm Hall (a men's residence in Victoria Park, founded by the Church of England in 1907). Mr McKenna, a member of the Registrar's Department, was in charge of the University Accommodation Office 1982–97.

By the late 1930s halls of residence were already playing a small but important part in the life of the University – small because most students came from the local area and did not live in, but important because both the University and the halls' own residents attached great significance to them. Perhaps tellingly, the only halls directly owned by the University were for women: Ashburne in Fallowfield and Ellis Llwyd Jones in Old Trafford. All the other halls intended exclusively for the University's students were owned by the religious denominations that had founded them, and were located in the fading grandeur of Victoria Park: Langdale, an Anglican foundation for women; Hulme and St Anselm, Anglican foundations for men; St Gabriel's, a Roman Catholic foundation for women; and the oldest purpose-built hall, Dalton, a Quaker foundation for men. Beyond these seven halls, a number of other mainly religious institutions accommodated a few students. And beyond them all were the homes of the large number of students

A tower block residence – part of the 'student village' of Owens Park in Fallowfield, opened in 1964.

Left: One of the eight modern blocks of the Richmond Park residencies located at the Fallowfield campus.

Bottom left: A modern student bedroom in Richmond Park.

Below: The buildings in Victoria Park to which the Anglican Hulme Hall moved from Plymouth Grove in 1907.

residence and to their role in students' experience. The University of Manchester and its wardens were fully engaged in this discussion. In 1955, the Vice-Chancellor suggested that Manchester's students, though intellectually excellent, were receiving too narrowly academic an education which was not adequately preparing them for the wider aspects of their later careers: "the only way to remedy this defect is to take steps to become ... a residential university," he concluded.

Manchester had good reason to be concerned about this issue. It stood at the forefront of the later nineteenth-century English universities, and both its reputation and its ambition were growing rapidly. Yet in its residential provision for students it fell below the national average, and well behind institutions which by status and standing it considered distinctly its inferior. Worse still, the great majority of Manchester's meagre provision was made not by the University at all but by independent institutions.

Most of Manchester's students lived either at home or in lodgings. For some students, this accommodation served them well; it was relatively cheap, and some were left with happy memories of devoted landladies. The contribution of the latter was acknowledged every year at the landladies' tea party, when the Vice-Chancellor and members of staff, all wearing academic robes, thanked them for their efforts. For other students, however, living at home or in lodgings

living in lodgings or with their families. All halls admitted students from all parts of the University.

The Second World War posed a particular challenge to the halls. They all had to make special arrangements for emergencies and for the safety of their students, and also had to impose endless wartime regulations while simultaneously coping with food rationing. In addition, men's halls lost a large proportion of their residents to active service, though many of their places were taken by officer cadets on six-month training courses.

One of the most long-lasting effects of the war was the wide-ranging national debate it provoked about education. Much attention was paid to the need for more university halls of

Dalton Hall was founded in 1876 by the Society of Friends and originally called Friends' Hall. A small male community whose motto was "nec solitudo nec tumultus" ("neither loneliness nor rowdiness"), it moved to specially constructed premises in Victoria Park in 1881. It was then renamed in honour of the Quaker scientist John Dalton. The programme for Dalton's Jubilee Social, celebrating the fiftieth anniversary of Owens College, was designed by Hamilton Irving of Huddersfield, who resided at Dalton from 1896 to 1901.

was restrictive and isolating, often involving long daily journeys and a lack of congenial study environments. Such circumstances were especially trying at weekends unless one took refuge in team sports or sought congenial company at the Saturday night Union dance. Life in lodgings was certainly very different from that of later generations who rent flats or houses; far from being a free agent, one was a guest in the house of a landlady, who supervised one's comings and goings. Crucially, the university experience of students who were home- or lodgings-based was largely confined to the working day and to fellow students studying the same course. Some rose above these restrictions by becoming heavily involved in the Students' Union or in one of its many societies. Others argued that, unlike those cloistered in a hall, they were learning to cope with the "real world". Yet many students agreed with their Vice-Chancellor in feeling that they were being short-changed.

The distinguished Niblett Committee of the UGC, which reported in 1957, believed that a hall should "mean far more than

a place in which to eat and sleep" and that it could have a "civilising and humanising influence" on its students. However, a hall would only become such "an instrument of liberal education" if it was put under the control of a sympathetic person who took the trouble to see that it developed in this way. Such a hall would be "full of life and ideas", and might have "debating societies, discussion groups, play reading and dramatic clubs, visits of outside lecturers, enterprise in social service", as well as music making, team sports, a small general library, and much else, so that a hall became "half the total influence of a university on a student". The Committee also concluded that the optimum size for a hall was 130 to 150 members.

But the reality of life in Manchester's halls was not always as high-minded as the Niblett Committee's expectations. Neither Rag nor ragging, traditions that survived from the 1930s, were particularly "civilising and humanising influences". Rag (which was strongly supported by the halls) was justified on the grounds that it was raising money for charity, and it appealed because it involved extroverted communal behaviour. It survived a declining existence into the 1980s, though its offshoot the Bogle Stroll continued to be prominent in hall life thereafter. Ragging was justified as team-building; it was a relatively mild form of initiation but could easily descend into bullying, and was encouraged into decline in the 1950s.

Yet there was plenty about Manchester's halls in the 1940s and 1950s that did correspond exactly to the ideal. Hall students held debates, staged plays, performed live music, ran history and science societies, sustained libraries and chapels, organised social service activities – and recorded these multifarious activities in hall magazines. They were headed by wardens who did take the trouble to foster their halls as "an instrument of liberal education". Students did learn that obligations went with rights, through a high level of involvement in their representative Junior Common Room committees. And out of this there developed a considerable sense of wider responsibility, as evidenced by the student work-parties which, at various points from the 1940s onwards, did voluntary maintenance work in halls during vacations.

Certainly by the later 1950s, the case for providing more hall accommodation for Manchester's rapidly increasing student population (from 5,205 in 1953–4 to 7,215 in 1959–60) had been made sufficiently convincingly for the University to embark on an ambitious, three-pronged expansion. First, it acquired from their religious founders the three men's halls (first St Anselm in 1956, then Hulme and Dalton) and the women's hall Langdale. Secondly,

A couple on the Bogle Stroll (Mancunion, 20 February 1975).

it embarked on a considerable building programme in all four halls, bringing St Anselm, Dalton and Langdale close to Niblett's recommended size, and taking Hulme a bit beyond it. Thirdly, it built two new residences for men, Woolton and Needham, which both opened in 1959; and the Vice-Chancellor encouraged the Roman Catholic Diocese of Salford to build a third new residence for men, Allen, which opened in 1961.

These seven halls, along with Ashburne, Ellis Llwyd Jones and St Gabriel's, were henceforth referred to as Manchester's "traditional" halls – though they would have been more aptly described as "collegiate" halls. Coordination of student activity between them was fostered by the Senior Students' Council, which organised *inter alia* an annual inter-hall Formal Ball. In them the characteristics of halls of residence were variously developed. Team-building through sport flourished, focused on the Behrens Cup for women but now on the Stopford Cup for men. Twinning arrangements between men's and women's halls facilitated amateur dramatics and music making, not least romance. Debating, journalism, intellectual and religious meetings, and the development of political skills occurred in some halls.

This great programme of hall expansion posed one serious challenge to the University: its high cost. Taking over the independent halls had not cost much, but putting them on a secure foundation and expanding them had been expensive. Building the new halls had been possible only because of an energetic appeal, led by the Chancellor and Vice-Chancellor, which had raised nearly £1m. All this outlay was justified by the need to raise the proportion of students living in University accommodation – yet it was still only a minority, and considerable further expansion in student numbers was imminent. Quite how considerable became apparent only with the Robbins Report in 1963. The University was under pressure to provide much more student accommodation and to do so rapidly.

At this point the changing mood and mores of society came to the University's financial rescue. The decline of deference made formal dinners less appealing. Slackening sexual norms created tensions when wardens upheld traditional values. Pressure to lower the age of majority made the presence of resident tutors seem less necessary. Thus the idea rapidly gained acceptance that the University might provide less structured, more open types of accommodation that focused less on communal life and facilities and so would cost less than collegiate halls. Indeed, the council of the future UMIST was considering as early as the mid-1950s providing accommodation that catered only for "the basic living requirements of students". It was against this background that the University and UMIST developed two new types of student accommodation during the 1960s and 1970s.

Bed and Board

The University's Student Accommodation Office was overwhelmed in late September 1961 with requests, mainly from freshers, for help in finding digs. Such was the pressure that staff did not have time to vet either property made available for renting or landladies offering board and lodging.

Along with forty-one other young males I had received correspondence from the University stating that, because demand for student housing was much higher than had been anticipated, temporary accommodation would be provided on a half-board basis at a private hotel. The proprietors also wrote to all concerned, and mentioned that the hotel was in the outskirts of Manchester but well served by public transport, with a games room with snooker and table tennis tables.

It sounded too good to be true. Our imagination ran riot. Reality soon destroyed those dreams. When Peter and myself made it to the second floor, we were shocked, just as everyone else must have been, to find out that there would be six to eight students per room. We dutifully chose a bunk bed and put our belongings on top of the mattress.

Breakfasts were always the same. Cereals followed by a greasy plate of either overdone or underdone rasher of bacon, a thin sausage, a hard fried egg, tinned tomatoes and fried bread. The evening meal and lunch at weekends consisted of three courses

but no choice. Sometimes we had the same soup two or three days running, leading to suspicions that the bowls which had been untouched had been emptied straight back into the vat-style saucepan. On one occasion we had the same soup for the whole week!

This led to a brilliantly organised protest. The front door was always locked at 11pm In order to get in after that the time the bell had to be rung. On the chosen evening about thirty of us arranged to arrive back at the hotel from midnight onwards at five-minute intervals. The manager was furious. It did the trick, however. We were united in expressing our dissatisfaction with the food and the pressure we exerted led to much better fare being dished out.

Despite the cramped conditions, petty restrictions and relatively awful food we had an enjoyable time. There was great camaraderie among all of the students and lasting friendships were established.

Keith Mallett
BA Admin 1971

> *I knew two men who had a flat, or rather the upper floor of a suburban house. The remarkable thing to them and everyone, much remarked upon, was that they had a fridge – an amazing luxury in the 1950s.*

Wendy McMullan

Top left: Arthur Armitage, Vice-Chancellor, with two landladies, Dora Somerville and Beryl Selbie, at the annual landladies' tea party (Manchester Evening News, 1971).

Top: Protesting landladies besiege the Student Representative Council (SRC) in 1904, alarmed at rumours that the University planned to build or license more halls and put them out of business. Sketch by Hamilton Irving.

The first new type was frankly experimental, and involved changing some but not all aspects of a collegiate hall. Not surprisingly, it took various forms, each one novel in a different way. The first form was created by UMIST and the University when they built a number of tower blocks in the middle of their respective campuses, Chandos and Wright Robinson Halls at UMIST and Moberly Tower at the University. These were single gender, headed by a warden but they had only basic facilities and their catering was to be cafeteria-style. A much more novel form was created by the University when in 1964 it opened a very tall tower block, initially referred to as the Fallowfield Student Village and later called Owens Park; this was mixed gender, had a Chairman of the Tutors instead of a warden, and was seven times Niblett's recommended size. It was similar to the first form in having cafeteria-style catering and relatively modest central facilities. The third form, slightly more cautious at least architecturally, was represented by UMIST, which opened a low-rise hall, Grosvenor Place, in 1972 adjacent to its campus. In many ways this adhered to the Owens Park pattern, but it did have a warden and was merely three times Niblett's recommended size.

Given the experimental nature of these various halls (the Vice-Chancellor of the 1960s said of Owens Park that it was a glorious experiment which might fail!), it is not surprising that the character of each evolved in the following years.

The second new type of accommodation was even less structured and cheaper to create than the first. This was the self-catered accommodation, which involved units of up to 1,000 student rooms which were arranged in flats of about eight rooms, each with its own front door and shared kitchen and bathroom. There were no resident staff, but instead a team of non-resident advisers drawn from University staff, who held surgeries, visited the flats assigned to them, and sought to encourage communal activities through the formation of Residents' Associations. Though such activities were handicapped by a paucity of communal facilities, as a living environment these halls were in the main more humane and sometimes more interesting than their 1960s predecessors. They appealed both to radical student opinion, which was influential from the late 1960s, and also to

Behrens House, Ashburne Hall. Originally The Oaks, Fallowfield, the home of Edward and Abigail Behrens, it was sold by the family on easy terms to the University after Behrens's death in 1906. The University rented it to the first women's hall of residence, Ashburne (founded in 1899), which moved to new buildings on the site in 1910.

University financial officers faced with the need to accommodate ever more students as cheaply as possible. In consequence, almost all accommodation built after the early 1970s was self-catered.

In this style the University built Cornbrook House and Whitworth Park (popularly known as the Toblerones) on the main campus, and Oak House next door to Owens Park. Similarly, UMIST built Hardy Farm (delightfully bucolic but hardly conveniently located, though provided with a resident warden) and converted its catered halls to self-catered. The absence of any daily meeting over dinner and the paucity of common facilities meant that self-catered accommodation produced relatively little in the way of regular sports teams and other communal activities, but many students enjoyed the sense of self-sufficiency it conferred.

An adaptation of this style of accommodation from the late 1980s was to provide the most luxurious student accommodation

James Buckle, porter (d.1896) and domestic staff at Dalton Hall, probably in the 1890s.

ever. It was initially provoked by a wish to cater for the vacation conference trade and was then fuelled by ever-rising student expectations. It led to the provision of blocks of en-suite self-catered rooms with resident tutorial staff. Sometimes these blocks were established as separate halls, e.g. UMIST's Charles Street Residence, later named Weston Hall (the first such hall, which doubled as an hotel) and Richmond Park. Sometimes these blocks were established as separate halls and run in conjunction with established collegiate halls, e.g. Canterbury Court administered by St Anselm Hall, and Sheavyn House administered by Ashburne Hall. And sometimes they were administered as integral parts of existing halls, e.g. Burkhardt House in Hulme Hall, and Pankhurst Court in Dalton Hall. Apart from a common avoidance of any bathroom crush, the student experience varied greatly across these halls, courts, houses and parks. Despite high rents, they were extremely popular, which sat awkwardly with a rising outcry over student poverty.

Independently of these developments, the character of Manchester's collegiate halls was being changed by two other developments. One concerned gender. Those running these halls (all single sex) had been expected to limit any intimacy within them between sexes. In practice, men's halls were turning a blind eye by the early 1970s, though women's halls still tried to hold the line (hence the "one foot on the floor at all times" rule). In the late 1980s, many wardens were in favour of having both sexes officially in their halls. The students, previously opposed to enforced separation, were now doubtful about total integration. In a number of cases, the student body was persuaded to agree to the change, but in the three cases where it was put to a referendum (two men's halls and one women's) it was rejected by majorities of 90 per cent. Most of the changes went ahead nevertheless, so that by the late 1990s most of the collegiate halls were mixed. Domestic bliss may have come earlier, but intra-hall communal activity struggled and the men's inter-hall Stopford sports league declined.

The second development concerned the length of time a student lived in University accommodation. Given the shortage of accommodation, should all students have a brief time in hall or should just some students experience hall but for a longer time? The

majority of expert opinion favoured the latter option, as halls dominated by one-year residents would be unable to fulfil a wider educational role. This opinion accorded with Manchester practice. However, in the 1970s, to strengthen its undergraduate recruitment, the University started reserving most hall places for first-years. Just as the post-war experts predicted, the policy posed a severe challenge to the collegiate halls, because an orthodoxy rapidly developed among students that one only lived in hall, any hall, for just one year.

One consequence of this first-year policy was to ensure that the vast majority of Manchester students had some experience of living outside hall. However, this was a very different experience from that of earlier generations. The proportion living at home was now small; landladies and lodgings had disappeared. Instead, students now lived unsupervised in housing they arranged for themselves. Usually this involved learning the harsh realities of dealing with a landlord, though sometimes it involved students (or their parents) buying property and becoming landlords themselves. This was a far cry from the ideals of the post-war planners, but no doubt still educational.

Up to the 1950s, students needing to live "in lodgings approved by the University authorities" were referred for information to the Warden of Men Students in Lodgings, or to the Adviser to Women Students. However, as lodgings gave way to less controlled outside accommodation, the Accommodation Office was developed to

Above: View across the Fallowfield residential campus from Owens Park tower.

Right: Burkhardt House, on the Victoria campus, is part of Hulme Hall and was completed in 1994.

maintain registers of such accommodation and to advise students in their dealings with landlords. This role was further expanded in the 1970s under the direct leasing scheme, whereby the Accommodation Office effectively leased and sublet properties, culminating in the formation in the early 1990s of Manchester Student Homes. Through these initiatives the Accommodation Office became a central part of students' university experience.

These developments enabled Manchester to offer students an exceptionally diverse range of accommodation. As each new type developed, it was added to the existing types, operating alongside them, rather than becoming the norm which was imposed upon earlier types. Thus collegiate halls, the half-way house of Owens Park, self-catered blocks, and the various en-suite recipes now combine to offer a wide range of choice. This is further supplemented by the choice for both men and women between mixed and single sex accommodation. Underpinning this wide variety are different types of management, offering students different levels of involvement in their hall's affairs. It is to be hoped that the new University continues to value this variety and to see it as a source of educational enrichment and opportunity.

Sport at Manchester

ALISON ODELL

The history of sport at Manchester can be traced back at least as far as the 1850s when there is mention of the sorry state of gym equipment provided in a rear room of Owens College in Quay Street. The 1860s proved to be a key decade in the development of sports. The first outside fixture took place in 1861, the following year saw the institution of an annual boat race on the Irwell, and by 1865 the first official Sports Day had been held and quickly became a major social fixture at the College.

By 1870 the College had adopted its first 'colour' of purple and straw, a choice of the Principal's wife. However, final agreement on the men's and women's colours was to be a matter of interminable debate into the middle of the twentieth century. It wasn't until 1884 that a sending-off was first recorded of an Owens player during a game of lacrosse – Mr Bell for hitting Mr Lewis. A second dismissal wasn't slow in coming – Mr Lewis for hitting Mr Bell.

The seminal event in the early years of sport at Manchester was the formation of the Athletic Union in 1885. Its founding four men's clubs were cricket, lacrosse, lawn tennis and rugby. The AU suffered many vicissitudes of fortune in its early years but survived sometimes against the odds to the present day. The Union contended not only with problems of finance and facilities, but also of general apathy amongst much of the student body. Most students lived locally, many preferred to play for local rather than College clubs.

Top: Women's hockey c1900 and 2000.

Right: The Firs Pavilion at the Fallowfield Sports Field in the first years of the twentieth century.

Far left: Men's rugby at Manchester.

Left: E.F. Fookes, who represented England at Rugby Union in the 1890s.

Right: The gymnasium.

In 1900 the Firs Pavilion and the Fallowfield sports grounds were officially opened, addressing a major need for better facilities. Apart from a period during the First World War when they were requisitioned as a POW camp by the army, the grounds have remained in constant use for sports to this day with the increasingly dilapidated Firs Pavilion providing the focus of much nostalgia amongst generations of sporting students.

The year 1900 also saw the establishment of a Women's Athletic Union (WAU) with hockey as its sole founding club. The need for segregation of the sexes was a fiercely entrenched view within the AU for many years despite periodic protests from the women on a number of *causes célèbres*. Indeed this separation of the sexes applied right up until the start of the 1980s. Segregation finally came to an end in 1981 with the formation of the UMAU,

under the Presidency of Dr Rosemary Mitchell, and later of Ron Unsworth.

The XXI Club was founded in 1932 and with it a long-standing sporting institution at VUM. Its membership consists of the elite amongst Manchester's student athletes. An 'active' member must have been awarded full colours and normally have achieved international representation, as well as being a current student at University or no more than one year down. Until recently election was only into the open places amongst the twenty-one active members. Originally founded for men, the Club started to admit women only in 1990. The members gather each year for an annual dinner, and 2007 will see the celebration of the seventy-fifth anniversary of the Club.

The AU at VUM played a key role in the original founding of the national inter-universities sport association, both the men's Universities Athletic Union (UAU) and the Women's Inter Varsity Athletic Board (WIVAB). Alongside the British Universities Sports Association (BUSA) competition, VUM has traditionally contested the Christie Cup each March across a range of sports in a three-way competition with the other two Victoria Universities of Liverpool and Leeds.

The history of the AU at VUM was long entwined with the history of sport at Tech and later UMIST. There has been much sharing of facilities down the years, and indeed the UMIST AU, formed in the late 1940s, voted to become fully independent of the VUM AU only in 1978. An aspect of the relationship between the institutions was that many UMIST athletes opted to play for Victoria University clubs, especially in sports where provision at UMIST was more limited. This arrangement became increasingly controversial leading to the UMIST AU enforcing a ruling that

Women's badminton.

The Manchester Aquatics Centre constructed for the 2002 Commonwealth Games.

UMIST students must only play for UMIST teams. Meanwhile, the UAU began to object (particularly after 1994 when UMIST began to award its own degrees), that Manchester would enjoy an unfair advantage in inter-varsity competitions if it were allowed to recruit its teams from separate institutions.

Following AU separation, UMIST appointed Dr Richard Cox as Director of Sport and increased investment in its own facilities and clubs. Much of this investment was made possible through strategic partnerships, for example with Manchester Metropolitan University (MMU) in developing the Sugden Centre from a squash courts and weights area facility with five-a-side pitch, into a fully-fledged centre with sports hall and activity rooms. Links with elite local sporting institutions were also forged, including Manchester United FC.

The building of the Armitage Centre in 1986 provided VUM with a modern sports/conference centre and was a key development which helped the institution to understand the commercial potential of such facilities, and enabled sport to be showcased more effectively both internally and externally. In the early 1990s a full integration of the management of clubs, facilities and programmes was achieved with the formation in 1993 of a Directorate of Sport. This brought together the Armitage Centre, the now defunct McDougall Centre, the AU and the sports grounds under one management structure for the first time.

The McDougall Centre originated as an equestrian centre but came to incorporate a 25yd pool built in the 1920s. It was taken out of use following the opening of the Manchester Aquatics Centre constructed for the Commonwealth Games in 2002 in a partnership between VUM, UMIST, MMU and the City of Manchester.

The McDougall was also important as the home of the Centre for Physical Education within the former Department of Education. The Centre began by providing training in physical education to school teachers in the late 1940s under the directorship of former Olympic hurdler Roland Harper. However, by the 1970s it had

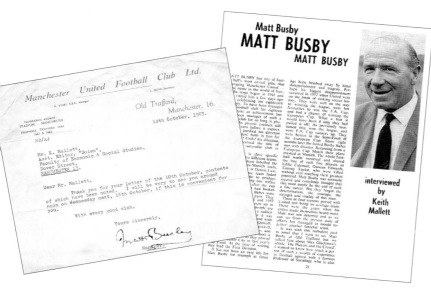

Keith Mallet, then Assistant Editor of Solem, successfully secured an interview with Sir Matt Busby in 1963 – the year that Manchester Utd won the FA Cup.

grown to develop the UK's first Masters programme in Physical Education, later complemented with a doctoral programme. Teaching continued until the late 1990s, when the Centre fell victim to a decline in demand for MEd qualifications as staff training budgets within the schools sector tightened.

During the late 1990s there was a growing emphasis on sports development in terms of improving the range and quality of service delivery to students at all levels of participation in sports activities. Scholarship programmes were instigated, a sports volunteer training scheme began strengthening the links with the local community, a well-being centre was started in partnership with the Counselling Service, health and fitness classes expanded to accommodate modern trends in maintaining healthy lifestyles, and the intra-mural sports programmes, a long-standing tradition amongst halls in VUM, were revamped to create a Campus Sport ethos across the expanded university by 2004.

At the same time the University attempted to improve the standard of its athletes by providing professional coaching and facilities and increasing the number of athletic scholarships. These tend to be awarded in "focus sports" where good facilities and coaching are available in the city. One happy result is that the University achieved its highest ever finishing position in the BUSA Overall National League table at the close of the 2005–6 season, finishing tenth out of 150 competing institutions.

The World Academy of Sport, an international education company, was established within the Manchester Business School in 2005. The two bodies are combining to train executives who will serve international sport federations, event organisers and educationalists throughout the world.

Above and left: Football and cross country at the University today.

Below: Owens lacrosse team c.1900.

A Family Connection

Above: Studying in Langdale.

Left: Langdale Hall friends.

I commenced University in September 1998 and graduated in 2001 with a degree in Human Communication Studies and Italian. I moved to Owens Park for my first year where I lived in the tower, a perfect location for making the most of the Bop! In my second year I was with friends in Mauldeth Road, returning to Fallowfield, Mabfield Road, for my final year.

I joined Manchester and Salford Officer Training Corps and spent three years undertaking some military training and a lot of socialising! I made the most of the sporting opportunities, playing for the women's rugby team and competing in the British Army Ski Championships on three occasions.

My family's connection with Manchester goes back to 1928, when my grandfather, Sidney Denham Austerberry and my grandmother, Eleanor Jane Naylor (Jennie), met there. Sidney was studying Theology and Jennie, English. They met at a party arranged between the halls on bonfire night, 1928: Jennie lived in Langdale Hall and I think Sidney lived in Hulme. Sidney

used to visit Jennie at Langdale Hall but of course they had to have a chaperone present!

They became engaged while Jennie was still at Manchester (she graduated in 1931) and the engagement ring was bought at Herbert Wolf Ltd, Piccadilly, Manchester. They married in 1934 and were married for 62 years until Sidney's death in 1986. Jennie died in 2000.

My cousin, Stephen Edward Tomlinson also studied Theology at Manchester, graduating in 1984. Another cousin, Michael

Right: The wedding of Sidney and Jennie on 22 May 1934.

Below: Whitworth Park.

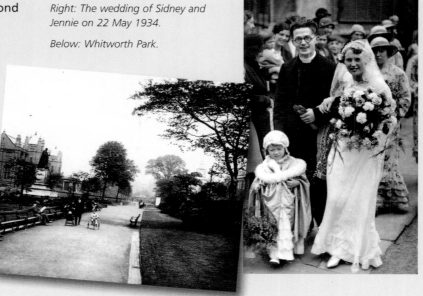

Above: Stephen Tomlinson getting his degree in 1984.

Right: My graduation in 1984.

Sidney Austerberry, graduated in Chemistry at Manchester in 1988 and continued with his PhD, also at Manchester, which he attained in 1992.

Last year I took my younger sister to Manchester to start her course in Art and Design – at Manchester Metropolitan rather than the University – but her stories of Freshers Week certainly brought back memories. And by the time she graduates, our family will have achieved an eighty-year association with higher education in Manchester!

Sarah Jones
BA Hons Human Communication Studies and Italian, 2001

Summer camp friends.

Jennie on graduation day in 1931.

Manchester University Women: Historical Reflections

SHEILA GRIFFITHS

This chapter describes the first cautious moves towards admitting women, setting up suitable establishments to receive them (including a common room, a separate women's union and a hall of residence), and eventually accepting them as full members of the University, entitled to read any subject for which they were qualified. Sheila Griffiths read History at Owens and Personnel Management at Tech in the 1950s. She is Secretary of the Ashburne Association of Past and Present Students, archivist of Ashburne Hall, and an Honorary Companion of the Victoria University of Manchester.

The intention of John Owens to endow a college in Manchester did not envisage the inclusion of women, but fortunately the city was blessed with prominent families who thought differently. What began in the middle of the nineteenth century as an eager desire to establish reputable girls' schools soon became a wish to give young women further opportunities.

In 1874, tentative Latin classes were held for seventy women; in 1877 the Manchester Association for the Higher Education of Women formally requested that Owens College admit women. The Court of the College showed some reluctance. Learned members perhaps feared the frivolity that girls would bring, the challenge to the gravitas of Owens, a possible hint of scandal. And where would they accommodate all those hats? Some medical authorities even doubted whether women had the stamina to cope with higher education. However, urged by some of the great men of the city, the Court proposed a compromise: the establishment of a separate women's college. Thus was born in 1877 the Manchester and Salford College for Women, at 223 Brunswick Street; its Honorary Secretary was Mrs C.P. Scott, wife of the

editor of the *Manchester Guardian* and a member of Girton College, Cambridge.

With the foundation of the Victoria University in 1880 women were admitted to degrees, and Owens absorbed the College for Women in 1885. Most of the women's classes, however, were still held in Brunswick Street, whence women students made a dash, as they said, across to senior classes in the University. A solitary woman was expected to be chaperoned by Edith Wilson, the Woman Tutor, but groups could venture unescorted across Oxford Road. College humorists jested that the College crest – a snake rearing to the sun with the motto *Arduus ad Solem* – depicted the College Principal as the sun, a face peering nervously

Helen Stephen, first warden, and the first residents of the women's hall opened in 1899, outside their house in Victoria Park.

over battlements, watching the advance of the snake women across Oxford Road, and declaring: Thus far and no further!

In 1887, the first edition of *Iris* appeared, the newsletter of the women's department, which was issued regularly until subsumed into the *Owens College Union Magazine* in 1894. *Iris* notes that the female presence was at first recognised only by the appearance of a hat-stand, outside the History Theatre. Then the women were given a room at the top of the main building, part of the Zoological Department of the Manchester Museum, and segregated like a nunnery. The women had to pick their way past a stuffed tiger, a gorilla and snakes, but soon the common room became their haven.

Iris reported in its first edition that out of an average attendance of sixty-one females, eighteen were reading for degrees. They were known as "women students"; the rest, attending only a few classes, were known as "ladies". The editor proudly delivered an account of the first four women to gain their degree in 1887: "Their wealth of hair was a source of great displeasure to the obliging costumier – the difficulty of finding caps!" On 3 November 1887, women students cut lectures and hurried to the ceremony at the Town

Hall, where the men were already in full voice. "Happily we were held back from too great exuberance by our sex's sense of decorum," but the editor notes that with the appearance of the first pale lady graduate, they joined in the cheers with the rest.

Iris continued to record the expansion of the women's department, and the networking that went on with other women's colleges, which sent letters of support to Owens. University College, Liverpool, wrote in 1888 that "unlike Owens, our women students are on an equal footing with men". Indeed, some Manchester professors refused to lecture to women and the indignity of chaperonage remained.

Since the flourishing Men's Union at Owens refused to allow the admission of women, in 1899 a small group met around the fire in the women's Common Room to discuss the formation of a Women's Union, which was set up in 1900. Its objects were "the promotion of intellectual intercourse, the provision of means of recreation and the development of social life among past and present students". The Council of the University took a lease on 248 Oxford Road and 170 members were enrolled. The size of the donations from the great and good must have won over some hesitant academics, the whole being crowned by Mrs James Worthington's offer to decorate and furnish the premises.

Given the steady progress made by the Women's Department over twenty years, it is not surprising that Manchester was closely identified with the Women's Movement in the early twentieth century. In 1904, Marie Stopes was the first woman to be admitted to the scientific staff. Mrs Pankhurst was prominent in the life of the city, Christabel Pankhurst was an Owens law graduate and Miss Horniman lit up the dramatic scene in her Gaiety Theatre. In 1909, women graduates in academic dress paraded through the city as part of the great Suffragette March. When women were finally given the vote on equal footing with men in 1928, prospective parliamentary candidates hurried down to the Women's Union and halls of residence to win support.

By the 1890s, the increasing number of women students was making accommodation an issue. Samuel Alexander, Professor of

The women's common room in 1901.

Philosophy, told by headmistresses that they did not think there were adequate safe lodgings for women, determined to establish a women's hall of residence. His lifelong support for the women's cause made him a much-loved figure. "Dear old Sammy," wrote one girl, "cycling down Oxford Road with his gown flying." After the Epstein bust of the professor was placed in the entrance to the Arts Building, for many years women students patted him before going into exams or even gave him a surreptitious kiss.

After a successful meeting in the Town Hall, £3,000 was raised and R.D. Darbishire, a lawyer, generously provided Ashburne House, adjacent to his own home in Victoria Park. Helen Stephen, daughter of a judge and from a family linked to most of the Victorian intelligentsia, was appointed Warden. In 1900, Mrs Sidgwick, Principal of Newnham College, Cambridge, opened the hall, which she described in her address as "a younger sister of Newnham".

The June 1905 edition of the *Manchester University Magazine*, commenting on Helen Stephen's move to a larger hall in Aberystwyth, referred to the establishment of Manchester's first hall of residence for women as initially "only a venture", but there was no doubt as to its viability and numbers grew steadily, necessitating additions to the building. Miss Stephen began writing a chronicle, a unique account of the development of this fledgling institution. In October 1899 there were eleven students, one high school mistress and the Warden. She comments:

> At that time, there were thirteen unconnected individuals, mostly knowing nothing whatever of each other, cast together to sink or swim. Without boasting, they have swum not sunk. Early on, a community was forged.

Nine of the original eleven students had some sort of scholarship, so the hall was not an elite finishing school, although male students soon referred to it as "the virgins' retreat".

Elizabeth Parker, one of the first residents and later assistant lecturer at the University, began to request articles for their house magazine, *Yggdrasill* – named after the Norse ash tree of existence, spreading its boughs over the whole universe. "The title," she writes, "is connected with the house and suggests an emblem." Early

Women at Manchester

Marie Stopes (1880–1958)

Famous as the British pioneer of family planning, Marie Stopes was voted 'Woman of the Millennium' by readers of *The Guardian* newspaper in 1999, itself a Manchester institution in inception.

Marie Stopes was born in Scotland and began her career as a palaeobotanist. Equipped with a first-class degree in botany from University College London, she took a doctorate at the Botanical Institute attached to the University of Munich, where she was the only woman among five thousand men. She was the first woman to be appointed to the scientific staff of the University of Manchester, as a demonstrator in botany in 1904, where her efforts to enliven the students – e.g. by appearing at a Biological Fancy Dress Ball as a tropical pink moth in a dress secured only by safety pins – earned her some disapproval. She extended her research into plant fossils, specifically those petrified in coal seams, to Japan in 1907–09, before resigning her lectureship in 1910.

Stopes is best known for her work subsequent to her time at Manchester. She opened her first family planning clinic, the Mothers' Clinic in Holloway, North London in 1921. The clinic offered a free contraception service to married women. She also edited *Birth Control News*, a journal offering anatomically explicit advice on sexual intercourse. This and her sex manual *Married Love* (1918), proved to be as controversial in its time as it was influential and earned Marie Stopes fierce criticism from the Churches in particular. In 1930 the national Birth Control Council was formed.

More controversial to the modern sensibility was Stopes's campaigning in support of policies of eugenics, outlined in her 1920 book *Radiant Motherhood* which advocated compulsory sterilization of those deemed unfit for parenthood. The memory of her pioneering work in family planning, breaking down sex taboos and improving reproductive health is perpetuated in the work of the Marie Stopes International Global Partnership.

Dr Phoebe Sheavyn (1865–1968)

Phoebe Sheavyn was born in Atherstone, to a family of drapers and became a governess. However, she was determined to go to university and aged twenty-two, won a scholarship to the University College of Aberystwyth. Later, in 1894–6, she spent two interesting years at Bryn Mawr College as Reader and then Fellow in English, being impressed by the comparatively generous provision for women's education in the USA.

After ten years at Somerville College, Oxford, where she worked with Professor Wright on the English Dialect Dictionary, Sheavyn was offered the post of Warden of Ashburne Hall and Senior Tutor to Women Students at Manchester in 1907. That same year she helped to establish the Federation of University Women. In 1912, she was given a seat on the Senate of the University of Manchester, the first and for many years the only woman so honoured.

During the First World War, Phoebe Sheavyn worked tirelessly as Deputy Commandant of the Voluntary Aid Detachment, training women students in nursing and accompanying them at night to welcome the troop trains full of wounded men coming into Manchester. This heavy work load resulted in her deciding in 1917 to relinquish the Wardenship of Ashburne, although she continued to be an active supporter of the Hall. She remained Director of Women Students and a member of the English department and Senate until her retirement in 1925. The rest of her long life was devoted to family, friends and former students. One of the wings in Ashburne Hall is named after her.

Women at Manchester

Drawings of Alison Uttley's inventions by her friend Gladys Llewellyn in Yggdrasil.

Alison Uttley (1884–1976)

Alice Taylor, later and better known as Alison Uttley, went to Manchester on a Major County Scholarship from her school in Bakewell, Derbyshire, and graduated with honours in Physics in 1906. She was a suffragette in her youth and a friend of Ramsay MacDonald, the first British Prime Minster to come from the Labour Party.

One of the early students in Ashburne Hall, Alison showed literary promise in her articles, poems and inventions written for the house magazine, *Yggdrasill*. Her dedication to physics was suffused with her belief that life is inherent in all the material world. She thought that time travel was possible and claimed to have foreseen one of the questions in her finals paper in a dream, as a result feeling herself forced to take another. A powerful imagination lay beneath the outward appearance of the ambitious young woman, whose children's stories and essays on country life were later to become so popular.

Uttley's early adult career as a physics teacher did not especially hint at the fame that was to follow. It was only on her husband's death in 1930, which left her in financial difficulties looking after a young son, that she began to embark on a remarkable and prolific career as a writer of some twenty adult books and forty children's books. Her *The Squirrel, The Hare and The Little Grey Rabbit* books, profoundly influenced by her rural upbringing in Derbyshire, were perhaps her most famous and best loved books.

As a farmer's daughter on a scholarship to the university, Alison never forgot her humble origins. She was a generous benefactor of her hall of residence, Ashburne, which enjoys one-third of the income from her literary property. Uttley was given an Honorary Degree by the University in 1970 in recognition of her literary achievement and there are two memorial plaques to her, one on the former physics building in Coupland Street and the other in Ashburne Hall.

Rt Hon. Ellen Wilkinson MP (1891–1947)

Ellen Wilkinson was born in Ardwick to a family of robust Methodists, her father a cotton operative who later became an insurance agent. She made her way by winning scholarships and entered the University as Jones History Scholar in 1910. Active in the University Fabian Society and the Socialist Federation, well trained by historians in the art of marshalling pertinent facts, she earned her first wages as an organiser of women's constitutional suffrage societies and then of a trade union for shop assistants and factory workers.

After flirting with communism in 1920 and serving as a Manchester City Councillor, she was elected with union sponsorship to represent Middlesbrough East in 1924, when she became one of four women Members of the House of Commons. Her far-left politics, auburn hair and diminutive stature earned her various nicknames, including 'The Elfin Fury', 'The Fiery Atom', 'Little Miss Perky', 'The Pocket Pasionaria' and, simply, 'Red Nellie'.

Active in the General Strike of 1926 (the subject of her novel *Clash*), Ellen Wilkinson lost her seat in the General Election of 1931. In 1935, however, she was elected as Member for Jarrow, a town fatally dependent on the fortunes of a single shipyard, Palmer's, as her book, *The Town That Was Murdered* (1939), was to relate. She walked much of the way to London with two hundred

Ellen Wilkinson walking at the head of the Jarrow March from Newcastle-upon-Tyne to London, in protest against unemployment levels in the north of England, 28 October 1936.

unemployed workers on the famous Jarrow March of 1936, allegedly taking three steps to the men's one.

She served in Churchill's war-time coalition government as a junior minister responsible for civil defence, including air-raid shelters, compulsory fire-watching and the conscription of young unmarried women into war work. In 1945 Clement Attlee appointed her Minister of Education with the formidable task of putting into effect the Education Act of 1944, which made secondary education available to everyone, and of raising the school-leaving age to fifteen by April 1947. She achieved this aim, but did not herself live to see it, dying prematurely whilst in office on 6 February 1947.

Baroness Mcfarlane of Llandaff (1926–)
Jean McFarlane was the nurse enlisted by Alwyn Smith, Manchester's Professor of Community Medicine, in his campaign from 1969 onwards to establish a degree in nursing and equip the profession with a graduate elite. She had taken a Master's degree in Manpower Studies and carried out research into nursing education on behalf of the Department of Health. Whilst on the staff of the Royal College of Nursing she had directed a course which had the capacity to train pupils to become nurses, or district nurses, or health visitors.

Miss McFarlane came to Manchester as a Senior Lecturer in 1971 and in 1974 became the first Professor of Nursing in an English university, a position which she held for fourteen years. Here she ran what was at first a small, intimate, collegiate department, which vigorously debated the problem of how to advance beyond practical vocational training and provide nurses with something more robust than a diluted course in medicine. The curriculum explored such topics as the theory and content of nursing itself, the processes of making decisions in patients' interests, and the ethics of such controversial matters as abortion and euthanasia. When Australian authorities, for example, decided to transform nursing into a graduate profession, they sent potential heads of departments to Manchester to 'get themselves made respectable academically'.

Professor McFarlane was the only nurse appointed to the Royal Commission on the National Health Service which sat from 1976 to 1979. Raised to the peerage, she took her seat on the crossbenches of the House of Lords, reflecting afterwards: 'I have never been a Political person with a capital "p", although I have been political with a small "p" – one can't live in an academic world and not be political!'

Baroness Mcfarlane has received two honorary degrees from the University of Manchester. In 2005 she was awarded a Lifetime Achievement Award by the *British Journal of Nursing*.

Rt Hon. Margaret Beckett MP (1943–)
Born in Ashton-under-Lyne, Greater Manchester, Margaret Beckett stayed in Manchester to study Metallurgy at UMIST and the John Dalton Polytechnic, before taking up a position in 1966 as an experimental officer in the Metallurgy Department at the Victoria University. In 1970 she left to begin a career as a political researcher in industrial relations for the Labour Party.

A party official and special adviser to minister Judith Hart in the early 1970s, she was elected MP for Lincoln in October 1974 and served as a government whip and then a junior education and science minister until she lost her seat in 1979. However, Beckett returned to the Commons as MP for Derby South in 1983 and has sat on the front bench since 1984, joining the Shadow Cabinet in 1989 as Shadow Chief Secretary to the Treasury.

Following the 1992 General Election Margaret Beckett was elected Deputy Leader of the Labour Party to John Smith, the first woman to hold this position, and following Smith's sudden death found herself Acting Leader of the Opposition for three months in 1994. She stood for leadership of the party but was beaten by Tony Blair.

Following the Labour General Election victory in 1997, Beckett returned to government briefly as Trade and Industry Secretary, before becoming Leader of the House of Commons in 1998, in a role which involved her overseeing much modernisation of Commons procedures. In 2001, she was appointed Secretary of State for Environment, Food and Rural affairs and in 2006 was made Foreign Secretary. She is only the second woman after Margaret Thatcher to hold one of the four great offices of state.

The Rt Hon. Margaret Beckett MP.

Covers of the Ashburne magazine Yggdrasill *spanning over seventy years.*

editions up to 1909 were hand-drawn and painted, giving us today a glimpse into the lives of these women, with sepia photographs and vivid art nouveau-style covers. Here we find the everlasting themes of lack of sleep, time and money, linking students of all generations.

Among these first redoubtable students was Alice Taylor, one of the first women physics graduates who later, as Alison Uttley, became a famous author. Her poems and inventions enlivened the pages of the magazine, with sketches of her leading her friends down to Owens on special skates and being whisked back in a

pneumatic tunnel. She even designed a teapot with a "nearly empty" alarm, doubtless having been late back from her laboratory on many a damp evening and missing a warming cuppa. Students today have cause to be grateful to Alison, since she left part of her literary estate for the benefits of students in need. Perhaps this reflects her own insecurity as a farmer's daughter, coming to the hall in 1905. "How wonderful," she wrote, "to open a parcel from home and smell with the apples inside, the fields and hedgerows."

The next two Wardens of Ashburne, Hilda Oakley (1905–7) and Dr Phoebe Sheavyn (1907–17), had experience between them of women's colleges in Canada and the USA; they brought with them both scholarship and a liberal attitude.

The formidable Dr Sheavyn was both Warden of Ashburne and Tutor to Women Students in the University. In 1912, she was given a seat in the University Senate, the only woman to hold this position until Dr Mildred Pope became Professor of French in 1934. Dr Sheavyn masterminded the move in 1908 to the Behrens Estate in Fallowfield, and the building of the Mary Worthington Wing. During the First World War, she acted as deputy commandant of the Voluntary Aid Detachment. Her women students trained as nurses, spending weary nights waiting for the troop trains to come into Mayfield Station, and then giving tea and cigarettes to the exhausted men (see p116).

With the increasing demand for places, the University decided to extend Ashburne Hall with a library, dining hall and Ward Wing. Lord Morley, Chancellor of the University from 1908 to 1923, bequeathed his library to the women students, asking that it be housed "in some such institution as Ashburne Hall".

In 1931, Ashburne was expanded with the Lees Wing. The University had already licensed a smaller women's hall (the Victoria Church Hostel, renamed Langdale in 1911), and after the war it established Ellis Llwyd Jones, which was originally for teachers of the deaf. St Gabriel's, a Roman Catholic foundation, was set up in Victoria Park. Thus, by the 1930s, when worsening economic conditions precluded further expansion, a firm residential basis existed.

With the outbreak of war in 1939, women students were encouraged to continue their studies, but had to do war service,

Suffragettes in Manchester, c1908; university women wear academic dress for the rally.

Women alone graduate in modern languages, January 1945.

such as making camouflage nets or fire-watching during air raids. Miss Middleton (Middy), the resident horticulturalist in Ashburne, acquired loads of tobacco, soaked by firemen in the Manchester Blitz, and with her student team dug it into spare ground, thus fertilising wonderful rhubarb for pies. Langdale students secretly suspected the largest women's hall of snaffling some of their coal ration. Twenty-first birthday parties continued somehow, but on one occasion a cardboard box was iced to represent a cake during food rationing.

Until the 1960s, women students tended to see a university education as a privilege rather than the right that it appears nowadays. Dealings with university staff were formal, and professors and wardens were seen as "gracious figureheads". "We were not expected to have problems, and if we had, we had to get on with it," was the common feeling. In the early 1950s, women represented some 20 per cent of students. Courses remained traditional, "with death by a thousand exams", but some new openings were appearing. After graduating in history in 1957, I went on to the Faculty of Technology (later UMIST) to do a postgraduate diploma in personnel management. Women were few and far between in Sackville Street. On registering, I was asked which was my first university. Knowing the rivalry, I said "Owens" in a whisper, but that one name seemed to echo round

the room and was greeted by much foot-stamping by the men. We were rare birds indeed, nor did we have many female role models. There were few women professors, and our union was one of the last to be de-segregated. It was a great day when Elva Corrie was elected first woman president of the joint union in 1960.

Women students today readily move into areas formerly dominated by men, such as journalism, finance and business. They have won protection from crude misogyny and sexism, and some provision is made for women with children. The female mature student is not uncommon, and many women live independently in shared houses. However, whereas my interviewees of the late 1940s and 1950s revelled in the independence given them by their government grants, today's students face considerable levels of debt. Nevertheless, I find women students today optimistic and committed. We have Anna Ford, one of our own graduates, as co-Chancellor. As companies and institutions continue to seek more highly qualified women, the new University of Manchester is well placed to fulfil those demands.

Staff House for women, 1944.

Students' Unions and Newspapers at Owens

BRIAN PULLAN

By the second half of the twentieth century, the students' unions at Owens were all-embracing organisations run by elected officers who could claim to represent students to the University and the world, to look after some aspects of their welfare, and to provide them with information, comforts and entertainment (they had no monopoly of any of these things, but contributed to all of them). Brian Pullan describes their development from modest nineteenth-century beginnings, and considers some of the activities that fell within their purview – from the carnivalesque rituals of Rag Week to mainstream student journalism and prize-winning student newspapers.

"Who killed Mr Tulkinghorn?" was one of the first questions that early students at Owens College chose to debate in their leisure hours. Bleak House was appearing in monthly parts in 1852 and 1853, and the shooting in Chapter 48 of Sir Leicester Dedlock's desiccated lawyer, "surrounded by a mysterious halo of family confidences", was a matter of public interest to the college's Dickens fans. The students' discussion club was as precarious as the college itself, but it had a continuous existence from 1861 onwards. Over the next fifty years it expanded to become not only a union of individual students but also a cluster of societies, an association that ran a clubhouse, and the proprietor of a magazine. In Edwardian days the Men's Union consisted of a Debating Society (mainly of interest to students of Arts and Law), and the Medical, Biological, Chemical, Physical and Engineering Societies. Students joined the union through one of these bodies until the session of 1905–6, when the process was reversed, so that entry to the union gave access to all its affiliated societies and the Debating Society became everyone's province.

Top: The Men's and Women's Union Building was opened in 1909 and demolished in the late 1950s to make way for the present-day Refectory.

"The invisible but impassable line", by J. Tynan, 1912.

UNION DEBATES.

A conspicuous feature of Union life is the series of fortnightly debates throughout the Michaelmas and Lent terms. As can be seen by a glance at the syllabus below, some of these are held in conjunction with the Women's Union, some are contests with debaters from elsewhere, and some peculiar to ourselves. This variety of form is enhanced, we make bold to claim, by the wide assortment of topics that have been proposed for the present session by an assiduous Debates Sub-committee. In a further effort to make it easier for members to attend and enjoy them, lunch-hour as well as evening debates have been arranged. It is hoped that members will take full advantage of these facilities and provide, by their own effort, what even the most considerate of committees cannot supply—a good and plentiful supply of speakers. Whilst rhetoric and fluency are bound to be appreciated, do not imagine they are indispensable. The debates are not intended as a display of oratorical talents, but as an occasion for members to exercise those powers of intellectual discussion, only too often exhibited over the coffee bar tables during rush hours. Will any member who is prepared to lead or oppose or second any of the motions please call and see the Debates Secretary in the Committee Room.

Joint Debates Programme, 1935-36.

MICHAELMAS TERM.

Friday Oct. 11 4.30 p.m.—"This house would welcome the break up of the British Empire."

Monday Nov. 4 12.30 p.m.—"This house commends the prescience of 'Guy Fawkes.'"

Friday Nov. 22 4.30 p.m.—FRESHERS' DEBATE. "That the University dims the diamond and polishes the pebble."

29

Below left: the Union Building of 1957, by J.S. Beaumont, seen from Oxford Road.

Far left: Eamonn De Valera, the Irish Prime Minister, speaking in the Union.

Left: A page from the Union Handbook, 1935–6.

Mutually distrustful and inclined, at least in print and at committee meetings, to spar with and jeer at each other, men and women students belonged to separate unions throughout the first half of the twentieth century. Custom dictated that at most social gatherings there was an 'invisible but impassable line', with men and women congregating at opposite ends of the room; doubting their own capacity for sparkling conversation about theatres and music halls, the men held themselves apart like the unreformed Darcy fighting shy of the Misses Bennet. Such arrangements were perpetuated by the architecture of the union premises off Oxford Road, built in 1908, which contained separate rooms for men and women, back to back, the men entering (or bursting in at the end of morning lectures) from Burlington Street, the women from Lime Grove.

The two organisations, as the women complained, did very similar things on either side of the partition wall even when social conventions had changed. Until the mid-1950s a strong body of masculine opinion strove to preserve the Men's Union as a

gentlemen's club with its own traditions of acceptable conduct (as late as October 1957 an associate member suffered expulsion for "behaviour unbecoming of a gentleman"). In 1954 the newly elected President of the Women's Union declared it "proud to be the only University Women's Union in England", but her rationalising colleague, the House Secretary, rejoined that "Manchester is the only University in the country which maintains this stupid segregation of the sexes". Separate unions could not survive the planning and construction of the new union building on Oxford Road, opened in 1957. After much discussion, the Men's and Women's Unions agreed to federate and set up a mixed administration for the new premises: the offices of President and Vice-President were open to both sexes, and most rooms were accessible to both sexes. The first woman President of the federation, Elva Corrie, was elected in 1960; the second, Anna Ford, who reigned in 1966–7, became the first woman to hold the office for a full session. Women distinguished themselves in union affairs, particularly as journalists and as administrators of its increasingly elaborate welfare machine.

By 1980 the union clubhouse, designed by the firm of J.S. Beaumont in what was sometimes irritably called the late Fascist style, was offering students a debating hall; venues for discos and dances; a large coffee-cum-snackbar; three drinking bars, and rooms in which to watch television, play games, hold meetings, read and enjoy silence. Available in the basement were ablutions and sanitation, two hairdressers' establishments, a travel bureau, a newsagent, a bank and a second-hand bookshop. Membership now opened the door to at least 150 affiliated societies. The union ran several organisations for the welfare of students, including an advisory and supportive service called Contact Nightline and a Legal Advice Centre, to say nothing of Community Action, which looked outwards towards the people of the city. For a time there was a child care society which ran a crèche for students' children, and when the city streets became more threatening the union began to supply a minibus which delivered women safely to their homes at night. Union officers became adept at nagging dilatory local education

The main Student Union bar in the Union Building.

authorities into releasing grant cheques and saving impecunious students from having to live on nothing until their money arrived.

In Edwardian days graduates often presided, at least over the Men's Union. Even in the 1950s, the office of president, filled by annual election, tended to fall to senior students on lengthy professional courses, especially in medicine, some of whom made a habit of failing examinations and prolonging their student lives. The poll was low and victory generally went to those who had made themselves known by being around for many years. A permanent staff of managers maintained continuity; some had served for thirty years or so in the union, starting their careers as boys in pillbox hats bearing coffee to the clientele. The Steward, later called the Union Manager, was vital to the solvency and stability of the place.

Electioneering, canvassing on the strength of personal manifestos for positions in the executive, was first practised in 1956. In and after the middle and late 1960s the union became increasingly politicised. As it expanded and grew more complex in the Robbins era, the principal elected officers were allowed to interrupt their studies and enjoy sabbatical years on salaries paid by the union in order to carry out their duties without jeopardising their degrees. Younger students taking shorter courses such as politics and modern history came to the fore. The responsibility for leading the union often fell to

members of political societies (usually the more disciplined and pragmatic bodies), who were sometimes rehearsing for political careers: Nick Brown, the beleaguered Agriculture Minister in Tony Blair's administration at the time of the disastrous outbreak of foot and mouth disease, had served an apprenticeship in Manchester in the early 1970s, when he was Vice-President responsible for liaison between the union in Manchester and the National Union of Students. In 1974 the system of presidents and vice-presidents, perhaps too redolent of hierarchy, was abolished in favour of collective rule by a small group of sabbatical officers – Manchester could now claim the only students' union in the country without a president.

For much of the 1970s and 1980s the union had a strong left-wing image, projected less by its executive than by the general meetings which determined union policy and could easily be dominated by bands of dedicated and intolerant politicos. But there were occasional swings to the right and a notable attempt in the late 1980s to "reclaim" the union for the average student. It was probably true at all times that most members were more interested in the services which the union provided than in the political views it expressed, although they gave general support to its protests against the steep decline in the value of maintenance grants and against the looming prospect that a system of repayable loans would take their place.

Jealous of its autonomy, aspiring to be a state-within-a-state or at least a major fiefdom within the University, the union lost some of its independence with the demolition of its old premises in the 1950s. Funds for the old building had been raised by appeal; the University owned the new one, financed by the UGC, and was therefore entitled to object to some of its uses. Membership became compulsory and local education authorities paid students' subscriptions to the University. From universal membership, the union derived a guaranteed regular income and authority to speak for the whole student body. But awkward questions arose concerning the proper use of public money; the high-principled Vice-Chancellor of the 1960s, Sir William Mansfield Cooper, occasionally reminded the union that, should it fail to impose discipline or appear to condone indecent behaviour, it might have to revert to the status of a voluntary organisation and be obliged to collect its own subscriptions. In 1980, Margaret Thatcher's government introduced a new system of financing unions from within the universities' block grants, in the belief that this move would enable, perhaps even force, universities to impose tighter control. Later in the decade, Conservative governments obliged all universities to ensure that students' unions observed charity law and respected free speech – the policy of "No Platform for Racists and Fascists", agreed by the National Union of Students and

Women at Manchester

Anna Ford (1943–)

Anna Ford, now Co-Chancellor of the University with Sir Terry Leahy, entered the Department of Sociology and Social Anthropology as an undergraduate in 1963. She left in 1970 with a BA (Econ.) degree and a Diploma in Adult Education – this she put to work for several years by teaching social sciences in a Belfast college, by becoming an Open University staff tutor, and by visiting the internment camp at Long Kesh to teach politics to political prisoners.

At Manchester she became, in 1966–7, the second woman President of the Students' Union and the first one to serve a full term in office, as "a militant determined to be moderate". There she made television appearances which foreshadowed her later career, one of them in a prophetic documentary film made for Granada by Mike Beckham about five Manchester students who appeared to "have the world at their feet". The University created for her a post in the Registrar's Department which effectively made her director of the International Society, and she had much to do with acquiring the house in Plymouth Grove, once the residence of the Victorian novelist Elizabeth Gaskell, which for many years served as the Society's headquarters.

Her distinguished broadcasting career commenced in 1974. She worked initially as a researcher, news reporter and later news reader for Granada Television and the BBC, before joining ITN as its first female newsreader in 1978. Later her career was to lead her back to the BBC in the mid-1980s where she presented successively the *Six O'Clock News* and the *One O'Clock News* on BBC One, and became a member of the BBC Radio 4 *Today* programme team from 1989, retiring in 2006.

Anna Ford has always had a keen interest in life outside of broadcasting and journalism and cited a desire to pursue other

interests while she still has the energy as the key to the timing of her retirement. Behind the newsreader image there has always lurked a sense of theatre and fun. As a student she toured Manchester's nightclub sets with a guitar for £5 a night, and always wished she could still be a nightclub singer, saying "You only have one life and it isn't a rehearsal. You may as well have fun."

Above and top: Anna Ford as a student in the 1960s, and today (left) as the first female Co-Chancellor of the University.

observed by individual unions, was becoming a pretext for howling down visiting Conservative politicians purveying unpopular views about such matters as immigration controls.

However, the Manchester Students' Union was justly proud of its ability to finance some of its activities by drawing on its trading income, and of its capacity for launching new and profitable enterprises. It was even able, in the late 1980s, to solve one of its most pressing problems, the need for additional space. Beaumont's 1957 building had been commissioned before the great expansion of the 1960s, with a far smaller student population in mind. The Academy, a large brick shed used by students for events and entertainments and by the University as a much-needed examination hall, was built by collaboration between the two bodies and erected on a plot hard by the union which had long been reserved for the union's eventual use. It is now one of the country's leading entertainment venues.

Slapstick and rough-housing, jolly japes, lewd songs chanted out of female earshot in the interests of male bonding, debaggings of bores and undesirables, feats of daring such as decorating the pinnacles of the Whitworth Hall with chamber-pots subsequently shot down by the Officers' Training Corps – these antics were quite compatible with the gentlemanly ethos of the Men's Union between the wars. Tribal conflicts broke out occasionally and a pitched battle between the rival unions of Owens and Tech during the session of 1928–9 called for police intervention, bringing Manchester students into disrepute throughout the north of England. For the most part, however, the citizens of Manchester suffered student high spirits, gladly or otherwise, only during Rag Week. This annual event culminated in the Shrove Tuesday procession, which seemed to mark the passage from Carnival to Lent like an ancient ritual designed to bring lasciviousness and gluttony to the surface, the better to purge them during the season of austerity and self-denial. Rag was, or came to be, organised by the Rag Committee of the students' union.

Three elements combined over the years to shape the festival. Patriotic torchlight processions in fancy dress had marked the Prince of Wales's visit to Manchester in 1887 and Queen Victoria's Diamond Jubilee ten years later. Processions to one of the local pantomimes had

taken place on Shrove Tuesday, and indulgent comedians quick at repartee, such as George Robey, Harry Lauder and George Formby, had invited students on stage and backstage. The practice of collecting for charities began in 1921 and imparted legitimacy to student capers, so that they became something more than a boisterous campaign to cajole the people of Manchester into reluctant laughter, and the spectators had the pleasure of pelting the performers with pennies. Union societies, academic departments and halls of residence devised tableaux and rode on lorries supplied by local firms to the Rag procession. During the fuel shortage of 1957, after the Suez crisis, "ten aged and dignified steam traction engines and kindred vehicles headed the procession". As the union paper testified, "all the other associated trappings were there – the showers of eggs, flour, water and other constituents of Shrove pancakes; the spivs along the route flogging paper hats and streamers; and the Shrove Queen riding in splendour in a very old car".

Rag always had critics among the students, who objected to its rowdiness, beeriness and contrived imbecility. A prominent target for the nice-minded was the Rag magazine, first launched in 1924. This was well described by the novelist Anthony Burgess, who contributed to it with "scabrous ingenuity" in the late 1930s, as "a male venture that was expected to skate about the black hole of obscenity". Demands that it be cleaned up, taken out of the hands of "nice girls" or suppressed altogether (its sale on union premises was forbidden in 1984) doubtless added to its allure.

With time, fundraising for charities during the Rag season began to be detached from the Rag procession. This ritual declined in importance from 1962 onwards with the rise of the University's great sponsored walk, the Bogle Stroll through the towns of Lancashire. In the 1970s the Stroll commonly accounted for about half Rag's income, and sales of the Rag magazine for another 30 per cent.

From 1867 onwards, the union published and to some extent controlled magazines and newspapers. These were, in varying degrees, literary journals carrying poetry, fiction, essays and criticism; parish newsletters complete with reports of meetings and events, gossip columns and letters of complaint; and commentaries on national and international issues affecting students. *The*

Far left: Cover of the Union's literary magazine.

Left: Manchester Independent, *18 March 1974.*

Serpent, named after the snake rising towards the sun in the University coat of arms, flourished or at least came out between 1917 and 1956, and had an office on the top floor of the union building. As Anthony Burgess remembered, "When the key to the office was mislaid, which was frequently, the only way into it was through its window, which necessitated a near-leap from a Joint Common Room window over a dizzying gap four storeys high. This was regarded as a test of journalistic courage." The literary *Serpent*, which reviewed Robert Graves's poems but would not handle *Finnegans Wake*, was eclipsed by the dully named *News Bulletin*, first printed in 1934. During the 1950s this veered between the solemnity of a broadsheet and a tabloid's avidity for scandal. At intervals, writers in *News Bulletin* attacked *Serpent* for objectionable cynicism and even for "nauseating filth", but it was *News Bulletin* that suffered suppression at the hands of the Vice-Chancellor in 1960. It had published scurrilous news stories with little attempt at verification, one attacking the University Bursar and another impugning the morals of students in lodgings. The paper was now widely circulated and assaults on the University's reputation were not quickly forgiven.

To deny the students a journal was inconceivable, however. A new paper, *Manchester Independent*, came into being in 1961. As its name suggested, it was detached from the union, and came to be controlled by a council of management including two members of the University staff, whose duty was not so much to censor as to remind the editors of the law of libel. During the 1960s the *Independent* acquired an excellent reputation for its content and presentation; in 1967 it won the highest *Daily Mirror* prize awarded to student papers, breaking the Oxford and Cambridge monopoly of the award.

Chastened by the crisis of 1960, the union ventured cautiously back into news in 1964 by putting out, albeit spasmodically, a modest free newssheet called *Mancunion*, designed to explain the activities of union officers and the council to their constituents. In the 1970s the *Independent*, plagued by financial troubles, began to founder and the *Mancunion*, swiftly acquiring many of the *Independent*'s good qualities and likewise offering features, reviews and sports reports, came forward to take its place. In these less paternalistic days there seemed to be no need for the *Mancunion* to be controlled by an outside body. At first resembling "a borrowed set of sociology notes" churned out by a photocopying machine, the *Mancunion* was professionally printed as a tabloid from 1975 onwards. Generally critical of the University establishment and inclined to accuse it of conspiring with the government against students' interests, the *Mancunion*, as the mouthpiece of "Union policy", sometimes infuriated many readers by its overt political bias – especially in 1982–3, when it could not advertise the Bogle

Rag Week

On Shrove Tuesday 1957, as part of the Rag Day "invasion" of central Manchester, Dalton Hall manned a float pulled by the traction engine *Pride of the Road*. The photograph was taken by me in Peter Street. The placard between the front wheels states: "From Yorkshire we bring Good Health, Good Luck, God Bless", showing that the engine had crossed the Pennines for the event.

G. Roberts
West Yorkshire

In 1953 a group of students, on the night prior to Rag Day, took a lorry to Llanfair PG in Anglesey. Under cover of darkness, they dismantled the name sign (famously the longest in Wales) at the local railway station and drove back to Manchester with it. By early on Shrove Tuesday morning, it had been erected at Oxford Road railway station – it met with no comment, but one wonders when the sign was missed at Llanfair PG!

David Davies
LLB Hons 1955

Nightlife in the 1990s

Life in Manchester was an hour's drive from home – far enough to live away, close enough to go home for laundry and catering at the weekend. My first year hall was in Victoria Park. I lived with ten other students, four of them British and the others ranging from American to Iraqi. Some of us are still in touch and we've travelled around the world to see each other.

Manchester has changed a lot since 1995 – before the IRA bomb, before the Printworks. The Deansgate Lock was still a canal lock whose only merit was that it was on the way to Dukes 92. Packs of dogs roamed the streets in Hulme. The Arndale was mustard coloured and Urbis was yet to grace an architect's pad. Piccadilly Gardens was still a garden, an oasis of grass, flower borders and cider drinkers.

I saw Marion live at the Haçienda for £1 entry fee, went to Prohibition nights in Club Underground at UMIST and Club Trop at the Academy. We played pinball in the students union at UMIST and pool in the Serpent Bar. Some Wednesday nights and the occasional Friday lunchtime were spent (along with a grant cheque – what a delight) at Manchester Met SU and I hazily recall waking up in McNally's bar at 3am one particular Saturday morning. I was hypnotised at a hypno-dog show in Freshers' week and amazed at the throngs of students on Oxford Road at 4am. There were beer festivals on the bowling green at UMIST and in the Manchester SU building. There were late night kebabs with lethal chilli sauce at Camel One in Rusholme. I remember seeing in the new year in the town hall square with locals wishing students a happy new year with a ubiquitous "nice one"…

I recall the struggle to get out of bed and make the trip to campus for 10am lectures, perhaps no surprise given my social life. Work could be hard, trying to understand quantum mechanics, enantiomers, crystal structures, synthesis and distillation. There were laboratory practicals and French classes on a Tuesday afternoon. We were using DOS-based email software and could check email or do other work on a computer, but not the two at the same time. I surfed the internet for the very first time on a computer in UMIST library.

University life let me meet my wife, live on the French Riviera for a year, have a job driving a busload of drunken students home around Manchester, write for the student magazine, be the Chairman of the Board of a company at only twenty-two, make lifelong friends and still get invited back to pen soundbites about life at university. What more could I have wanted?

Will Morley-Brown
MChem Hons 1999

The Academy.

Stroll without calling the event "politically redundant" and suggesting, "Save your boots for a Grants Demo instead." But the paper itself and some of its editors and feature-writers won national prizes and helped the *Mancunion* to equal or surpass the record of the *Independent*. In the late 1980s and early 1990s it was more inclined to publish good-humoured satires on the posturing of left-wingers and cheerful accounts of student hedonism, as prospects for graduate employment improved – drink, rave and be merry, for tomorrow we start a career.

Members of the union have always been members of the University. But, collectively, they have also formed (in dry legal terms) "an unincorporated association" "constitutionally separate from the University", even though partially dependent upon it in varying degrees for accommodation and finance. More trenchantly, the union was once described as "a large theatre workshop for those interested in politics and administration to practise their talents". Its task has been to represent students to the University and to the world; to entertain, inform and advise them; to attend to their welfare, adding to the pastoral care afforded by academic departments and halls of residence; to express their political opinions, or at least those of the minority most passionately interested in politics; and to campaign both for better pay and

Music, Drama and Entertainment

ANNE PULLAN

Amateur theatricals, concerts, fancy dress parades and visits to the pantomime and music hall always enlivened student existence. Student papers carried ample reviews of plays, music and films presented in the University and the city, and from the 1960s the University had a permanent theatre and a Department of Drama as well as a much older Faculty of Music. Anne Pullan explores some of the links between Manchester student life and the subsequent careers of alumni who became famous as novelists, composers, playwrights, musicians, actors and entertainers (some read music or drama or English, and others did not). She has a first degree in English from Manchester Metropolitan University and an MA in Arts and Heritage Management (specialising in Theatre Management) from the University of Sheffield.

Throughout the twentieth century, the performing arts have enhanced the quality of life in Manchester, home to the Hallé Orchestra and Miss Annie Horniman's Gaiety Theatre (where the first repertory theatre company took to the stage) and now to the Royal Exchange Theatre, the Bridgewater Hall and The Lowry. The city continues to play host to opera and musicals, classical and contemporary music, dance and drama productions. Students have often been at the heart of cultural activities, both as audiences and as amateur and professional performers, and alumni of the University of Manchester continue to have a huge impact on music, drama and entertainment.

Long before the inception of a drama department, the students of Owens had opportunities to perform in a variety of venues. The ambition to provide an environment that would generate well-rounded graduates, both socially and academically, encouraged students living in traditional halls of residence to produce annual plays and concerts, with men's and women's halls twinned for this and other social purposes. The Stage Society and the Settlement Players were two drama groups, made up of students and staff, who performed at the Round House in Ancoats where the Settlement policy actively encouraged students and graduates to live as neighbours with local inhabitants, provide entertainments and organise community projects. This was a deliberate attempt to put something back into the city, as if to compensate for the University's impact on the community around Oxford Road, which was acknowledged to be deprived and susceptible to being pushed out by a growing population of privileged students and their space-hungry University.

The Stephen Joseph Drama Studio, for many years the main laboratory of the Drama Department, housed in a former German Protestant church which probably dates from the 1860s.

Left and above: The Contact Theatre.

Right: Ashburne students in a performance of She Stoops To Conquer, *1928.*

Anthony Burgess recalls in his autobiography, *Little Wilson and Big God*, that the Round House on Every Street in Ancoats played host to the radical theatre producer Joan Littlewood, who founded the Theatre Workshop Company at the Theatre Royal in the East End of London. Promoting theatre as a tool of social revolution, Joan apparently pressed the "local unemployed and their wives, many of them with their false teeth out" to present the main theme of the first movement of William Walton's First Symphony as an angry working-class polemic. This opened the eyes of Burgess and his fellow students to the possibility that theatre could be something other than High Art.

During the rapid expansion of the University precinct and the building projects of the 1960s, the Students' Unions of the University and UMIST continued to host performances by societies and individuals of music, annual revues, comedy and drama. Students of all departments could perform in the Studio Theatre and additional space could be found at UMIST Students' Union and the Renold Theatre. From the 1960s, the new mixed forms of large-scale student accommodation (such as Owens Park village in Fallowfield) also gave the students the chance to display their talents to largely student audiences. Entertainments and drama were often incorporated into student protest and campaigning. A prime example was the imaginative use of drama to entertain protesters in an occupation of Whitworth Hall in 1970 – in the name of free speech, the hall was home to a captive and enthusiastic audience for a fortnight of sketches and plays by the group Occupational Hazard. Indeed, the sit-in was prolonged for a day to enable the protesters to see the last episode of a soap opera which had been left on a cliff-hanger.

The greatest innovation came in 1965 when the new University Theatre was opened by Dame Sybil Thorndike. Detached from nearby academic buildings, it was intended for use by a resident professional company, by departments (especially the Drama and Language departments), by university drama groups and by visiting companies. The theatre offered technical innovations to enable multiple staging arrangements, and the acoustics and intimacy of the space favoured a more naturalistic style of performance. University Theatre was directed by the first head of the newly formed Drama Department, Professor Hugh Hunt, and delivered a mixed programme of music, drama, dance and comedy to its target youth audience. In 1972, Hugh Hunt also formed a youth theatre company, called Contact, when the Sixty-Nine theatre company moved to its new home, the state-of-the-art Royal Exchange Theatre. This venture was not entirely to the liking of the drama students, but Professor Hunt had had the foresight to realise that mass entertainment media such as television could have a negative impact on attendance and the long-term survival of live theatre. He sought to engage young people from the local area in participating in performing arts, well before the rise of modern marketing, audience development studies and the education departments of today's professional organisations. Renamed and rebuilt, the Contact Theatre continues to cater successfully for the under-twenty-five market, offering workshops and writing opportunities from which to launch careers.

The Contact Theatre adjoins the former site of the Royal Manchester College of Music, founded by Sir Charles Hallé. This institution merged with the Northern College of Music and was re-housed to become the Royal Northern College of Music. The former premises of the college became known as the Squat (in memory of a student occupation which saved the buildings in 1973) and provided much-needed space for the union until they were demolished in 1982. It was to be several years before the union won the right to build a new extension and remodel its existing building to provide a large enough central space for its entertainments and meeting requirements. Other students' unions in Manchester and Salford had versatile, self-contained, large spaces as venues for night-clubs, comedy or popular music, serviced by bars. Later, the Students' Union at UMIST was quick to utilise its proximity to Manchester's "gay village" when Manchester Pride began in the 1990s, hosting some of the events across the annual August *Mardi Gras* weekend festival. The University of Manchester Students' Union solved its problems with the opening of The Academy in 1990.

Following the model of the Contact Theatre, the Academy was opened as a separate building, situated between the Union and the theatre. In addition, the Union building was remodelled with bars and additional smaller spaces which offered extremely flexible venues for bands from all genres of music; the student bop, and city-wide festivals of drama, poetry, dance and comedy. The Academy has built a major reputation as a popular and professional venue for audiences of students and the general public, and also hosts and promotes local bands, taking over the role from the popular but insalubrious Boardwalk near Deansgate, which was converted into flats in the 1990s.

The most recent addition to facilities has been the Martin Harris Centre for Music and Drama, situated within the oldest part of the University. Bringing together two existing buildings with a modern, light foyer, the centre provides state-of-the-art teaching facilities and incorporates the John Thaw Studio Theatre and the Cosmo Rodewald Concert Hall. In recognition of the prevalence and innovations of new technologies in music production, the centre also runs a joint project with the Royal Northern College of Music, providing studios for computer-generated music.

The Martin Harris Centre for Music and Drama.

Internet access to tickets and performance information enables the Contact Theatre, the Academy and the Martin Harris Centre to satisfy a wide range of tastes in performing arts for audiences from across the social spectrum. Access to such audiences provides excellent opportunities for all students to build on experience and knowledge and to be at the forefront of innovation in their given fields. However, it is not just the twenty-first-century student of the University who has the opportunity to make a significant mark in the arts; over the last century, many alumni have distinguished themselves as playwrights, composers, musicians, actors and novelists.

Anthony Burgess (1917–93) graduated in 1940 with a BA (Hons) in English Language and Literature. A local boy, Burgess aspired to be a composer, librettist and musician but was unable to gain the qualification in physics which was then essential to music students at the University of Manchester. However, his Catholic education and musical expertise led to an intense interest in linguistics, which was furthered by the strict linguistic curriculum of the English Department and became the hallmark of his novels, criticism and music. Burgess is best known for his cult futuristic novel, *A Clockwork Orange*, for which he invented a hybrid language for the young protagonists exploring the nature of evil.

So dark was the novel, the director Stanley Kubrick withdrew his 1972 film of it after claims that it inspired copy-cat violence. Burgess's most critically acclaimed novel was *Earthly Powers*, "a Tolstoyan saga of the twentieth century", and his *Enderby* cycle of comic novels is commonly understood to be based upon his own life, travels and diversions. Aside from his career as a novelist, Burgess continued to compose, adapt and translate, and to write for the theatre and screen. He was also a teacher, essayist, broadcaster, travel writer and prolific journalist, who disguised neither his desire for pecuniary reward nor his aversion to paying taxes.

Burgess's keen intellect and colourful character contributed enormously to the University in the late 1930s. He was on the committee for the Stage Society and also regularly performed recitals and adapted plays for the Men's Union. He wrote music for recitals and incidental music for the plays of the Stage Society, displayed his talent for student journalism in his role as chief reviewer and committee member of *The Serpent* and became involved in the political life and debating of the University.

Against a background of the Depression, the Spanish Civil War and the Second World War, it is hardly surprising that the performing arts were highly politicised, not least by the young socialist Robert Bolt (1924–95), playwright and Oscar-winning screenwriter, who graduated in history in 1949. Born in Sale, Bolt was brought up in a household given to constant social and political debate. After a short period in an insurance office, he started on an economics degree at Owens in 1943 and joined the Communist Party. His studies were interrupted in 1944 by his call-up papers, but an action-free stint in South Africa enabled him to spend his time with theatrical people, musicians, artists and other left-wing intellectuals. When he returned to Manchester, Bolt switched to history and became a pupil of the great Professor Lewis Namier. Like Burgess, he sought the constant stimulation of political debate, particularly within University societies and at Caf, the refectory cafeteria where men and women could most easily meet to socialise.

Robert Bolt began his career as a teacher in the newly reconstructed state education system, which allowed him to introduce drama and new teaching methods to a primary school in Bishopsteighton and then to Millfield public school. To supplement his earnings, he began to write radio plays and

adaptations for the BBC, which paid modestly but regularly. His *A Man for All Seasons* was first aired on BBC radio on 26 July 1954, televised on New Year's Day in 1957 and debuted on stage in 1960. It launched the professional career of Ian McKellen in 1961, and a new version was screened on television in 1964. The play is a study of individuality through the figure of Sir Thomas More, Henry VIII's Lord Chancellor, who chose execution rather than compromise his personal convictions. The Oscar-winning screenplay was filmed starring Paul Schofield alongside Orson Welles, John Hurt and Corin Redgrave in 1966, and a television film version was produced in 1988 starring Charlton Heston, John Gielgud and Vanessa Redgrave.

Bolt's political convictions sealed a long-lasting friendship with the radical Redgrave acting dynasty. He was jailed for his activities as a founder member of the Committee of 100, a militant breakaway group from CND that campaigned fervently for the abolition of Britain's weapons of mass destruction. His play *The Tiger and the Horse* dealt with the protagonist's dilemma between speaking out against nuclear weapons in support of his family principles, and the potential costs of this action to his career and thus his family's future. Bolt had secured, and wanted to wait for, Michael Redgrave in the lead, so it was a coincidence that both *The Tiger and the Horse* and *A Man for All Seasons* ran concurrently in the West End in 1960. *Tiger* was a rewrite of a radio play, *The Last of the Wine* (16 July 1955) which was initially called *Dandelions*. Interestingly, the original script of *Dandelions* had been sent to Hugh Hunt at the Arts Club in London in 1953, well before Hunt's arrival as Professor of Drama at Manchester University. Hunt forwarded the script to Peter Ustinov but the play was not produced, much to Bolt's disappointment. Bolt is also remembered for his screenplays for *Lawrence of Arabia* (1962), *Doctor Zhivago* (1965), *Ryan's Daughter* (1970) and *The Bounty* (1984), for which his early work for radio must have prepared him.

Like Bolt, the socialist playwright Trevor Griffiths (BA in English Language and Literature, 1955) was initially a teacher. He is known for his television dramas *All Good Men* (1974), *Comedians* (1979) and *Sons and Lovers* (1981) and for his script

Women at Manchester

Meera Syal
(BA Hons English and Drama 1983, Honorary LittD 2006)
Interviewed by Alison Utley

The oft-heard criticism that arts students have too few lectures worked in favour of Meera Syal. A student of English and Drama in the early 1980s who, after achieving a double first, has gone on to become a prolific and multi-talented writer and performer, Ms Syal says her tutors encouraged her to be creative by leaving her alone.

Reflecting on her work as a writer and performer in numerous film, television and theatre productions, Syal acknowledges that her sense of personal discipline was developed while studying and has been the foundation of her hugely successful career:

"I remember my time at the University with great affection," she says. "The drama department was thriving and I had chosen a really quite unique course." Academically she recalls the course was very hard work, particularly during the first two years when she was effectively studying for two degrees.

"But I loved what I was doing and I was very active," she says. "We were doing shows all the time, as well as experimentation and improvisation. It's where I cut my teeth and it was a very good grounding for what I later went on to do. Looking back it was as good as drama school."

Most importantly though, the degree course encouraged Ms Syal to become creatively self sufficient.

"I have always generated my own work and as the tutors largely left us alone it instilled in me the discipline of writing. The number of lectures was a joke in some ways and if you wanted to you could spend all your time in the pub, but actually for me that was the course's great strength."

Whilst an undergraduate Syal wrote and acted in *One of Us*, a play about a young Asian girl who runs away from home because she wants to be an actress. The character rejects her parents and becomes intoxicated with her white friend, Carol. She took the play to the Edinburgh Festival, and that same year it won the National Student Drama Award. A London theatre director saw her in the play and offered her the chance of an Equity card. It was time to abandon her plans of going on to study for an MA and start to act for a living.

For seven years after leaving university Meera Syal acted in London at the Royal Court Theatre, before receiving a call from the BBC who were looking for an Asian woman to co-write a script. Despite having no experience of television she went on to write *My Sisterwife*, a three-part BBC television series on marriage, before launching such enormously well received shows as *The Kumars* and *Goodness Gracious Me*.

As if that wasn't enough Ms Syal is also a highly acclaimed novelist – her first book *Anita and Me* draws on her childhood experiences growing up in a small mining community near Wolverhampton and was shortlisted for the Guardian Fiction Prize and won a Betty Trask Award.

Meera Syal was awarded an Honorary LittD by the University at a special graduation ceremony in 2006. Presenting the award, Professor Viv Gardner spoke of "her innovative and radical work in television, film and literature, her perceptive and witty comedy, her passionate commitment to racial equality and multi-culturalism, and her standing as one of the great storytellers in contemporary Britain."

for *Reds*, directed by Warren Beatty (1981). Griffiths is currently concentrating on writing and directing for the stage.

The pattern of crossover between genres in the arts, illustrated by Burgess, Bolt and Griffiths, is also reflected in the careers of more recent alumni. The anarchic comedy partners, Richard (Rik) Mayall and Adrian (Ade) Edmondson, both graduated with BA (Hons) in Drama in 1978. Rik Mayall was apparently a slacker at school and only got into Manchester on the strength of a good interview. He met the long-haired Edmondson by respectfully standing up at his first lecture on the arrival of Professor Prudhoe, only to be berated by Edmondson, much to the amusement of their fellow students. "Good Boy" Mayall and "Laconic" Edmondson formed a theatre company, 20th Century Coyote, with three others, performing at the Edinburgh Festival and around Manchester clubs. It was eventually whittled down to just Mayall and Edmondson, and as a duo they launched their comedy careers at The Comedy Store in London before setting up The Comic Strip. According to *The Times* in 1991, Mayall thought the late 1970s was a "dour time" for creativity "when everyone was doing their political theatre and being very puritanical". He and Edmondson would counter this depressing tendency at university with cries of "Showbiz! Showbiz! We're going to be stars!", dressing up at every opportunity and making mock phone calls to agents.

Anyone who has rented a room in shared accommodation will recognise the characters and setting of *The Young Ones*, their most celebrated alternative comedy television sit-com, broadcast in 1982 and 1984. Apparently written to mock the futility of raging against the state and trying to bring down the government of Margaret Thatcher by marching and wearing badges, the series was based on their experiences in Manchester. With a trademark of gratuitous violence, the pair have been prolific writers and performers on television and on the stage, with Mayall branching out into a straight performance in the drama series *All About George* in 2005.

Perhaps one of the "serious, politico" students that Mayall and Edmondson were railing against in *The Young Ones* was Ben Elton, who graduated in 1980 in Drama. In his mock autobiography, *The Rik Mayall: Bigger than Hitler Better than Christ*, Mayall claims to have taken the young Elton under his and Edmondson's "wing". However, it is rather more likely that this nephew of the eminent historian G.R. Elton had his own ideas. Ben Elton's comedy career began when

A student using the drama studio's mixing desk.

he followed Mayall and Edmondson to The Comedy Club and co-wrote *The Young Ones*. His public profile as a stand-up comedian was enhanced by a regular slot on the BBC's *Saturday Live* as a card-carrying member of the Labour Party, deeply cynical about the Conservative government of the day and the Prime Minister, Margaret Thatcher.

Ben Elton is a highly acclaimed comedy screenwriter for television. He combined a grasp of historical fact with a comedic understanding of human relations in the second series of *Blackadder*, first broadcast in 1986. Brought in by Richard Curtis to rejuvenate the quirky series, Elton worked with Rowan Atkinson, Tony Robinson and Rik Mayall, with a repertory cast of Britain's best comedians. Elton has been heavily involved in the Comic Relief organisation, which has campaigned for

Right: (Left to right) Nigel Planer, Rik Mayall and Adrian Edmondson on the cover of the DVD for their BBC series 'Filthy, Rich and Catflap', written by Ben Elton (left).

A student takes advantage of the latest technology to create music.

an end to poverty and for social justice, since Christmas 1985. He is also a novelist, actor, director and playwright and, most recently, a writer for musicals, co-scripting Andrew Lloyd Webber's *The Beautiful Game*, and writing the musicals *We Will Rock You* and *Tonight's the Night*, celebrating the music of Queen and Rod Stewart. This move to the popular musical genre is in keeping with his left-wing credentials, celebrating as it does the positive contribution of popular music to life in Britain and the resurgent popularity of musical theatre.

Students from across the University have regularly devised and performed drama at festivals across the country. The National Students Drama Festival (NSDF) has been running since 1956 and hosts competing student groups from schools, colleges and universities, awarding prizes for all aspects of theatre production. The golden age for students from Manchester was between 1978 and 1986, when the Manchester Umbrella Theatre Company flourished. Comparable with the Cambridge Footlights of the 1960s, the company was highly successful both in producing revivals and in writing and performing new scripts. These were transferred to the Edinburgh Festival and toured under the sponsorship of British Petroleum. The company first performed in 1978 at the NSDF, competing against two productions from the Manchester University Drama Department. In 1981, Manchester Umbrella Theatre Company was awarded four prizes for the production of Ben Jonson's *The Silent Woman* and one for a new play. In 1982, the company received six honours, which included the award for Best Incidental Music written by Sophie Aldred for *The Dog in the Manger* by Lope de Vega. Sophie Aldred graduated with a BA (Hons) in Drama in 1983, landed the part of Ace in the cult series *Dr Who* and has contributed enormously to children's educational television programming, with a specific emphasis on music.

An outstanding success for the Umbrella Theatre Company was *One of Us*, entered in the NSDF in 1983. Jointly written by Jacqui Shapiro and Meera Syal, the one-woman show traces the experience of a British Asian girl who runs away from home to become an actress. The play won the Scottish Arts Council Award, and Meera Syal also won the BP Best Solo Performance Award. Despite graduating with a double first in English and Drama in 1983, Meera Syal's expectations were coloured by frustration at not getting the best parts at university, which led her to devise her own role in *One of Us*. The show transferred to Edinburgh and went on tour, which attracted the attention of the BBC and led directly to further screenwriting. She has gone on to write novels, plays and screenplays, such as the highly acclaimed *Anita and Me* (1996). Her public profile soared with her comedy writing and performances in the Asian sketch shows, *Goodness Gracious Me* (1998), which began as a radio comedy show, and *The Kumars at No. 42* (2001). Like her novels *Anita and Me* and *Life isn't all Ha Ha Hee Hee*, these groundbreaking BBC shows shine a spotlight on both the British Asian experience and the flaws of the host society. The popular sketch featuring a group of young Asians "going out for an English [meal]" reveals an uncomfortable truth about the antics of the average student in the Asian restaurants of places like Rusholme.

Manchester has also produced internationally renowned musicians, singers, composers and conductors. Studying at both Owens and the Royal Manchester College of Music (RMCM) in the 1950s, Sir Peter Maxwell Davies and Elgar Howarth worked alongside Harrison Birtwistle, Alexander Goehr and the pianist John Ogdon (1937–89). Maxwell Davies had a particularly strained relationship with the University's Professor of Composition, Humphrey Proctor-Gregg, opting to study Indian and early music

Sir Peter Maxwell Davies.

The Chemical Brothers performing on stage in Trieste, Italy, July 2005.

for his thesis, possibly to challenge Proctor-Gregg's rigidly conservative view of "worthy" music and composers. Birtwistle, Howarth and Goehr studied composition under the rather more progressive Richard Hall at RMCM, experimenting with the new European style of composition. Together they formed what was briefly known as the New Music Manchester Group, which sought to compose and perform contemporary music, expanding the rather safe boundaries of classical composition for academics, musicians and audiences alike. Sir Peter Maxwell Davies currently holds the highest public position as Master of the Queen's Music (appointed in 2004), and the irrepressible Goehr, Birtwistle and Howarth remain highly influential in contemporary composition and performance. They still collaborate at intervals, producing chamber, orchestral, musical theatre and opera work which continues to challenge academics and audiences with a modernist aesthetic.

Harrison Birtwistle was particularly influenced by a 1954 BBC concert of Olivier Messiaen's *Turangalîla Symphonie*, conducted by the celebrated Walter Goehr, Alexander's father, and written for the ondes-martenot, the first successful electronic keyboard instrument (patented 1928) which is still used in orchestras today. The cyclical reworking of a section of music in Messaien's work is also a central motif of Birtwistle's music; a good example is his study of "Time and the Seasons" in his opera *Gawain*, commissioned and staged by the Royal Opera House in 1991. The opera is based on the Arthurian medieval poem *Sir Gawain and the Green Knight* and involved innovative special effects to present the headless Green Knight. Incidentally, a version of the poem published by Manchester University Press was, according to Anthony Burgess, "one of the most beautiful books ever published ... the handling of which was a profound physical pleasure". A revival of *Gawain* in 2000 saw the return of Elgar Howarth as conductor and starred the renowned bass Sir John Tomlinson as the phantom Green Knight. Tomlinson is

another notable alumnus, who graduated in 1967 with a BA(Hons) in Civil Engineering before taking up a scholarship at RMCM.

Careers in music have often led on from other studies, as witness those of Ed O'Brien, a self-taught guitarist for the alternative rock band Radiohead, and later Tom Rowlands and Ed Simons, digital and clubbing music specialists who form the Chemical Brothers, winners of two Grammy Awards in 2006. Ed O'Brien graduated with a BA (Hons) in Economics in 1990 and rejoined his former musical schoolfriends in On a Friday (later renamed Radiohead) on his return to his home town of Oxford. O'Brien and Radiohead have pushed the boundaries of modern music and been likened in influence to Pink Floyd, R.E.M. and the Beatles. Highly acclaimed for their composition and astute lyrics, the band utilise all genres of music including classical, jazz, blues, reggae, rock, hip-hop and electronic music. Most notably, Radiohead count Messaien as a musical influence, with Jonny Greenwood playing the ondes-martenot among other instruments. Likewise, the Chemical Brothers sample and utilise many genres of music in producing modern electronic and digital dance music. Manchester, nicknamed Madchester in the late 1980s and early 1990s, was briefly the centre of popular music production and innovation. As a result, Tom Rowlands and Ed Simons were both attracted to the city, and juxtaposed studies of medieval history with DJ slots at Manchester's nightclubs, including the Hacienda.

From the days of Disraeli's *Cottonopolis* and Friedrich Engels, Manchester has been at the heart of social activism and this is reflected in the city's contribution to the arts. As the facilities and teaching at the University have evolved and modernised, the students have had growing opportunities to innovate. The political messages may be presented in more diffuse ways through contemporary opera, popular music and comedy, but the University's alumni continue to challenge the status quo with radical culture for a radical city.

Student Protest

BRIAN PULLAN

In the 1950s and early 1960s many university students were highly critical of government policies and especially of militarism. They marched in protest against Anthony Eden's Suez adventure in 1956; they joined the Campaign for Nuclear Disarmament (CND) and sometimes the Committee of 100. Student politics took a new turn in the late 1960s, however, when students began to criticise their universities and some resorted to direct action in an attempt to force the universities to listen. Brian Pullan gives a brief account of the heyday of student protest in Manchester, the local version of a general phenomenon.

In late February and early March 1970 a strange 'happening' brought together hundreds, even thousands, of Manchester students in a mass occupation of the Whitworth Hall and the University's administrative offices. Many students normally unmoved by the fashionable "scattergun radicalism" of the times braved the chill of unheated buildings and partied by candle-light, briefly enjoying a kind of free university with impromptu seminars and teach-ins, folk songs and dramatic performances, punctuated by occasional reports on negotiations with the University authorities. To some senior members, the sit-in was a gross violation of law and order, noisome and unsavoury, the cause of unforgivable distress to an enlightened Vice-Chancellor, Sir William Mansfield Cooper. Others, including the Anglican chaplain, saw in the protest, more cheerful than any before or since, "an immense liberation and camaraderie … one vast experimental workshop", where the standard of discussion proved to be far higher than in the University's classrooms.

At the root of the sit-in lay unsubstantiated rumours that the University had been recording information about the political activities of student militants. Immediately, the protest was against the Vice-Chancellor's use of injunctions to stifle a debate in the Students' Union. His intention had been to stop certain members of the Socialist Society from inciting fellow students to commit an act of trespass which could have led to something worse – an attempt to break into the University's files. Visiting the protesters, Jack Straw, the future luminary of Blair's Britain, then serving as President of the National Union of Students (NUS), called the Vice-Chancellor's actions the greatest denial of free speech that he had ever seen.

The SRC (Student Representative Council) petitions the Court of Governors. Sketch by Hamilton Irving, early twentieth century.

Students protest against Anthony Eden's Suez adventure, 1956.

Principled student radicalism in the late 1960s, widespread in Europe and the USA, depicted universities as the tools of amoral capitalism: what were they but "knowledge factories", instruments of social engineering, churning out technocrats to serve industrial and commercial societies engaged in the oppression of Third World countries? They appeared to be easy targets, unused to serious challenges and relying unduly on a degree of student deference which was now evaporating. They could be disrupted, their routines paralysed, especially if their bosses could be provoked into over-reacting and thereby antagonising moderate students and academics. Sir William's nerve had been shaken by the tactics of a small group of between thirty and fifty militants, who were said to have a following of about two hundred. Dissent was fiercest, it seemed, among students of the social sciences and in certain parts of the Arts Faculty, quiescence most prevalent among the followers of vocational courses. But many intelligent, questioning students were not interested in tearing the University apart, for their wishes were more modest and attainable: for a role in decision-making,

for more competent teaching, for a fairer system of examining, for more acknowledgement of their new-found adult status, for a more liberal regime in halls of residence. No doubt the end of National Service in the early 1960s had weakened the habit of outwardly deferring to authority while inwardly cursing it; very likely the public emphasis on the country's need for graduates had increased students' self-esteem, raised their expectations and sharpened their critical sense.

To some extent the heads of universities blunted criticism and contained rebellion by establishing consultative machinery (boycotted by true radicals and considered ineffably tedious by some academics). More pragmatic than his predecessor, Sir Arthur Armitage, Vice-Chancellor from 1970 to 1980, was well described as a master of "repressive tolerance". Direct action became the speciality of small groups of activists for whom the struggle was an end in itself, especially members of the Socialist Workers' Party and the Revolutionary Communist Party. Throughout the 1970s, however, there was much principled opposition, among academics as well as students, to the

Left: Manchester Independent,
*3 March 1970, reports NUS President Jack Straw's visit to
the sit-in. Straw later went on to hold high Cabinet office
under Prime Minister Tony Blair.*

*Above: Sir William Mansfield Cooper: an unsympathetic
portrait provided by Insitter.*

University's investment in companies that had interests in southern Africa and could therefore be taxed with condoning apartheid. Most of the agitation was aimed at severing all economic ties with South Africa, and was directed at the businessmen who sat on the University Council and controlled its investments policy. Committed to maintaining a balanced portfolio, on which the pensions of the non-academic staff depended, they themselves denounced apartheid but preferred the strategy of "constructive engagement", which allowed them to press companies to pay better wages and establish more reasonable working conditions. There was no meeting of minds, for student moralists dismissed this tactic as a

*US Civil Rights
leader Malcolm X
during a visit to
Manchester
University in
1964.*

Insitter: *A pamphlet commemorating the occupation of the Whitworth Hall in February–March 1970.*

I believe and hope that everyone is prepared to make a reasonably clear distinction between confidential files and 'secret' files .... Anyone who wrote to me asking whether X was a Conservative, or Y a Trotskyist, or Z had a signed picture of Jeremy Thorpe over his bed would be told the quickest way to the lake ... our Administration did not, does not, and will not keep political files.

Lord Bowden replies to
the students, *Insitter*, 1970

From the 1970s onwards, when inflation began to erode student maintenance grants, there was always another, less idealistic strain in student protest, a form of trade unionism more narrowly concerned with protecting students' economic interests – in effect, with securing them decent wages and social security benefits and protecting them against exorbitant rents. In the face of mounting indebtedness it was this type of protest that tended to prevail after the late 1980s. Stiff competition for jobs in a market saturated with graduates, a concern with good qualifications and the need to do part-time work in order to survive economically – none of these things favoured idealism or fostered a strong political consciousness.

Top: Folk songs at the sit-in of 1970.

mere palliative, a patronising act that might prolong the life of an oppressive regime.

Left-wing student opinion was strongly internationalist and objected to the imposition of immigration controls and to demands that international students pay higher fees. Opposition to "fascism", a term never tightly defined but useful for general abuse, came to embrace not only extremist groups such as the National Front but also prominent members of the Conservative Party. The NUS policy of "No platform for racists and fascists" exposed universities to charges of attacking free speech – the concept vigorously defended by the sitters-in of 1970 – and substituting the chanting of slogans for reasoned debate. Events in November 1985 led to unaccustomed conflict between the University and the union and again provoked student occupations. Uncouth behaviour in the union, designed to silence a Home Office minister, David Waddington, caused the University to challenge the union's autonomy and punish the offenders through disciplinary tribunals of its own.

International Students

ALEX J. ROBERTSON

Owens and Tech were originally intended for a local and regional clientele, but from early days their reputation in certain fields enabled them to draw students from other countries. Alex Robertson describes the ebb and flow of recruitment from abroad, analyses the provenance of Manchester's growing contingent of international students, and considers the arrangements made for them when they arrived at the University. After some years teaching Economic History at the University, Mr Robertson joined the Registrar's Department with special responsibility for the recruitment of students from overseas.

Today the University of Manchester attracts a high proportion of international students but things were not always thus: the modern University's ancestral institutions – the Mechanics' Institution of 1824 and Owens College of 1851 – had both been set up unequivocally for the benefit of the inhabitants of Manchester and its surrounding industrial districts.

By the 1870s, however, a few international students were to be found in both institutions. There were, for example, the Japanese. Yamanobe Takeo, having trained in the technology of cotton manufacturing at the Mechanics' Institution and in local mills around Manchester, returned to set up and manage the Toyo cotton mill in Osaka in 1883, importing not only his machinery from Manchester but even the bricks from which the mill was built.

Students from overseas remained, however, only a modest presence on the eve of the First World War. But by 1928–9, just before the Great Depression, the University of Manchester and its Faculty of Technology included 134 students from abroad, constituting some 4.5 per cent of total student registrations. Of

David Beckham (left) and Prime Minister Tony Blair MP (centre) talking to Dr Tim Westlake, Head of the Division of International Development, at an international student fair.

these, 59 were from India, mostly registered in Technology. Next in numerical importance came 21 Egyptians, chiefly in a special course in Pharmacy which had apparently been set up by arrangement with the Egyptian government. The remaining 54 students came from no fewer than thirty different countries.

In the post-Depression period, international student numbers began to grow fairly rapidly. By 1938–9 they numbered 232, representing nearly 7.5 per cent of student registration in the

A Student Perspective

We have a problem-based learning system at The University of Manchester. Each week they give us a different medical case and we have to work out what is wrong. We call it "differential diagnoses". Within that case, you'll study all the areas. For example, if you're studying a case involving gastric ulcers, you'll study the whole digestive system – anatomy, physiology and related pharmacology. The system is really good. In other traditional universities, it is more lecture-based but our system makes you think about it and there is always a teacher on hand if you are getting stuck. You then have the chance to ask any questions. I am in my third year now and I work in the hospital. I have to work out what is wrong in a real-life environment, so it is really good training.

Jakibai Kimis from Malaysia
Studying Medicine

University and Faculty of Technology. Indian and Egyptian students remained in the forefront, with 76 of the former and 23 of the latter. Indeed, the Faculty of Technology now had a large enough body of Indian students – 80 per cent of the total – to persuade the Government of India to fund an Adviser to Indian Students, paid £100 per year through the India Office in London. Another prominent group in 1938–9 were students from Germany, who numbered 22. A significant proportion of these were refugees from the Nazi regime, though others had come to Manchester via student exchanges which the University had set up with the universities of Göttingen and Greifswald. After them in numerical importance came eighteen students from Poland.

Life on the wartime campus was not always easy for the German and Austrian students. Classed as "enemy aliens",

despite the fact that they or their parents had fled from Hitler's Reich to escape persecution, several were interned by the British authorities in 1940. The Vice-Chancellor, Sir John Stopford, seems to have made considerable efforts to secure their release in order to let them continue their studies, and when one medical student was indeed released – but only on condition that he immediately join the British Army's Pioneer Corps – Stopford sought to have the condition annulled on the grounds that the student would be of more use to the country as a doctor than as a military navvy.

International student numbers quickly recovered after the Second World War. By the early 1950s, the international student contingent fluctuated around 6.5 per cent of total registrations, with Indian students still the largest single group, followed by the Egyptians. It was notable, however, that the range of countries from which significant numbers of students were drawn to the University was much wider than ever before: Norway, Greece, the USA, Iraq, Nigeria and Pakistan were now prominent within a catchment area of sixty or so countries, nearly twice as many as before the war. Numbers had grown to more than 1,000 international students from 82 different countries, accounting for nearly 9 per cent of their joint student bodies. India remained the most important source, with 143 students, followed by the USA (79), Iraq (74), Pakistan (60), Nigeria (58), Egypt (56) and Malaysia (35).

It was at this point that the presence of international students in British universities first became a serious political issue. Until then, neither the British Government nor the universities had drawn any distinction between students from the British Isles and those from other countries. After 1966, all this changed, as did attitudes to international students, their recruitment and their significance to the universities. These were times of increasing economic stringency for Britain, in the face of which the government of Harold Wilson introduced a sharp differential between the fees paid by British students and those paid by students from abroad. The fees paid by international students rose from about £60 a year in 1966–7 to £250 in 1967–8. There they remained for ten years, before being ratcheted up by a series of annual fee increases that took them to £1,165 (£1,525 for postgraduates) by October 1980. At that point, the Thatcher government decreed that international students would in future meet the full cost of their education in British universities.

Fee increases did not halt the growth in international student numbers which had taken place since the mid 1950s. These peaked in 1976–7 at 1,165 (11.2 per cent of total registrations) for the University and 1,314 (34.7 per cent) for UMIST. Thereafter the upward trend of the previous twenty years was reversed; so that by 1984–5, international students numbered a mere 767

(4.9 per cent of total registrations) in the University and 879 (19.9 per cent) in UMIST.

Despite the problems caused for international students by the steep rise in fees, and especially by the introduction of "full cost" fees in 1980–81, there were groups whose enrolments in the University and UMIST during this difficult period actually increased. Students from Hong Kong, for example, grew from 92 in 1974–5 to 476 ten years later, and Nigerian student numbers increased from 94 to 196 over the same period.

UMIST was the first British university to appoint, in 1983, a member of staff – Dr Iain Bride – specifically "to market to potential overseas applicants the range of courses, facilities and opportunities we have to offer". Others gradually followed suit, though it was not until January 1988 that the University of Manchester authorised the establishment of an International Office with functions similar to those of the UMIST international students' Liaison Office. With these arrangements in place, the two institutions set about making good the losses they had sustained in their international student enrolments since 1976–7. To achieve this, they began to participate on a regular basis in student recruitment fairs overseas which were organised by the British Council or other contractors. Close relations in the form of credit-transfer arrangements, for example, began to be fostered with schools, colleges and universities abroad. UMIST took a lead in the establishment of the Northern Consortium (NCUK) of twelve universities in the north of England (including the University of Manchester) to develop "in country" delivery of first-year undergraduate studies in subjects such as engineering, computer science, law, architecture, accountancy and business studies, in partnership with local institutions such as the MARA Foundation in Malaysia and Braeburn School in Kenya.

As a result of these initiatives, the decline in international student numbers of the period 1977–85 was turned around. The international presence on the two campuses became more prominent than ever by the beginning of the twenty-first century. The Higher Education Statistics Agency (HESA) credited the University with a complement of 3,865 international students in 2000–1, representing nearly 15 per cent of the student body; UMIST had 2,050, representing nearly 30 per cent of its student population.

The process of recovery from the trough of the mid 1980s was by no means smooth. It had depended to a very large extent on increased student recruitment from the developing countries of East and South-East Asia whose economies were severely affected in 1997–98 by an abrupt fall in the exchange values of their currencies. Governments cut back sharply on their scholarship programmes for study overseas.

In the case of Malaysia, this decline turned out to be permanent, but students from some of the other places affected, such as Hong

Students from Italy, France and Egypt gather at a welcome reception for international students.

Kong and Taiwan, came back in their previous numbers after a couple of years. And both UMIST and the University benefited from the phenomenal rise in the numbers of students coming to Britain from mainland China after 1999. The numbers registered in the University alone increased from 79 in 1998–9 to 230 in 2000–01 and to 650 in 2002–03, by which time they were by far the largest single group of international students on the campus. The next largest group, Malaysian students, numbered only 217.

The rise of mainland China and the downgrading of Malaysia represented the most substantial changes by far in the geographical pattern of international student recruitment in the period 1998–2003 for both the Victoria University and UMIST. Otherwise, the pattern remained fairly consistent: both institutions recruited students from a very wide range of countries, 144 in the Victoria University's case in 2000–01, but the ten leading countries contributed something approaching half of the total of international student registrations at any given time. This "Top Ten" group consistently included Malaysia, Hong Kong, the USA, Cyprus, Singapore and Kenya throughout the period, with India, Iran, Japan, Korea, Nigeria, Pakistan, Taiwan, Turkey and one or two others hovering on the fringes of the group. Since 1990, too, the countries of the European Union have come to figure more prominently in the scheme of things, rising from 14 per cent of the joint University/UMIST cohort of international students in 1989–90 to well over 20 per cent in 2004–05.

EU students had been reclassified by the British Government in 1983, in terms of the fees they paid, as equivalent to British

An Alumni Perspective

I was born in Nicosia, Cyprus in August, 1978. I am of Greek origin and both my parents are refugees from the 1974 Turkish invasion of Cyprus.

It was the persistence of my parents (especially my mother) that persuaded me to study in the UK. After the invasion of 1974 my parents were left with nothing other than their university education. Therefore I learnt from them that a good education is paramount. I knew that UMIST could offer this, as it was one of the UK's top institutions. In addition, I had heard that Manchester was the best city for students with an overwhelming, vibrant atmosphere. How true that is!

My younger brother, Alexandros Mantis, came to visit me at Manchester for the first time a few years ago when he was going for an interview at Cambridge University. He was fascinated by the student life in Manchester and especially the state-of-the art Aquatics Centre, as he is a keen athlete who trains at least four hours every day. Eventually he chose to study for his BEng and MSC at UMIST rather than Cambridge.

Stavros Mantis from Cyprus
MEng Electronic Engineering 2003

for example, the warden of Ellis Llwyd Jones Hall remarked that "their presence and enthusiasm has widened our outlook and enlarged our interests". The sentiment remains valid: students from other countries, cultures and intellectual traditions bring to bear on the academic work they share with their British colleagues, and in general on the corporate life of their colleges and universities, different insights and perspectives which often challenge indigenous assumptions. British students (and, one might argue, academic staff) can only be enriched by such exposure.

There were, in any case, powerful practical advantages to rebuilding the international student presence on the campuses of both the University and UMIST after the decline of 1977–85. The point has already been made that nearly one-third of the University's and two thirds of UMIST's postgraduate students in 1976–77 were from abroad. As the Principal of UMIST remarked in 1984, international students were "an indispensable part of UMIST life, particularly at the postgraduate level where they make a marvellous contribution to our research programmes". Without their presence, the credibility of the two institutions as centres of research and postgraduate study – vital to their academic standing in the world – would have been seriously compromised.

From the 1960s onwards, there was a dawning recognition that international students needed help and support both on arrival in Manchester and throughout their courses in ways that indigenous British students did not. Efforts were increasingly made to provide adequate support, typically with the universities building on initiatives taken by individual departments or faculties or by the Students' Unions. Thus, for example, by 1992 all single international students newly arrived in Manchester were guaranteed accommodation in University and UMIST halls of residence, a provision initiated in the 1960s by the Faculty of Economic and Social Studies. By that time, too, the University and UMIST provided, through the International Society (established as a private organisation with university financial support in 1966), a week-long orientation programme to introduce newly arrived students from abroad into the mysteries of everyday student life in Manchester. The International Society itself provided a valuable social focus for international students, as well as ongoing welfare and advice services.

Today, the University attracts more applications from international students than any other British university and is home to more than 5,300 students from over 180 countries. International student recruitment and partnerships are overseen by a team of professionals in the Division of International Development, headed by Dr Tim Westlake. A specialist International Advice Team provides welfare support and the International Society continues to provide an exciting social programme

"home" students. "Full cost" fees applied thereafter only to students from outside the EU. Many of the EU students came to Manchester in any case as participants in student-exchange programmes sponsored by the European Commission, and therefore did not actually pay fees to their British host universities.

There were broad "cultural" advantages derived by the institutions from the recruitment of students from abroad. In 1929,

Part 4
The Future

A Vision of the Future

AURIOL STEVENS

The new University of Manchester, born on 1 October 2004, set itself an ambitious goal: to build on existing strengths and create a new style of world-leading university for the twenty-first century.

To realise its ambition, the University appointed an Australian historian, Professor Alan Gilbert, as its leader, now to be called President and Vice-Chancellor, a title more generally recognised internationally than the traditional Vice-Chancellor.

Professor Gilbert brought to Manchester a wealth of experience as a university leader and manager. He had presided over the merger of the University of Tasmania with its rival the Tasmanian State Institute of Technology in the 1990s and then moved on to Melbourne, where in his nine years' tenure that university's reputation both in Australia and abroad rose spectacularly.

He arrived in Manchester believing that universities, like companies, are now engaged in a global competition and that the merger created "The best opportunity for any university community anywhere in the world to really think through what it wants to be and to reinvent itself and produce something that's really important for the northwest of England and for the UK as a whole and in some ways to have a real world impact."

The Manchester "merger" was the product of strategic thinking and driving ambition. The two legacy institutions were both successful, research-led universities. Both had reasons to be confident about the future, and the merger was not in any sense a last resort for either. It was strategic opportunity, not survival, that shaped the thinking behind the creation of the new University. The defining metaphor was "step change". Those driving the merger saw within their grasp an opportunity not just to create a single institution greater than the sum of the component parts, but to

Above: Professor Alan Gilbert, President and Vice-Chancellor.

build in Manchester an academic powerhouse whose international recognition and academic performance would place it among the world's greatest and most influential universities.

With Professor Gilbert's arrival in February 2004 detailed planning began. The University decided to take full advantage of the opportunity created by the "fresh start" by devising new ways of conducting its day-to-day business, rather than adopting by default the processes bequethed by the two parent universities. The mission: "To make The University of Manchester, already an internationally distinguished centre of research, innovation, learning and scholarly inquiry, one of the leading universities in the world by 2015."

In 2005, the new President and Vice-Chancellor set out the underlying philosophy. "The new University of Manchester is engaged in two related experiments. Firstly, we are testing the hypothesis that through ambitious, well-executed strategic planning it will be possible over the course of the next decade to turn what is already the largest and, on many commonly adduced criteria, the strongest 'Big Civic' university in England into one of the top 25 research-intensive universities in the world."

"The second, overlapping experiment, relates to the economic and social future of the Manchester City Region." Recent government initiatives, he said, "reflect a genuine concern in the UK that the long-term dynamism of the economy as a whole may well depend on the emergence of one or more globally important sub-economies outside London and the Southeast."

Of Britain's old industrial heartlands, Manchester, he said, had the best chance of developing into "The kind of self-sustaining, innovation-led, knowledge sub-economy characteristic of places like Silicon Valley, Boston's Route 128 beltway or the research and development precincts of San Diego, Singapore, Bangalore and Shenzhen.

"If the ability to attract and add value to 'knowledge workers' is the most important single competitive advantage in a knowledge economy, as Robert Reich and others have predicted, then a university that operates internationally as a magnet for such people, as scholars, researchers, research students and undergraduates, is a crucial contributor to the economic strength and competitiveness of its city region. If access to a continuing supply of new intellectual property and creative people is central to innovation-led economic growth, then large, research-intensive universities, as hothouses of intellectual creativity, have critical roles to play."

This then is the role the new University chose for itself. The strategy for turning aspiration into reality, *Towards Manchester 2015*, was published in the autumn of 2004. It reaffirmed timeless academic values and advocated robust modern management.

The aims of the new University would surely appeal to all who had watched England's universities struggle in recent decades with growing central government direction and shrinking funding per student.

The Nowgen Centre, the new multi-million pound, Manchester-based centre for genetics in healthcare.

The new University would be a dynamic institution engaging scholars in pioneering research, transferring its products to the market, drawing in bright students from the region and from around the world and ensuring that they "learn to respect the disciplined pursuit of truth" and engage with the community around them.

Further, the university would be a liberal institution "where rational inquiry remains unfettered" and "academic freedom is protected": an independent institution which while "discharging its formal accountability obligations" to government and others "remains essentially autonomous".

Links would be forged with other universities at home and abroad, with local authorities and agencies and with companies. Stress would be laid on community engagement and on providing a good, modern learning environment for students.

If the ends commanded universal approbation, the means were open to debate. High standing around the world and freedom of action at home do not come cheap. The University authorities recognised that their efforts had to be focused. New structures were needed to allow flexible programmes and efficient administration.

Precise goals and demanding performance indicators were agreed. The University's structure was streamlined. Schools and Departments of the two founder universities were reorganised into four massive Faculties: Humanities, Medical and Human Sciences, Life Sciences, and Engineering and Physical Sciences, made up of more than twenty Schools. Inevitably some people were not comfortable with the new structure. There were early retirements and some disappointments when staff found themselves competing for jobs. Management techniques involving regular staff, student and stakeholder satisfaction surveys and performance reviews for Faculties, central administration and senior executives, were somewhat unfamiliar. New IT and operating systems took time to bed in. Nation-wide salary re-grading and industrial action over pay impeded progress. The first year of the new university's life seemed to many long and frustrating.

Professor Gilbert's first annual "warts and all" Stock Take Report to the Board of Governors in February 2006, picked out some disappointing areas – postgraduate enrolments, internal communications and international student recruitment in particular – but he concluded that "overall progress of the University in 2004–5 was remarkable. This Stock Take of our first year provides grounds for justifiable confidence that the Manchester 2015 agenda is actually achievable."

In an interview in May 2006, Professor Gilbert felt able to assert that, "the merger has really worked to the point where I think it's over." A £600m capital investment programme was showing results as buildings went up on the University's sites. Knots had been teased out of the administrative system. New staff were coming in. The campus was abuzz.

High priority was given to improving conditions for students. One of the strategic goals was to improve the resources dedicated to each student by 50 per cent, a welcome change in a British university where so called "unit costs" have been driven down for decades.

This resolve was tested early on. Manchester with its vibrant youth culture attracts some 60,000 applications a year – more than any other UK university – and the merger increased its appeal.

The University has, however, resisted the temptation to go for an unfettered expansion of student numbers. Quality not quantity is the aim. High-flying home applicants are offered generous bursaries and scholarships so that they can come to Manchester whatever their circumstances and the University is seeking to attract more able students from overseas.

By 2006, Manchester was already the UK's top location for international students, but it was keen to expand its appeal. Links were being forged particularly with China, one of the most

important sources of international students. Its appeal was no doubt helped by the Chinese government's decision to establish in Manchester one of only two Confucius Centres in the UK. These centres provide training in language, culture and business etiquette for the whole community. "Equity and Merit" scholarships – up to 750 of them by 2015 – are being offered to qualified students from educationally deprived backgrounds in developing countries.

The University has recently signed a partnership agreement with the Open University, the world's leading expert at online teaching, to develop distance learning courses around the globe and to help modernise the University's teaching on campus as well as off. "The generation of young people who will come into the University in the next decade are going to be used to getting information, analysing information, communicating with other people, in other words living a substantial part of their lives and not just in educational terms but in social terms, in professional terms, online", Professor Gilbert says.

"What I am saying to the University is 'We have to become a university which can operate in the same cognitive space as the

Above: The SCAN building under construction in 2007.

Left: The Incubator Building is a state-of-the-art biotechnology research and development centre.

students and that means learning to apply pedagogic techniques with which our students will feel at home.'"

Because of this commitment to teaching, unusual for a university with major research ambitions, it will be possible to develop a career at Manchester, and become a professor, on the basis of teaching ability.

And there is further, more concrete evidence of the importance of students as customers. The drum shaped SCAN building going up on Oxford Road, planned in consultation with the student union, will bring all student services together in one student "hub". Registration, welfare, grants, careers advice will all be here along with new accommodation and teaching spaces. It will also attract conference business out of term time.

Students may be some of the University's most important customers, but there are other customers too. The Manchester Leadership Programme is designed to turn out graduates who will be more informed citizens, able to help build sustainable, civilised societies as well as becoming attractive employees. Piloted in 2005–6 with eighty students and with 300 in 2006–7, the programme offers

students who undertake sixty hours of community work in the year credit towards their degrees. They also get, as one of the first cohort, Benjamin Lambert, put it after working at an HIV/AIDS charity in Ardwick, "different perspectives, not just on topics covered in the unit, but on life in general".

Attracting excellent students and looking after them well is one part of the University's strategy. Attracting excellent new staff and providing unparalleled career opportunities for those already here is the other.

Here one of the strategies is to target "iconic academics". "We will try to put packages together in our chosen areas which will persuade some of the world's intellectual giants to relocate, wholly or partly, to Manchester and bring colleagues and both post-doctoral and doctoral students with them. We don't mind sharing them with other institutions so long as we join the leaders in this field of research," Professor Gilbert says.

The University has set aside £20m a year for salaries and facilities to back the recruitment drive, a drive concentrated on areas where the university was already strong, where interdisciplinary work could flourish and where there would be some impact on the local economy, such as cancer, world poverty, and nuclear engineering.

There are no academics more iconic than Nobel laureates. The University has set itself a goal of having five on its books as full or part-time members of staff by 2015. Within two years of its inception it has succeeded in attracting one Nobel laureate. Former World Bank chief economist, Professor Joseph E. Stiglitz has become chairman of the University's new Brooks World Poverty

The Dalton Nuclear Institute

The launch of the Dalton Nuclear Institute in July 2005 signalled The University of Manchester's intention to be the UK's leading university in nuclear research and education and one of the principal international players in this field.

It is highly fitting that the University is taking another step towards the advancement of nuclear technology; after all it was at Manchester that Ernest Rutherford began his work on the nucleus of the atom. The Institute perpetuates the name of John Dalton (above), the Quaker meteorologist and chemist who lived in Manchester from 1793 to 1844 and was a leading figure in the Literary and Philosophical Society. In 1803 he began to communicate to the Society the ideas which soon became known as the Atomic Theory and imparted a new degree of precision to chemical analysis.

The Dalton Nuclear Institute boasts some of the UK's most advanced university-based nuclear research facilities, including the Centre for Radiochemistry Research and the Materials Performance Centre.

Dalton's research encompasses the whole spectrum of the nuclear fuel cycle from reactor technology and fuel performance to decommissioning, waste treatment and disposal. The Institute is also involved in policy and regulation, nuclear medicine and fusion.

The Institute works closely with industry. A strong example of this is Dalton's collaboration with the Nuclear Decommissioning Authority to establish a new research facility in West Cumbria. Each organisation will invest an initial £10m to provide specialist research equipment and facilities, including access to the British Technology Centre. The facility will be the home of two new research centres in radiation sciences and engineering decommissioning and will drive forward the Institute's other research agendas.

The Institute has been a leading player in the establishment of NTEC – a consortium of UK Higher Education Institutions offering postgraduate education in nuclear science and technology – and hosts its coordination centre. It also coordinates the UK's first doctorate (EngD) in nuclear engineering.

Nationally, Dalton is linking with the government, industry, sector groups and learned societies to address the nuclear skills shortfall, identified in a number of studies including the DTI's report on Radiological Skills and the HSE's Report on Higher Education in Nuclear Training.

Dalton is beginning to collaborate with scientists in many foreign countries, including the US, China, India and South Africa. International collaborative research programmes include the Generation IV advanced reactors, and these will ensure that the UK maintains access to international know-how, technology advances and teaching material. The Institute also supports educational initiatives such as the World Nuclear University.

Institute, which was set up with a gift of £1.3m from former student Rory Brooks and his wife Elizabeth. The Institute brings together the University's expertise in development economics, development studies, social anthropology, sociology and politics.

The University is keen to develop the entrepreneurial skills of its academic staff. Professor Gilbert: "We think we have the most generous intellectual property policies anywhere, so one of the offers we are making to possible new recruits is that if they can find more generous terms elsewhere then let us know and we will match them. What we think is worth doing is to say to really top people internationally 'If you want to be a creator and you want to exploit your inventive ideas, then come here.' It's an enormous incentive."

Manchester Cancer Research Centre

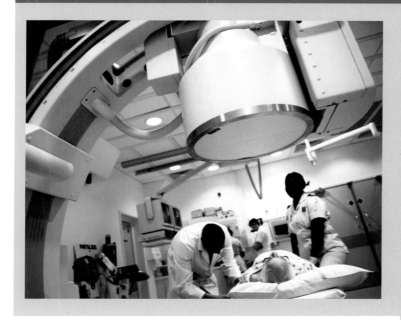

Heralding "a new era for cancer research", the Manchester Cancer Research Centre (MCRC) was launched in November 2005. The Centre brings together researchers from the University's Faculties of Life Sciences and Medical and Human Sciences, the Paterson Institute for Cancer Research (PICR), which became part of the University in January 2006, Christie Hospital and Cancer Research UK.

Professor Nic Jones, Director of the Manchester Cancer Research Centre (MCRC) said: "We are looking forward to expanding our basic research efforts and applying the knowledge we gain to the development of better and more specific therapies – and, therefore, to the benefit of patients".

While Manchester already has an enviable reputation for cancer research, the development of the MCRC will create outstanding facilities where scientists and doctors can work much more closely together than at present.

The joint aim will be to gain a greater understanding of how cancer develops and apply that knowledge to developing new diagnostic tests, potential treatments and better ways to predict the outcomes. These multi-disciplinary activities will involve basic research scientists, biologists, chemists, pharmacologists, physicists, computer experts and cancer doctors.

Success breeds success and it is hoped that the creation of the MCRC will enable the partners to continue to recruit the best researchers, consolidate and amplify the strong links with industrial and research partners, and sustain investment in facilities. There are now about forty principal investigators overseeing cancer research programmes in the Manchester area. This number is expected to increase to over eighty over the next few years.

Such activities are not new to Manchester. In 2006, husband and wife team Professors Ruth Matthews and James Burnie made a small fortune for the University and for themselves when they sold their biotech drugs company, NeuTec Pharma, to a Swiss multinational, Novartis, for £300m. The company was set up to develop commercial drugs from their pioneering work on genetically recombinant antibodies ("grabs") for treating life-threatening infections, such as fungal candida and MRSA.

Commercial activities are concentrated in the Incubator Building. Opened before the two universities came together, it houses sixteen research laboratories equipped with the infrastructure vital to the rapid development of a fledgling biotech business. The building is managed by the University of Manchester Incubator Company (UMIC) and is also home to the University's exploitation company – University of Manchester Intellectual Property Limited (UMIP).

The £27m Core Technology Centre, launched in 2006, located next to the Incubator Building, will "hothouse" joint work between academics and biotech companies on treatments for diseases such as HIV and cancer. It will also house the North West Embryonic Stem Cell Centre, which produces cells for tissue engineering and treatment of degenerative diseases.

Exploiting intellectual property involves high risks and not all enterprises turn into lasting companies. But there are jewels in the crown. Renovo, founded by Professor Mark Ferguson and Dr

Sharon O'Kane, has a potential multi-million pound market for products which prevent scarring and help to heal chronic skin wounds. And D-Mist Technologies Ltd's equipment, which allows cameras to film through fog, mist, rain or smoke, has excited the interest of operators in fields which range from security to navigation.

If commercial attitudes are encouraged, so is interdisciplinary working. Take the Manchester Interdisciplinary Biocentre whose glossy new building opened in 2006, bringing together 500 academic and support staff and 85 research teams. It includes, for example, the Centre for Excellence in Biocatalysis,

Brooks World Poverty Institute

Nobel Laureate Professor Joseph E. Stiglitz was appointed to chair the University's Brooks World Poverty Institute in November 2005. The Institute was generously funded by £1.3m from the Rory and Elizabeth Brooks Foundation. Mr Brooks, former Chairman of the Alumni Association, is a long-term supporter of the University and previously funded a Chair in Enterprise.

The Institute was formally launched in February 2006, when Professor Stiglitz came from New York to give the Inaugural Lecture. He was Chief Economist and Senior Vice-President of the World Bank, 1997–2000, and was Chairman of the Council of Economic Advisers in the Clinton White House.

The Brooks World Poverty Institute is a multidisciplinary centre of global excellence researching poverty, poverty reduction, inequality and growth. Well over a billion people – about a fifth of the world's population – live in absolute poverty.

The BWPI will encourage new ideas and knowledge, as well as new approaches to poverty research, which are urgently needed to develop the world's understanding of the dynamics of poverty, and to help the development and improvement of strategies and processes to combat poverty.

Manchester has traditionally been a centre for the creation of ideas and knowledge that have profoundly influenced global patterns of poverty and well-being. In the post-war period, the

Nobel Laureate, Professor Joseph Stiglitz (right), with Rory Brooks a former chairman of the Alumni Association.

university gained a global reputation for research on social and economic change, crowned by Sir Arthur Lewis's Nobel Prize for research on development economics.

The Institute is building on this tradition and in particular on the work carried out by the Chronic Poverty Research Centre within the Institute for Development and Policy Management. It also involves staff from elsewhere in the School of Environment and Development.

Biocatalytic Manufacture and the UK Centre for Text Mining, which offers services to the national academic community working with the new bioscience industries.

"Our work here seeks to abandon the traditionally qualitative and descriptive approach to bioscience and to develop a research programme underpinned by theory and methodology from the physical sciences and engineering," according to its Director, Professor John McCarthy.

Such developments need young researchers. In 2006 the University won £2.7m for research fellowships from Research Council UK, each worth £125,000 over five years for work on such matters as culture, cohesion and conflict; complex modelling and computation for the twenty-first century; physiological systems; health sciences and technology at the extreme. And the Department of Health awarded the University funding for eleven special programmes to train Academic Clinical Fellows in medical research, programmes designed to increase the research capacity of the National Health Service.

Medicine, in particular cancer, is a target area for development. Early in the new University's life, the Paterson Institute for Cancer Research, based at the Christie Hospital in Withington, joined the University, sparking an ambitious development of the University's commitment to cancer research. The new Manchester Cancer Research Centre brings together the Paterson, the Christie, Cancer Research UK and staff from the University's Faculties of Life Sciences and of Medical and Human Sciences to work in multidisciplinary teams on the causes and progression of cancers, the translation of new knowledge into novel treatments and state-of-the-art patient care.

Although the University's priority is its own research excellence (and the 2008 national Research Assessment Exercise will be a major test of success) there is also determination to join forces with other institutions in supporting the economy of the region.

The £10m Joule Centre for Energy Research, funded by the Northwest Regional Development Agency, is home for a partnership between universities in the region, regional industry,

The Core Technology Centre.

commerce and energy users. Its principal concern is with low carbon technologies and energy efficiency.

The Northwest Composites Centre provides a focus for University research in aerospace. The hope is that its work on new, low cost, low energy ways of manufacturing polymer composite materials as strong as steel but half the weight of aluminium will lead to lighter, more fuel efficient and therefore "greener" aircraft, a hope which has led to the Manchester Seattle Composite Partnership with the University of Washington in Seattle, home of the Boeing Corporation.

When this book went to press the reborn University was just two and a half years old, but already the ambitious agenda and investment was bearing fruit. Although not quite half way through the £620 million capital programme, an impressive new campus was taking shape. The total number of staff employed by the University in March 2005 had increased by more than 2,800 from the number that was inherited from VUM and UMIST in October 2004, the substantial majority of whom are involved in frontline teaching and research activities. In such buoyant circumstances, all the key indicators of academic and research performance have been positive. Research activity has grown rapidly, exceeding expectations; undergraduate applications and postgraduate research enrolments remain buoyant; undergraduate student satisfaction continues to trend upwards; and the University was named "University of the Year" by the *Times Higher Education Supplement* in 2005 and both the *Sunday Times* in 2006. The great dual experiment described by the President was on its way.

Whether the University will succeed in realising its inspiring vision, remains an open question. If it does, it will set a new pattern for universities in Britain. It will raise not only its own already high reputation but that of all its former graduates. But more important still it will boost the regeneration and economic and social development of the Northwest and bring new balance to the national economy. Manchester's bold experiment deserves – and needs – the help and support of all the founding universities' many friends.

Manchester and Harvard Join Forces

Harvard University and The University of Manchester have joined forces to help Britain and America better understand the challenges of contemporary society.

"Social Change: A Joint Project of Harvard and Manchester" is directed by Professor Robert Putnam, Peter and Isabel Malkin Professor of Public Policy at Harvard's Kennedy School of Government, who is renowned for his influential research into community ties known as "social capital".

As part of the project, Putnam has taken-up a part-time Visiting Professorship at the University for five years. His activities will include a series of collaborative projects, graduate summer school coursework and postgraduate programmes.

Named one of the *Guardian's* Top 100 Intellectuals of 2005 and a member of both the American National Academy of Science and the British Academy, Putnam charted the thirty-year decline of social connectivity in the US and described the atomised nature of modern life in his book *Bowling Alone*.

Since its publication in 2000, this work has been the subject of heated debate among politicians and commentators, including Tony Blair, Bill Clinton, and George Bush.

Researchers from the two universities will conduct a series of transatlantic comparative studies on topics such as inequality, immigration, religion, the changing workplace and civic engagement.

They will investigate what drives social change, how it relates to the well being of members of society and the implications for policy makers – issues which confront political leaders on both sides of the Atlantic. The research will be conducted by academics from Manchester and visiting academics from Harvard.

Professor Putnam said: "There is a long and fruitful history of collaboration between British and American scholars in learning across our similarities and differences in order to tackle important social issues. It builds on a foundation of exceptional expertise in both Manchester and Harvard, as well as elsewhere in our two countries."

The University of Manchester already hosts a number of centres of excellence specialising in the exploration of social change and is home to the £3.7m Centre for Research on Socio Cultural Change funded by the Economic and Social Research Council.

Nobel Laureates

Manchester is proud of its association with Nobel laureates over more than a century. The list on this page gives details of the subjects and awards, organised chronologically.

Physics 1906: J.J. (Joseph John) Thomson (1856–1940) for 'the theoretic and experimental study of the conduction of electricity through gases'. Student, Owens College, 1871–6 (certificate and prize in engineering); Cavendish Professor of Experimental Physics, Cambridge, 1884–1918; President of the Royal Society, 1916–20; Master of Trinity College Cambridge, 1918–40.

Chemistry 1908: Ernest Rutherford (1871–1937) for 'investigations into the disintegration of the elements and the chemistry of radioactive substances'. Langworthy Professor of Physics, Manchester, 1907–19; Cavendish Professor of Experimental Physics, Cambridge, 1919–37; President of the Royal Society, 1925–30.

Physics 1915: William Lawrence Bragg (1890–1971), jointly with his father William Henry Bragg for 'their contribution to the study of crystal structures by means of x-rays'. Langworthy Professor of Physics, Manchester, 1919–37; Cavendish Professor of Experimental Physics, Cambridge, 1938–53; Director of the Royal Institution, 1954–66.

Physics 1922: Niels Henrik David Bohr (1885–1962), for 'the investigation of the structure of atoms, and of the radiation emanating from them'. Visiting scholar, Physical Laboratories, Manchester, 1912–13; Schuster Reader in Mathematical Physics, 1914–16. Professor of Theoretical Physics, Copenhagen, 1916–62; founder and Director of the Institute of Theoretical Physics, 1920–62. Leader in developing the field of quantum physics.

Medicine and Physiology 1922: A.V. (Archibald Vivian) Hill (1886–1977) for 'his discovery relating to the production of heat in the muscles'. Brackenbury Professor of Physiology, Manchester, 1920–3; Jodrell Professor of Physiology, University College London, 1923–5; Foulerton Research Professor, Royal Society, 1926–51.

Physics 1927: C.T.R. (Charles Thomas Rees) Wilson (1869–1959) for 'his methods of making the paths of electrically charged particles visible by condensation of vapour' (by inventing the Wilson cloud chamber). B.Sc. Owens College, 1887; University Lecturer in Experimental Physics, Cambridge, 1901–19; Reader in Electrical Meteorology, 1919–25; Jacksonian Professor of Natural Philosophy, Cambridge, 1925–34.

Chemistry 1929: Arthur Harden (1865–1940), jointly with Hans von Euler-Chelpin for 'investigation on the fermentation of sugar and fermentative enzymes'. B.Sc. Manchester, 1885; lecturer and demonstrator in chemistry, 1888–97. Chemist to the Lister Institute, 1897–1930 (Head of the Department of Biochemistry from 1907, Professor of Biochemistry in the University of London from 1912).

Physics 1935: James Chadwick (1891–1974) for 'his discovery of the neutron'. B.Sc. Manchester 1911; M.Sc. 1912; demonstrator and research fellow, Physical Laboratories. After his release from internment in Germany, 1914–18, accompanied Rutherford to Cambridge, 1919, and worked with him at the Cavendish Laboratory 1919–35, from 1923 as assistant director of research. Lyon Jones Professor of Physics, Liverpool, 1935–48; Master of Gonville and Caius College Cambridge, 1948–58.

Chemistry 1937: Walter Norman Haworth (1883–1950) for 'researches into the constitution of carbohydrates and vitamin C'. B.Sc. Manchester 1906; research fellow 1910–11. Professor of Organic Chemistry, Armstrong (later King's) College Newcastle 1920–5; Mason Professor of Chemistry, University of Birmingham, 1925–48.

Chemistry 1943: George Hevesy (1885–1966) for 'work on the use of isotopes as tracer elements in researches on chemical processes'. Researcher at the Physical Laboratories, Manchester, and the Vienna Institute of Radium Research, 1911–14; researcher at the Institute of Theoretical Physics, Copenhagen, 1920–6, 1934–43; Professor at Freiburg, 1926–34, and at Stockholm, 1943–55.

Chemistry 1947: Robert Robinson (1886–1975) for 'research on certain vegetable products of great biological importance, particularly alkaloids'. Professor of Organic Chemistry, Manchester, 1922–8, and at University College London, 1928–30; Waynflete Professor of Chemistry, Oxford, 1930–55; President of the Royal Society, 1945–50.

Physics 1948: P.M.S. (Patrick Maynard Stuart) Blackett (1897–1974) for 'his development of the Wilson cloud chamber and his discoveries therewith in the field of nuclear physics and cosmic radiation'. Langworthy Professor of Physics, Manchester, 1937–53; Professor of Physics at Imperial College of Science and Technology, London, 1953–65; President of the Royal Society, 1965–70.

Physics 1951: John Douglas Cockcroft (1897–1967), jointly with his former colleague Ernest Walton, who built a linear accelerator with him at the Cavendish Laboratory, Cambridge, for their 'pioneer work on the transmutation of atomic nuclei by artificially accelerated atomic particles', first accomplished in 1932. Read mathematics at Owens 1914–15 and electrical engineering at Tech 1919–21 after war service, Royal Field Artillery; college apprentice, Metropolitan-Vickers; M.Sc. Tech., 1922. Jacksonian Professor of Natural Philosophy, Cambridge, 1939–46; Director of the Atomic Energy Research Establishment, Harwell, 1946–58; Master of Churchill College Cambridge, 1959–67; President of Manchester College of Science and Technology (later UMIST), 1961–7.

Chemistry 1954: Linus Carl Pauling (1901–94) for 'research into the nature of the chemical bond … and its application to the elucidation of complex substances'. Visited the Department of Physics, Manchester, as honorary research fellow, 1930, when working in x-ray crystallography and sharing W.L. Bragg's interest in silicates. Taught and researched at Caltech (the California Institute of Technology), 1925–64 (full professor from 1931); established the Linus Pauling Institute of Science and Medicine, 1974, especially concerned with the use of vitamin C as treatment for cancer.

Chemistry 1957: Alexander Robertus Todd (1907–97) for 'contributions to biochemistry and to understanding of the gene'. Sir Samuel Hall Professor of Chemistry, Manchester, 1938–44; Professor of Organic Chemistry, Cambridge, 1944–71; Master of Christ's College Cambridge, 1963–78. President of the Royal Society, 1975–80.

Chemistry 1961: Melvin Calvin (1911–97) for 'research on the carbon dioxide assimilation in plants' [photosynthesis]. Research fellow, Manchester, 1935–7; thereafter teacher and researcher, University of California at Berkeley (Professor from 1947 and Director of the Laboratory of Chemical Biodynamics 1960–80).

Peace 1962 (awarded 1963): Linus Carl Pauling (see above) for his writings and lectures on the dangers of radio-active fallout in weapons testing and war.

Physics 1967: Hans Albrecht Bethe (1906–2005) for 'his several contributions to nuclear reaction theory, with special reference to the energy production of stars'. Lecturer in Manchester 1933–4. Professor of Theoretical Physics, Cornell University, NY, 1937–75.

Economics 1972: J.R. (John Richard) Hicks (1904–89) for 'pioneering contributions to economic equilibrium theory and welfare theory'. Professor of Political Economy, Manchester, 1938–46; Drummond Professor of Political Economy, Oxford, 1952–65.

Physics 1977: Nevill Francis Mott (1905–96), jointly with P.W. Anderson and J.H. Van Vleck for their 'fundamental theoretical investigations of the electronic structure of magnetic and disordered systems'. Lecturer, Manchester, 1929–30, responsible for expounding wave theory; Melville Wills Professor of Theoretical Physics, Bristol, 1933–54; Cavendish Professor of Physics, Cambridge, 1954–71; Master of Gonville and Caius College, Cambridge, 1959–66.

Economics 1979: (William) Arthur Lewis (1915–91) in recognition of his 'lifelong concerns with poverty and growth, agricultural and human development in developing countries'. Stanley Jevons Professor of Political Economy, Manchester, 1948–58; Principal, later Vice-Chancellor, University College, later University of the West Indies, 1959–63; Professor at Princeton, 1963–83, with three different titles in succession (Public and International Affairs; Political Economy; Economics and International Affairs).

Chemistry 1986: John Charles Polanyi (b. 1929), jointly with D.R. Herschbach and Y.T. Lee, for 'contributions concerning the dynamics of elementary chemical reactions' (he used chemiluminescence, his co-laureates other methods). B.Sc. Manchester 1949; M.Sc. 1950; Ph.D. 1952. Professor of Chemistry, Toronto, since 1962.

Chemistry 1993: Michael Smith (1932–2000) for his development of oligonucleotide-based, site-directed mutagenesis, a precise technique for manipulating DNA with wide implications for protein engineering. B.Sc. Manchester 1953; Ph.D. 1956. Research associate, Medical Research Council of Canada, from 1966; Professor of Biochemistry, University of British Columbia, Vancouver, from 1970; founding Director of the Biotechnology Laboratory, 1987–97; Director of the Genome Sequencing Centre of the British Columbia Cancer Agency, 1997–2000. The Michael Smith Building at the University of Manchester was named in his honour.

Economics 2001: Joseph Eugene Stiglitz (b.1943) for his analysis of markets with asymmetric information. Famous for his critical view of the privatisation and liberalisation policies pursued by the International Monetary Fund and the World Bank, he stepped down in 2000 from the position as Senior Vice-President and Chief Economist of the World Bank which he had held since 1997. Chairman of the Brooks World Poverty Institute, University of Manchester, since 2006. Professor of Economics at the Columbia Business School, Columbia University, since 2001.

List of Subscribers

With grateful thanks to the subscribers listed below, whose generosity has made this book possible.

Samir Mahmoud Abdulhadi		Alison M. Ashworth	1979	John C.F. Berg	1961	Ian Brooks	
Aisha Abu	2002	Neil Ashworth	1984	Ian Berry	1990	Vic Brooks	
Edward Michael Adams	1951	Robert Aspinall		Dr Robert W.H. Berry	1955, 1958	Eric Broome	1943
J. Richard Agg		Koustoulidis Athanasios		Dr J.P. Bickford	1953	James W. Brophy	1985
Omar A. Aggad		Than Athanassiades		J. Bina	1959	Dr David Brown	1963
Tony Aggarwal	1995	Sahdia Waheed Awan		D.G. Bindon		George E. Brown JP	
Tawhid Ahmad		Alan Geoffrey Axon	1959	Norah H. Binns	1937	Miss M. Jean Brown	1950
Dr Mukhtar Ahman		Audrey Axon (née Shaw)	1960	Ann Birch	1978	Warwick Brown	1980
Alastair S. Ahmed		David Axon	1968	R.H. Bird	1947	Norah J. Browning	1948
Dr Ali Ahmed		Hans S. Baartveit		Dr G.I. Birley		Dr B. Bruckshaw	1949
W.H. Aikman		Olufemi Akinyemi Babalola		David Paul Bishop	1966	Dr Mark Brundrett	
David Ainsbury		Talat Nader Baddar	1954	Derek Black	1980	J.R. Brunskill (Robin)	
Anna-Lisa Ainsorth	1997	Edward Bagley		R. Geoffrey Blain	1938	Steven Bryant	
Marjorie E. Ainsworth		Hjördis Maguire Bailey	2006	Norman Blakebrough		Stephen Bryce	
Tayo Akingbehin	1975	M. Hugh Bailey	1974	Mark Blakemore	1986	Alastair Brydon	1984
Dr Alan Akrigg	1966	Harry Baines		John L. Blakey	1954	Edward George Buck	1963
Dr Jane Alcock		Michael Bale	1953	Walter Norman Bland	1957	Chris Buckle	1971
Desmond B. Aldren		Andrew Balfour		George Blankson	1975	David D. Buckley	1984
Pat Aldridge	1956	Aileen Ball	1969	Paul Bloom	2006	M.A. Buckley	Staff 1966–94
Mike Alexander	1969	W.B. Ball		Margaret N. Blount	1951	Norman Buckley	
Ahmed Ali		Claire Baumforth	1996	David and Karen Bluff		Jeffrey Budimulia	1989
Ibrahim A. Al-Kalbani	2004	Georgios Banasakis		Neil Blunt		David A. Bullock	1968
Dr Anne E. Allan		Anna Carolyn Bannister		E. Boardman	1947	Warren S. Burdock	
In memory of Ken Allan	1947	Frank B. Bardsley		Angela Bogg	Staff	Tracey Burke	
Alham Jassim Al-Langawi		Stanley J. Barett	1974	Barbara Bolton		Dr Antony J. Burkhardt	1956
Patricia M. Alldred		Clive Barker	1982	Harold Bolton		John Geoffrey Burnell	1999
Dr Josephine Allen (née Rudge)	1964	Dr Colin T. Barnes	1999	Dr G. Boocock	1952	W. Derek Burns	1947
Caroline Allison	1984	I.T. Barnish	1963, 1966	Dr P. Boocock (née Levesley)	1956	David Bury	1964
Martin Allison	1984	Dr Robert Barr		Barbara C. Boone	1982	Roy Butler	1952
B.O. Allwood		Janet Barratt		Javier Bordaberry		Tom Butler	1976
Klinger Marcos B. Alves	1980	José Augusto Lima Barreiros	1989	Raymond A. Boulter	1945	Dr Donald R. Buttress	
Dr Colin E. Alvey	1974	Dr Harold Barrington	1970	Prof Chris Bounds	1976	Bill Byers	1964
Mian Muhammad Amjad		John Barry		Dr Ann Bowden (née Webb)		Gwyn Cabral	Staff 1965–
Michelle Anderson		Revd B.J. Batchelor		Ian Bowie		Zane Vincent Cahill	2000
Sir James Anderton	1960	Pauline Bate (née Horsefield)	1954	Tony Boyd		Dr Barry Caldwell	
Paul Rodger Andrews		Ian Bates		Joan M. Brabin	1977	Donald William Cameron	
In Memory of Geoffrey Anlezark	1941	Maher Emile Batrouny	1992	Andrew D. Bracey	1976	Jennifer E. Capes (née Paine)	1958
Christian Antretter		Ian Batsford	2000	D.M. Bradbury	1954	Agustin Cardenas R.	
Raja Ali Raza Anwar	1994	Dr Brian Beagley		Patricia Bradley	1970	Paul Carhart	1989
Arthur Appleton	1943	David W. Beak	1977	Norine Napier (née Braithwaite)	1972	Philip Carnelley	1978
T. Jacqueline Appleton	1945	Roger Beastall	1973	P.A. Branton	2002	Dr B.J. Carroll	
Andreas Araouzos	2001	Kathleen Beavis (née Atkin)		Debbie Brereton	2004	Dr D.H. Carroll	1956
Menelaos Costa Aristodemou		Kenneth Beckwith	1952	R.E.S. Brimelow		Dr Elin M. Carson	1946
Paul Arnold		Godfrey Bedford	1960	Revd. Canon Frances A. Briscoe	1974	Jean Carter	
Jonathan S. Arthur		Craig Beedie	1972	Dr T.E. Broadbent		Hannah Cartmell	2006
Vimall Arumugham		Ivars J. Bekeris	1972	Professor John Brocklehurst CBE		Mrs Pat Case (née O'Gara) CBE	1954
Dr Adrian Ashdown		John D.C. Bennett	1979	Egan R. Brooks		Sarah Cawley	1998

Patricia Ceballos	2003
Brian Centrone	2006
Eric Chadwick	
Katie Chalk	1999
Dr Gabriel Ka Po Chan	1989, 1996
Chan Ho Chung	1989
C.C. Chang	1969
Jaesung Chang	2002
Derrick F. Chapman	
Dr Roy Chapman	
Revd Ted Chapman	
Irene Charalambous	2002, 2003
Dr Graham C. Charters	1990
Dimitrios Chatzigeorgiou	
Dimos Chatzipanteliadis	1999
Chee Koon Long	
Hung-Hsin Chen	
Dr Hua Chen	
Jason S. Chen	
Sheung Hun Cheng	
Heather Mary Cherryman (Baddar)	1953
S.M. Brockhausen (née Cheshire)	1998
K.F. Chew	1991
Gavin N. Childs	
Michael Childs	
Dr Peter Chivers MBE	1946
Ellen Y.M. Chok	
Anthony Peter Choppen	
Suzanne Choppen (née Fuller)	
Tom Choularton	1974
Charlotte A. Churchman	
Michele Cianci	
Amy-Louise Clark	1999
Kristine Brodie Clark	
Mike Clark	1964, 1967
Geoffrey A.W. Clarke	1962
R.F. Clay	1941
Dr Pamela Clayton	1966
John Clements	1968
Dr Alan J. Cockbain	1954
Margaret Cocker (née Jacques)	
Jim Cohen	
Dr Phil Coles	1974
Dr Paul F. Coley	
Dr M.M.F. Collier	
James Collins	
Mair Collins (née Thomas)	1951
D. Collison	
Andrew W. Colman	
Dr Richard D. Colwill	1997
Jose Luis Conde	1991
Eamonn Connolly	1979, 1983
Dr J.A. Connor	1965, 1994
Alessandro Conti	2003
Paul Conway	1991
David S. Cooke	1960
Peter A. Cooke	1955
Brian Cooper	
Mr Brian W. Cooper	1975
Dr Fiona Cooper	1986
Julia Cooper (née Davenport)	
Brian Oliver Corbett	1953
John D. Corcoran	
Robert S. Cornish	
Francis Costello	
Alan Cottam	1973
Dr John Lawrence Cotton	
David Coulstock	1966
Kay Coulthard (née Hall)	
In memory of Allen Coxon	
Dr Shirley Willis Coy	1976
Thomas Cragnolini	
William H. Craig	1968

Miss M.M. Crawford	1945
Brian F. Crawley	1960
J.E. Creamer	
Andrew Kevin Cregan	2005
Joy Crispin-Wilson	1965
Dr J.P. Critchley	1954, 1958
Karen Critchley	1991
Dr T.A. Critchley	1964
W.C. Critchley (née Jackson)	1959
Diane Croasdell	1966
James R. Crossley	1959
Dr J.B. Crummett	1955, 1957, 1972
S. Crummett	1957
Dr Gordana Anic Cubric	
Reverend Averil Cunnington	1973
Adrian Curtis	1969
Gordon E. Cusick	1953
Brian Dale	
Manaf Khalid Abdulla Damluji	1978
Martin Dancey	1967
George Keith Daniels	1935
Susan Daniels	
Chris Darlington	1995
John and Hilda Davenport	1945
Keith Davey	
Dr Katherine E. Davidson	
D.L. Davies	
David G.M. Davies	1955
John Y. Davies	
Martin Davies	
Patricia Davies (née Dutton)	1954
Professor Rodney D. Davies FRS CBE	1956, Staff 1976–97
Wilbert Henry Purton Davies	1953
Maev Crompton De La Guardia	
Bill Deas	1957
John Dekker	
Jérôme Demange	2000
D.W. Denning	Staff
Cesar J. Deschamps	1994
Ted Dew-Jones	
Clive Dickinson	1999
June M. Dimelow	
Professor Gerald Dix	
Roger Dix	
Peter L.S. Dixon	
Dr K.L. Dobbs	1976
Dr Stefanos Dodouras	2000
Harry and Olwen Dolphin	
Louise Donovan	1978
Peter J. Dore	1962
John V. Doris	1980
Dr Janet Double	1970
J. Patrick Dougherty	2001
Professor Ken Douglas	
Dr Patricia Downes (née Anderson)	1951
Simon Drakeford	
Mrs A.E. Driscoll	1963
Dr J.L. Driscoll	1966
Professor Alan Dronsfield	1969
Evelyn Duckworth (née Rushton)	1928
Jan and Stuart Duffield	1970, 1974
Richard Duffield	
Robert D. Durrad	1941
Chris Dyckhoff SJ	1970
T.R.P. Dyer	
Tadeusz Dziurman	1972
Nigel C. Earnshaw	
Tony Easter	1962
Margaret Eastwood	1967
John Eaton	
Peter J. Eccles	1972, Staff 1971–
Margaret Edwardson (née Nestor)	1963

Dr Michael Efthymiou	1977
Edwin Ejima Egbuniwe	1981
Dr Martin F. Egerton	
Professor Emeritus Harry Elliot CBE FRS	1941
Dr Andy Ellis	1966, 1970
Dawn Ellis	
Dr Katherine E.S. Ellis	1996
Philip S. Ellis	1939
Ronald G. Ellwood	
Ahmed M. El-Mokadem	1969
Revd and Mrs W.J. Else	
Selina Elton	1936
Emeritus Professor Alan E.H. Emery	
Dr Jonathan England	
David N. Entwisle	
A. Patricia M. Entwistle	1945
Richard G. Erskine	
Alun Evans	1990
Miss Audrey Evans	1953
Karen Evans (O'Reilly)	
Dr Rotimi Oluseyi Ewedemi	
Harry M. Fairhurst	
Brian Falder	
Andrew Fallis	1970
Jane Fallis (née Auty)	1971
Professor Paddy Farrell	
Gerald Farrow	
Barbara M. Fawkes (née Henley)	1949
Susan Fay (née Jaynes)	1965
Hannah Fearn	2003
Jacquie Featherstone	
Graham Fehrsen	2003
Robert J. Fenton	
Margaret Ferrario	1988, 1990
Revd Dr Donald Firth	1972
C.B.R. Fish	1947
Sarah Louise Fisher	2002
Sid Fisher	1958
Stephen W. Fitzpatrick	
Alex and Maureen Fitzsimmons	1963
Sean D. Fleming	1963
Lord Flowers	
Dr P.J. Ford	
Iain Forsyth	1959
Allan B. Fox	
David Franklin	1964
Joseph Fray	
Richard Freebury	
Avis A. Freeman	
Jamie Freeman	2004
Dr Paul I. Freeman C.B.	
Emma French	
John French	
Frank Fricker	1950
Andrew Frith	
Geoff Frost	1963
Simon Fry	1993
Fu Chong	2005
Shohei Fukuda	2004
Richard J. Fullard	
David Michael Fuller	1969
P.F. Fuller	1974
Sachie Funahashi	
Siu Hung Perry Fung	2000
Walter Fung	1965
Yin Wo Erica Fung	1999
Dr B.N. Furber	
Michael Gadd	1962
Professor Charles S.B. Galasko	
Ken Galloway	
Abid Iqbal Ganaie	
Alan Gardner	1947
Sheila Garry (née Coupe)	1952

John Garside	
Kate Williams (née Garstang)	1968
G.C. (Bill) Garton	
Susan Gaukroger (née Coath)	
Peter Gavagan	2000
Dr A. Denise George	1963
Julian George	1978
Dr T. Adrian George	1963
Revd Patrick H. Gerard	1986, 1988
Ms Abibatu Ibironkeh Gerber	1965
Christine Gibbs (née Bailey)	
Anita Gidumal	
Dr Owen Gilbert	1948
John L. Giles M.Ed	1975
John M. Gill	1949
Nancy E. Gill (née Sutton)	1946, 1948
Professor Iain E. Gillespie	
Jan Gillett	1968
Helen Gilman	1991
Gordon Henry Harper Glasgow	2002
Dr Cyril S. Gledhill	1952, 1966
Michael Glendinning	1985
Arokiasamy Gnanapragasam	
P.J. Goddard	1978
I.D.F. Godden	
Dr Jon Goldin	1992
Dr Trevor Goodwin	1971
Dr F.P. Gopsill	1967
Dr Lynne Gornall	1988
Mark Steven Gould	1996
Leo Govier	Staff 1976–82
Brian G. Gowenlock	1946
Alexander James Graham	
H.J. Graham (née Bateman)	1969
Mark Hugh David Graham	
William T. Graham	1978
Lesley Grainger (née Cook)	1966, 1970
Delphine Gratrix	1971
Dr Walter Grattidge	
John Greenhough	
David M. Greenwood	1973
Dr Mark Greenwood	1986, 1994
Penny Greenwood	1967
Cdr. Brian D.B. Gresham OBE, R.N	1949
R.E. Griffin	
Joe Griffiths	1940
Sheila Griffiths (née Chapman)	1957
Walter J. Griffiths	
Francis J. Groark	1970
Avinash Grover	1981
David Groves	1966
Laura Guerrero	2003
Roger Guest	
Dr Mohan Gunaratnam	
Derek Gunnell	1956
John A. Gwillam	
Bernhard G. Gyssler	
Helen Hackney	
Constantinos Hadjipavlou	
Samji Halai (Patel)	1980
W.A. Hale	1968
Eduardo Andrew Peloche Halkyard	1999
Dr Daphne Hall	
Gordon Hall	1981
Dr Sally Hall	1980
Norman Halliday	1988
Joy Hallsworth	1974
Elsie Hamilton (née Howell)	
Dr Maurice Hamilton	1967
Mark Daniel Hammill	1993, 1994
Dr Michael J. Hammond	1995
Dr Keith Hamnett	
Hanisah Han	1997

H.R. Hancox	1942	Hork Hau	1990

H.R. Hancox 1942
Professor Harold Hankins
T.R.G. Hanlon 1995, 1998
Bruce Hannay 1969
Johan J. Hansen 1974
Graham H. Harding 1975
Robert Hargreaves Staff 1984–94
Claire Harper (née Goddard) 1996
Adele Harris
Susan E. Harris
Stephen M. Harris 1971
Suzanne Harrison 2006
Gerry Hartley 1957
Michael G. Hartley
Pat Hartley 1958
Susan V. Hartshorne 1958
Ian J. Harvey 1976
Stavros Hatzis 1999
J. Haworth 1949
Gregory F. Hazzard 1986
Michael E. Heard and Elaine Heard
(née Taberner) 1961, 1963
T.S. Hearn 1975
Dr Paul J. Heath
Noel T. Heaton
Chee Teck Hee 1982
Frederick S. Heeley
F.G. and H. Helps
William B. Hemingway OBE 1952
Dr Richard Henchman
Robert H. Henson 1966
Katherine Herbert (née Beswick)
Professor Gordon Heron 1967
Don Hesketh
Dr D.G. Hessayon OBE 1954
Frank Hewson 1964
Yee That Hian
A.J. Hickox
Professor Peter J. Hicks and Ruth H. Hicks
Robert Higginbottom 1958, 1960
Professor Nicholas J. Higham 1982
Sheila Mary Higham (née Duckworth) 1975
Miss A.M. Hill 1981
Bernie Hill
J. Hazel Hill 1951
Julia Hill 1964
Sean Ronnie Hill
Susan L. Hill
J.E. Hillidge 1963
Dr Angela Hilton 1965
Mr Clifford P. Hilton
Kenneth A. Hilton 1940
Pamela Hirst (née Duxbury) 1978
Brian Hitchon 1952, 1955
Cedric Hitchon 1954
Yoon K. Ho
Noel V.A. Hobbs 1962
Steven Hockaday 2003
Geoff Hodson 1983
Ian Holland 1948
Ralph Holland 1942
David S. Hollas 1964
K.E. Holman
Dr Jennifer E. Holmes
Philip Holmes 1972
Penelope Holroyde
E. Winifred Holt (née Knight)
John N. Holt 1958
Emeritus Professor Kenneth S. Holt
Margaret E. Holt 1966
Dr Koay Cheng Hong
D.J. Hood 1960
Wendy K.M. Hopkins 1976

Hork Hau 1990
Judith Horsfield
Dr John Houghton 1961, 1972
Anthony Houndsworth
Sue Howe (née Fargher) 1973
Peter Howells 1961
D.J. Howes (née Harvey) 1950
Dr Tim Howes
Robin Howie
Emma Howland
James R. Howlett
C.E. Hoyle 1953
Errol Hudson 1954
Ann Hughes 1968
Dr Derek Hughes
David H. Hughes 1974
J. Eryl Hughes
Paul C. Hughes 1986
Peter Edward Hughes 1960
Bernard Hulcroft 1968
John Hullah 1968
David Hulse
Ross Hunt 2001
Rowena Dixon 2002
Angus M. Hunter
David B. Hunter
S.G. Hurd 1972
Aidan Hurley
Norman Hurst
Christopher T. Husbands 1966
Professor Roland Ibbett 1962
Airlie Inglis (née Carver) 1990
Peter A. Ingram
Verina Ingram 1989
Betty Irons (née Knibbs)
Marjorie E. Isaac (née White) 1941
Hedy L. Isaacs
Karan Israni 1978
Alan Jackson 1983
Dr Robin Jackson 1977
Hazel Jacques
Johan Jainudin
Helen Nicola James (née Parr) 1992
Dr Ian G.V. James 1974
Timothy Mark James 1989
Yervant Artin Jamgochian
Geoffrey and Marcia Jaques
Damini Jawaheer 1991, 1995
Girish Jawaheer
Sanjaye Jawaheer 1957, 1960
Dr Laurent F.C. Jeanmeure
Dr Gordon Jefferson 1958
Judy Jeffryes
David Jellis
Dr M.K. Jenyon 1953
Ade Johal 1991
Per Wollert Johansen 1970
Wyndham M. John 1949
Carl R. Johnson
David F. Johnson
Henry Johnson
Professor W. Johnson 1943
Sara Johnston
Patrick Jolliffe 1959
Ann Jones
Arthur S. Jones 1952
Christopher Martin Jones 2002
Emeritus Professor Derry W. Jones 1948
Dr E. Malcolm Jones 1972
Geoffrey Jones 1951
Keith Jones 1965
Mark Hadyn Jones
Dr Michael J. Jones

Professor Norman Jones 1961
Ros Jones
Ruth M. Jones 2003
Sarah Jones 2001
Dr Trevor J.D. Jones 1979
R.R. Jordan 1998
S.L. Josephs 1948
Dr H. Peter Jost CBE
Ma Jun 2004
Hon. Usman S.A. Kagbo JP MP
Tarlochan Singh Kalsi
Mr A.C. Kannenberg
Joyce Kappes
Dr David R. Karsa
Daniele Kay 2002
Brian S.B. Kear
John Keep 1971
Adrian J. Keetley 1979
Brian Kevin Kelly 1981, 1998
Sir Christopher Kelly KCB 1970
Dr D. Kelsall
Dr Andrew S.C. Kelsey 1975
Colin Kempthorne 1954
J. Derrick Kendrick 1952
Christopher L. Kenyon 1967
William Khoshaba
R.M. Kilby 1962
Judith Kilgallon 1996
Sung-Hun Kim 2003
Professor Ian Kimber
R.D. King 1957
Ron King
Professor Terence A. King
Asher Kiperstok 1994
Susan M. Kirby 1976, 1988
Douglas T. Kirk
Earl Kitchen 1987
Ken and Ann Kitchen 1995
Mrs Enid Kitney
Mr Wilbert Kitney
Azam Kiyobekov 2005
Asta Klimaviciene
Robin Knipe 1964
Dr C.B. Knowles 1947, 1948, 1951
Amarylis Kocbuch 1973
Nicholas Kolarides 2006
Charles Ho Jung Koo 1969
Gosia Kubiak 2003
Siv Tove Kulbrandstad Walker 2002
Kristel Priscille Tang Fee Chin Kung
Kwun Cheung 1999
Dimitrios Kyrkilis
Chee Yan Lai 1974
Esther B. Laing 1962
William V. Laing 1962
Kenneth Kar Yan Lam
Lam Ngai Kun 1993
S.J. Lancashire 1971
A.J. Lane 1986
Kath Lapsley
L.J.M. Lawrence
Revd Gary A. Lawson
R.S. Lawson 1969
Eric Layland 1952
Lisa Yang Layzell
Professor Paul Layzell 1978
Colin M. Lea 1981
Dr J. Leary 1944
Catherine Rose Lee
Graham Lee 1968
Hiew Siew Lee
Pei-Hsuan Lee
Peter T.C. Lee 1976

Sydney Lee 1994
Victoria Jane Lee
Dr B.H. Lees 1946
David L. Leete 1963
Dr David S. Leitch
Angeliki Lekka
Anthony Lenten 1973
John Leong 1972
Lord Peter Levene
Barbara R. Lewis 1968, 1971
Susan Lewis (née Butterworth)
T. Ian Life 1970
Dr John D. Lilley 1962
E.J. Lim 1983
K.S. Billy Lim
Dr Leonard M. Lines
Ann G. Lipson 1959
Ralph Lissok 2004
David Lister
Kexing Liu 1987
Rosemary Kusensela Liywalii
Chris and Lyneth Lockwood 1966
Sheila R. Lockyer (née Mudie) 1991
Sandra Loder
Gerald Loh 1998
Elaine M. Longley (née Fleming)
Robert J. Loosmore 1946
Jo Lowe 2002
Dr Peter Lowe
Miss Stella J. Lowe
Professor John Lowry CBE 1963, 1970
Dr David Lucas 1959
Eileen Lucas
Gordon F. Lucas 1954
Richard M. Lucas
Dr Michael Lumb
Gillian A. Lund 1970
Philip J. Lund 1963, 1969
Simon W. Lunt
Dr Stan Lynch 1969
Dr David Lyon 1970
Dr Mary Lyon 1970
Henry Innes MacAdam 1979
Tatiana Macfarlane 2000
Jacqueline Macleod (née Groocock) 1964
W. Ross Macnab 1993
Derek W. Maddocks 1949
Robert Maguire 1967
His Honour Terence Maher
Denys Mahon 1949
Keith Mallett
Malcolm Mallins
Rob Mammen
Parveen Mann
Maz Mannan
Gerry Margiotta
Dr Jeffrey Marks
Dr Paul H. Marriott
John D. Marsden 1962, 1964, 1967
J. Kevin Marshall 1967
Steven C. Marshall 1982
Nicolas I. Martakis
Helen C. Martin 1992, 1994
In memory of Ronald G. Martin 1953
Stephen Martin
H.E. (Ted) Mason 1949
Lesley Mason (née Kendall) 1963
Paul Edward Mason
Graham Matthews 1968
Paul Matthews 1977
Julia Maynard
Patrick Mbaya
Russell McAndrew 1966

Dr Damian McAreavey	
Dr Eric J.B. McArthur	1952
M. Howard McCann	1960
Doreen McCarthy	2003
Julian McCollin	
Jonathan Richard McDermott	
Dr Richard John Willersley McDermott	
Dr Helen McElroy	
Mary C.S. McFarlane	
Siobhán McGonigle	
Brenda McGregor	
Diana A. McGregor-Brown	1976
Damian McHugh	1990
Hector McIntyre	1977
D.C. McKie	
William McLaughlin	1973, Staff 1975–
Wendy McMullan	1956
John McNair	1970
H. Meakin	1947
John Meeks	1957
P.A. Meek-Welsh	
John Gordon Mellor	1962
Dr Michael Mellor	
Lucy M. Mensah-Forson	
Christine Mera	1995
Nick Mercieca	1995
Paul Metcalf	
Victor Middlemas	
Dr Benedito Geraldo Miglio Pinto	1980
Malcolm F. Miles	
Dr Roy Millington	1975
Doreen Millns	1959
Anthony Mills	
C.R. Milne	1943
Charles B. Milne	
The Revd Catherine. L. Minor	1986
Andrew Mitchell	1968
Sarah Mitchell-Cameron (née Moore)	1966
Professor Peter Mittler CBE	
Dr John Mogan	
Dr Peter D. Mohr	1969
Glenn Mollan	1977
William Trevor Molloy	
Pedro Monteiro	
Linda Montgomery	1976
Andrew P. Moore	
John Moore	1965, 1966, 1971
Julia A.R. Moore	
Trevor Moore	1980
E. Moores	
Dr P.J. Moorhouse	1979
Ann Moran	1992
Patrick J. Moran	
Professor D.H.J. Morgan	
Dr Judith Anne Morgan	2002
A.G. Morrell	1948
Alan P. Morris	1980
Moira Morris	
Helena Anne Morrison (née Marsden)	1942
Rosemary M. Morrison	1959
Sandra C. Morrison	1994
Dr Marianna J. Morris-Worrall	
Ed Morton	1960
Steven C. Moschidis	
John E. Moseley	1962
Margaret Moss	1968
John C. Moult	
Kathryn M. Mowatt	2001
I.S. Moxon	
Ms Remija C. Mponzi	
Roger Mudge	1970
Dr T.P.C. Mulholland	
Conceição D. Guirro Murphy	

Jean M. Murray	
Professor G. Musgrave	
Michelle Mycock	2004
Colin C. Myles	1966
Dr J. Nagington	1947
Michael Napier CBE. QC. LL.D	1967
Dr R.B.E. Napper	1964
Dr Asif Ahmad Naseem	
Peter G. Nash	1964
Graham John Naylor	
Helen G. Naylor (née Parker)	1953
Dr John G. Naylor	1973
Malcolm P. Neill	1991
Sandra Neillie (Darlington)	1968
Brian Nelson	1956
Adrian Newberry	
John Newton	1974
Fat-Yeung Ng	1979
Russell Nimmo	1971
Dr Mbugwile S. Nkolokosa	1977
Geir Åge Noven	1988
Brian Nugent	
Frank R. Nunn	1955
Richard H. Nurse	1970
John Nutt	1960
Tom W.B. Nuttall	1948
Professor E.I. Nwogugu	
Pauline I. Obi	2004
Peter James O'Connor	
Mark Odgers	1990
The Revd Eric Ogden	Staff 1968–89
Hamish Ogston	
Olumuyiwa Ayodele Ogunyode	
Sarah O'Keefe	1996
Dr Sam Oleesky	
Dr Richard J. Oliver	
Ruairi O'Neill	1998
Revd Joseph A. Onwudiwe	1984
Eddie Orme	
Pieter J.H.M. van Osch	2002
Pippa Ovey (née Knight)	
Elaine Owen	1955
Branavan P.	
Yvonne C. Pachmayer	2001
Stewart J. Page	1974
Theo Pakos	
Sheila Palmer (née Ridley)	
Mr R.K. Pandey	1966
Dr Kok-Fu Pang and Dr Jenny C.Y. Liu	
Saleel Panthakkalakath	2004
Claire Papadi	
George Papadimitriou	
Bhupendra M. Parekh	
Dr Daniel Park	1970
Joan Parker (née Marland)	
Professor M.S. Parker	
Mr M.D. Parker	
Steve N. Parker	
Tanya Parker (née Sansom)	1964
Andrew Parkinson	1983
John Parr	1969
Linda Parry	1964
Christakis Partassides	
Dr F.R. Partington	1960
Alan Passmore	1962
Ashok Patel	1968
Dr Ghanshyam Patel	1978
Andrew Patterson	1998
Derek Patterson	
Marios A. Pavlides	
D.R. Payne	
Douglas Payne	
Roy Peach	1956, 1957, 1960

Professor A.R. Peaker	
Tim Pearce	1970
Nancy Peel (née Hopkinson)	1954
Alan G. Pendleton	1949, 1951
Patricia A. Penney	
B.O. Percival	
Mr and Mrs M.D. Pereira-Mendoza	1994
Sergio A. Perez-Huerta	1995
Katina Maria Perkin	1998
Brian Peters	
Mark H. Peters	
Mrs Petroff	
Dr Eugenia Petropoulou	
Dr W.J. Pettit	1973
C.J. Phillips (née Kiddle)	1963
Matthew D. Phillips	
Paul Phillips	1980
Robin A. Phillips	
Christopher Phoenix	1968
Professor John A. Pickett CBE FRS	1972
Alan Pigott	1950, 1952
Dr J.R. Pilley	
Fred Robert Pittman	
Odile M. Plantevin	
A.J. Pockley	1960
Robert Pope	1963
Graham R. Porter	1955
Vernon Porter MBE	1969
Margaret Portman (née Buxton)	1948
R.J. Postlethwaite	1970
Jeremy L. Poulter	1993
Bill Pound	
Professor James A. Powell OBE	
Jack G. Powles	
Fay Poyser	2004
Dyah S. Prabandari	
Marios Prapopoulos	
Roger Preston	
M.D. Pride	1966
Les Priestley	
Maureen Pritchard (née Nathans)	1957
Rick Pritchard	1965
Graham S. Proudlove	1978
Wyn Pugh	1971
Dr M.N.M. Punter	
Richard Purdy	1951
Shirley Purdy (née Wright)	1950
Edward Pysden	1969
Dr Robert Quayle	1970, 1973, 1982
Colin Rand	1995, 2004
Brian Ratcliffe	
Dr F.W. Ratcliffe CBE	
Peter Raymond MBE	
Dr Bryan Read	
Greg Read	1979
Grace Christine Plant Reader	1964, 1972
Dr Barry Redfearn	
Carl S. Redpath	1979
Robert U. Redpath	
Willian Reed	1966
Robert Rees	
Sheila Rose Regan	
James Christopher Reid	
Dr Edward Reid-Smith	1965
Martin Renshaw	
Stephen J. Reyes	1984
Bob Reynolds	
Sheila R. Reynolds	
Professor John Rhodes	
Lynne Rich (née Marrable)	1976
Professor B. Richards	
Geraint Richards CBE	
Alex Richardson	

Bert Rigby	1956
Brian K. Rigby	1956
Toby Riley	2003
John Rimington	1947, 1968
Dr Peter Risdale	
J.K. Roberts	
Professor A.P. Roberts	1951
Jo Robertson (née Bowers)	1952
Emeritus Professor David Robinson	1992
Dr John Malcolm Robinson	1974
Martin S. Robinson	1978
Dr Peter W. Robinson	1974
Michelle Roche	2003
Jane Roden	1976
David Rogers	1948
Carlos Romualdo-Torres	1996
Kevin J. Rooney	1972
Gerald Henry Roose	
Izaias Rosenblatt	1981
The Revd F. Ian Ross	1956
John Rothwell	1960
Dr James John Rothwell	2002
W.K. Roughton	
Gavin Rouse	2002
Aldyth Rowe	
Dr Derek John Rowlands	1958, 1961, 1984
Malcolm J. Rowley	1957
Dr Janet V. Rubner	1982
Dr Eric Rushton	1965
Andriny Rusman	
E. Moira Russell	1953
Denis Ryan	
Dr James Ryan	
Amar J.P. Sabberwal	1958
Shakeel R. Saeed	
Margaret P. Salmon	
Revd Eileen Sambrooks	1979
George Sams	1967
Colin W. Sanderson	1974
Montserrat Santandreu	1994
Charles Sara	
Gorka Sarasa	1998
Theodoros A. Savvides	
Yvonne Scales (née Hampson)	
Consul General Gilbert M. Schlaefli	
Felix Schwarz	1944
Oldrich Schwarz	
Graham W. Scott	1965
Jim Scott	1975
P.M. Scott	1951
Patrick J.H. Scott	1971
Phillip and Brenda Scragg	
Dr C.J. Scully	1978
Dr W.A.L. Seaman	
Stephen Sears	
Jane Lila Seddon	
Roy D. Seddon	1969
Nicholas E. Segal	
Lily M. Segerman-Peck	1977
Dr H. Selcon	1950
Brian Sellers	1960
Ang Koh Seng	1980
Pradip Kumar Sengupta	1968
Gordon Senior	1950
A.M. Shafi	1996
Jayesh Shah	1997
Sachit Shah	1985
Albert W. Sharpe	
Peter H.M. Sharrock	
Carole A. Shaw	1973
Dr Duncan F. Shaw MBE	1951
Don Shearman	1953
Janet Shearman MBE (née Paterson)	1954

Amy Sheldon
Emeritus Professor T.Y. Shen — 1950
Peter John Shennan — 1972
Alan Shenton 1954
Andrew John Shepherd — 2003
Paul C. Sherlock — 1972
Hazel Sherwin (née Isherwood)
Jin Shi — 2005
Anthony Shires — 1968
Dr David J. Shirt
Dr Alexander P.W. Shubsachs — 1968
Chan Tak Shun
Diana Simmons (née Hurlock)
David Sims — 2003
Dr A. Sippert
Michael Skidmore — 1982
Svein Skoglund
Philip Sladen
Dr Conrad and Mrs Josephine Slater
— 1957 and 1961
Geoffrey Smethurst — 1970
Arnold N. Smith — 1988
Anthony Smith — 1979
David J. Smith — 1976
Debbie Smith — 1987
Ian Peter Smith — 1966
Dr J.K. Smith — 1959
Jeremy Smith — 1969
Kenneth H. Smith — 1943
Lilian Smith (née Higham) — 1941
Lorraine Hamilton Smith — 1997
Malcolm David Smith — 1960
Marion Smith — 1973
Neil Smith — 1983
Nicholas H. Smith — 1978
Norman H.A. Smith — 1952
Peter John Smith — 1961
Dr R.A. and Mrs K. Smith — 1957
William J. Smith
W.V.R. Smythe
J.M. Snowdon — 1957
Andreas Solomonides
Edward Somerville
Walter S. Sondhelm — 1939
Sangham Raj Soni — 1963
S.R. Soni
Dr James G. Speight
Brian Spence — 1965
George D. Spithouris — 1997
Thomas Spooner — 2005
Mary Isobel Springett — 1992
M.R. Spry (née Curtis) — 1949
Maria Stachowiak — 1973
Professor Derek Stafford TD, DL — 1954
Pam Stanier — 1970
David H. Starbuck — 1962
Steve Starling — 1989
Graham Starmer
Angela Staton (née Armstrong) — 1967
Roger Staton — 1967
Mike Staunton
Dr John Steed
Carl Anton Stenling — 1988
Dr Philip Stephens — 1974
Leslie Stevens CBE — 1948
Peter Stevenson — 1975
Judith Ann Stewart
L.J. Stewart — 1961
Dr T.W. Stewart — 1955
Dr Angela Strank — 1980
John Stratton
Kenneth G.H. Stubbs — 1971
Marc Stuessel

Patricia Mary Stuttard (née Chadwick) — 1954
Roy Stuttard — 1955
Kazuhiko Suga — 1996
Dr David Sugg — 1988
Danette I. Sullivan
Ian Summers — Staff 1966–1992
Dr Gerald Sumner
Harminder Singh Sura
T.J. Surridge
Michael Sweeney — 1969
Ferry Syarifuddin
Carlos G. Taborda-Monton — 2000
Hironori Takabayashi — 2003
Tan Kang Hai — 1986, 1989
Y.P. and C.Y. Tang
Anna Taraschuk — 1974
Andrew Tarcy
Christopher W. Tarry — 1964
Caroline Elizabeth Tate
Lyn Tattum
Dr John B. Taylor — 1941
John F. Taylor
Sir Jonathan Taylor
Roger W. Taylor — 1965
Francisco D.B. Teixeira E Melo — 1994
K. Thangavadivel
Mrs M.M. Theodorides — 1973
Peter F. Thewlis — 1979
N.J. Thistleton B.D.S. — 1967
Alan E. Thomas — 1947
J.S. Thomas — 1972
Margaret Thomas — 1944
Robin Neal Thomas — 1985
Tommy Thomas
David Samuel Charles Thompson — 1993
Paul Thompson — 1999, 2004
Mrs P. F. Thompson — 1961
Anne-Marie Thomson — 1987, 2000
Christina Thomson
G.R.M. Thomson
Mike Thorn
Jim and Chris Thornton — 1967
Dr Tom A.J. Thorp — 1949
Dr Deanna Thorpe — 1963
Revd Dr P.N. Tindall — 1934
Kung-Yi Ting — 2003
Marjorie Tivey (née Alderson) — 1943
Prof A. Ray Toakley
Dr John F. Tomlinson — 1952
Shiu-Kin Tong
Helen Tonge
Dr Zoe C. Tootell — 1968
Professor Derek Torrington
Emeritus Professor C.R. Tottle
Paul Townley
Arthur Train — 2003
Dr Peter Travis — 1967
Group Captain R.C. Travis MBE — 1951
Elaine F. Treloar — 1983
Dr Michael J. Trenouth — 1967
Eva Julia Trickey (née Lengyel) — 1965
Mario Borba da Trindade
Andy Tseng
Dr E. Tsiliopoulos
A.J. Tucker — 1966
Gordon and Judy Tuff — 1961
Kevin Tuhey — 1973
Lord Turnberg
Angela Turner (née Flanagan) — 1959
Professor John D. Turner
Richard Turner
Dr Susan B. Turner
Ian Tuttell

J. George Tyror OBE — 1952
Annabella Tysall — 1981
Margaret Tyson — 1988, 1993
W.J. Tyson — 1968
Mazi M.N.A. Ukabam
University and College Union
Jenny Upson (née Birkitt)
David Uren — 1975
Francis Vale — 1982
In Memory of Professor
Azeglio Valgimigli — Staff 1898–1932
The Duke of Vallombrosa — 1957
Belkis Valdman
Peter Van Cauwenbergh — 1996
Elena Vassiliadou
Joan Eileen Vawdrey
Sir Alan Veale
Andrew Veitch — 1999
Glyn Veitch — 1970
Colin Vickerman OBE — 1965
Professor C.F.H. Vickers — 1950, 1960
O. Ola Vincent
Martin Vlietstra
Barbara Vollands (née Fidler) — 1961
Chun Yung Voon
Rosemary Vracas — 1977
Dr A.A. Wagland and Dr J.M. Wagland
Dr David Waite — 1963
Brian Wake
Neil Waller
J.D. Walsh — 1950
John Jarlath Verdon Walsh — 1963
John Patrick Walsh — 1940
Dr Maeve Lucy Walsh — 2003
Peter Walsh — 1972
Simon P. Walsh — 1998
Malcolm Walter
Peter Walthall — 1955
Keith S. Walton — 1956
Peter Warburton — 1948
Stephen R. Warburton — 1988
Dr Bill Ward
David M. Ward — 1993
Dr Eric Ward — 1968
Harold E. Waring
James Waring
Paul Waring
Professor Tom Warnes — 1962
Dr James R. Warren
John Warren — 1967
In memory of Paul Loraine Waters — 1934
Roger Waterworth — 1960
Fran Watson — 2004
Susan Watson
Sarah Watson
Eric I.N. Waughray
Dr P.N. Waughray — 1927
Professor Colin Webb — Staff 1979–
Ian P. Webb
Arthur Webster — 1957
Professor George Wedell
Rosemary I. Weinstein (née Fountain) — 1967
Brett Welch — 1994
John R. Welch
Lucy Welch (née Shepherd) — 1995
Martyn West — 1978
Ian J. Westbrook — 1978
Desmond A.R. Weston — 1964
Kevin Weston — 1975
James Whidborne — 1992
N. Whitbread
Estelle White
Dr Norman A. White — 1948

Rosemary White — 1975, 1982
Anthony Whitehead — 1948
Prof J.C. Whitehead
Kim Whitehouse — 1980
Major John Wiggell MBE
David Wightman
Dr A. Wightmore
Arthur Wilcox
Tony Williams — 1961
Dr Robert G. Wilkins — 1977
Anthony Willats — 1969
Allan P.O. Williams — 1957
Dave Williams — 1970
George F. Williams — 1957
J.G. Williams — 1985
Jill Williams (née Martin) — 1972
Kate Williams — 1995
Ninoslava Ana Williams
Richard J.W. Williams — 1995
Revd Dr Roger T. Williams — 1976
Dr Tom A. Williams — 1962
Trevor Cyril Williams — 1974
Professor Andrew and Eileen Williamson
Ashley G. Williamson — 2003
Ian Willis — 1970
Michael T. Wilmot — 1977
R. Windsor
Harry Winstanley — 1958
Denis Wise — 1954
David Witham
James Withers — 1991
Stuart Withnall — 1967
Dr Allan Withnell
Angelina Wong — 1990
Brendan Shing Huen Wong — 1981
Dr Eddie Moon Chung Wong
Nicholas Wong — 1998
Paul Kam Chung Wong — 1985
Rupert K.C. Wong
Yee-Khow Wong
Christopher Wood OBE — 1969
Sir John Wood and Lady Sonia Wood
Lady Wood (née Sonia Farrant) — 1950
Dr Nigel D. Wood — 1981
Wilfred Raymond Woodfine — 1980
Chris and Brenda Woods
P.N. Woods — 1970
Chris Woolford — 1991
L.B. Woolford — 2004
Anne Woolley (née Preece) — 1974
Jonathan Wray — 1977
Elizabeth Wright — 1997
Michael Wyatt — 1997
Graham M. Wybrow — 1969
Barbara and David Wynn
Humphrey Wynn — 1948
Yin Xu
Dr Nicolas Yannacopoulos
Tiong Peng Yap
Michael Yelland — 1951
Tan Ley Yen — 1981
Henry Wai-Chung Yeung — 1995
Chin Ching Yim — 2001
Dr P.K. Anthony Yiu — 1982
Yong Chin Wah
James Young — 1974
S.H. Young (née Smith) — 1957
W.J. Young — 1972
Al-Amin A. Yusufari — 2000
Paul I. Zairis
Dr Hisham Zakaria — 1960, 1963, 1973
Zibin Zhang — 2004
Paul Zickel

Index

Bibliography

General Histories of Owens and the Tech

Alderman Joseph Thompson, sometime Treasurer and Chairman of the College Council, wrote a bulky official history of *The Owens College, its Foundation and Growth* (Manchester, 1886). *The Owens College, Manchester,* by P.J. Hartog (Manchester, 1900) provides a snapshot of the institution at the turn of the century. *Chapters in the History of Owens College and Manchester University, 1851–1914* (Manchester, 1937) is a concise and entertaining work by Edward Fiddes, who was Registrar (1904–20) and later held a chair of History (1926–31). Two essays by Colin Lees and Alex B. Robertson, giving further details of the early days, have appeared in the University's learned journal, *Bulletin of the John Rylands University Library of Manchester:* see vol.78 (1996), 155–72, for 'Owens College: A.J. Scott and the struggle against "prodigious antagonistic forces"'; vol. 79 (1997), 161–94, for 'Early students and the "University of the Busy": the Quay Street years of Owens College, 1851–1870'. *Portrait of a University 1851–1951,* by H.B. Charlton (Manchester, 1951), designed to celebrate the centenary of Owens, does not purport to be a history but sets out to trace the evolution of John Owens's ideal and its realisation by 'shaping spirits'. It contains invaluable photographs, plans, lists and statistical tables. For one 'shaping spirit', Professor of Chemistry 1857–86, see *The Life and Experiences of Sir Henry Enfield Roscoe, Written by Himself* (London, 1906). For illustrations of university life around 1900, see *University Sketches,* by the medical student Hamilton Irving (Manchester, 1904). Vivid reminiscences and other

material on the Second World War appear in *The University of Manchester at War, 1939–1946,* by Eric E.Rowley with Colin Lees (Manchester, 2001). Two detailed volumes, *A History of the University of Manchester 1951–73* (Manchester, 2000) and *1973–90* (Manchester, 2004), were written by Brian Pullan, formerly Professor of Modern History, with the assistance of an oral historian, Michele Abendstern, who interviewed former staff and students. For students in the early 1960s see Ferdynand Zweig's comparative study *The Student in the Age of Anxiety. A Survey of Oxford and Manchester Students* (London, 1963). For lively impressions of the University and UMIST towards 1970 see *The Exploding University,* by Christopher Driver (London, 1971), pp. 25–43, 318–23.

There is no substantial continuous history of the Tech, but D.S.L. Cardwell, a historian of science, edited seventeen interesting essays under the title *Artisan to Graduate* (Manchester, 1974), to mark the 150th anniversary of the foundation of the Manchester Mechanics Institution, from which UMIST is descended.

The University and the City

There are two lively accounts of the University Settlement, produced for its fiftieth and its hundredth anniversary respectively: *Fifty Years in Every Street,* by Mary D. Stocks (second edition, Manchester, 1956), and *Everything Went On at the Round House,* by Michael E. Rose and Anne Woods (Manchester, 1995), which is amply and imaginatively illustrated. For one prominent benefactor and his legacy to the city and the

University, see *Joseph Whitworth. 'The World's Best Mechanician',* by Norman Atkinson (Stroud, 1996) and *The Whitworth Art Gallery. The First Hundred Years,* edited by C.R. Dodwell (Manchester, 1988). The best source for the history of the Library is its own publication, the *Bulletin of the John Rylands Library.* For essays by D.A. Farnie, a historian of the cotton trade in which John Rylands made his fortune, see vol. 71 (1989), 3–38 (on Mrs Rylands) and vol. 75 (1993), 3–103 (on John Rylands himself). Frank Taylor, formerly Librarian in Deansgate, covers the years 1936–72 in vol. 71 (1989), 39–66, and Peter McNiven the period 1972–2000 in vol. 82 (2000), 3–79. A trenchant and sometimes critical account of the exploits of University architects and planners appears in *Manchester,* by Clare Hartwell (Pevsner Architectural Guides, London, 2001). The piece on the John Rylands Library in Deansgate is by J.H.G. Archer, formerly of the Department of Architecture (see pp. 96–101). For the University, UMIST and the local and regional economy, see *The Economic and Social Impact of Greater Manchester's Universities,* a report issued in 1995 by a group of urban geographers, Brian Robson, Ian Deas, Neville Topham and Jim Twomey.

Arts and Theology

The first volume of Samuel Alexander's collected works, *Philosophical and Literary Pieces* (London, 1939; reprinted Bristol, 2000), opens with a memoir of Alexander by John Laird (pp. 1–96). *Lewis Namier: a Biography* (London, 1971) is an intimate personal account by his second wife, Julia Namier.

For intellectual portraits of Namier and his allies and critics, see Ved Mehta's *Fly and the Fly-Bottle. Encounters with British Intellectuals* (London, 1963), pp. 171–214; *The History Men,* by John Kenyon (London, 1983), pp. 251–69, and *Lewis Namier,* by Linda Colley (London, 1989). In *A Personal History* (London, 1983), Chapters VII and VIII, A.J.P. Taylor describes life as a junior academic in Manchester during the 1930s, with recollections of Alexander and Namier. See also *Troublemaker. The Life and History of A.J.P. Taylor,* by Kathleen Burk (London, 2000). *On Art and Nature and Other Essays,* by Eugène Vinaver Whitstable, 2000) is a posthumously published collection preceded by a memoir of Vinaver by the editor, W.R.J. Barron. See also the brief life by Philip E. Bennett in *Dictionary of National Biography,* new edition, vol. 56, pp. 528–9.

For the adventures of John Burgess Wilson (Anthony Burgess) when reading English in the shadow of the Second World War, see Part III of *Little Wilson and Big God. Being the First Part of the Confessions of Anthony Burgess* (first published 1987; Vintage Books edition, London, 2002), with recollections of H.B. Charlton, L.C. Knights and others. See also Andrew Biswell, *The Real Life of Anthony Burgess* (London, 2005), pp. 40–78. In *Not Entitled: a Memoir* (London, 1996) a distinguished critic, Frank Kermode, recalls at pp. 205–10 his career from 1958 to 1965 as a professor in the English Department. *The Great Betrayal. Memoirs of a Life in Education,* by Brian Cox (London, 1992), is the autobiography of a forthright campaigner for structure and discipline in education who was Professor of English Literature (later John Edward Taylor Professor) from 1966 to 1993.

The *Proceedings of the British Academy,* available in most large libraries, contains biographies of several members of the Faculties of Arts and Theology who became Fellows of the Academy. For one of the founders of the Faculty of Theology, see *Arthur Samuel Peake: a Biography,* by J.T. Wilkinson (London, 1974).

For an overall view of the Faculty of Theology, see *Seventy-Fifth Anniversary Papers of the University of Manchester Faculty of Theology, 1979,* edited by David Pailin (Manchester, 1980). There is nothing comparable for the much larger Faculty of Arts, but there are one or two accounts of departments. See, for example, the comparative piece by Peter Slee, *Learning and a Liberal Education: the Study of Modern History in the Universities of Oxford, Cambridge and Manchester, 1800–1914* (Manchester, 1986). *Reflections on 50 Years of the Manchester School of Planning and Landscape, 1952–2002,* edited by Christopher Wood and Stephen Jay (Manchester, 2002), is a volume of reminiscences. There is an unpublished *History of the Department of French Studies. One Hundred Years of French 1896–1996,* by Christine Hill.

Physics and Radio Astronomy

Rutherford at Manchester, edited by J.B. Birks (London, 1962) contains personal recollections of Rutherford by eminent friends and colleagues and also prints correspondence between Rutherford and Schuster. An early 'official' life is *Rutherford,* by A.S. Eve (Cambridge, 1939). Two lively recent biographies are *Rutherford. Simple Genius,* by David Wilson (London, 1983) and *Rutherford, Scientist Supreme,* by John Campbell (Christchurch, New Zealand, 1999). For the intellectual and personal lives of two of the youngest members of Rutherford's department, see *H.G.J. Moseley. The Life and Letters of an English Physicist, 1887–1915* (Berkeley and Los Angeles, 1974), by J.L. Heilbron, and *The Neutron and the Bomb. A Biography of Sir James Chadwick,* by Andrew Brown (Oxford, 1997). See also *Niels Bohr. A Centenary Volume,* edited by A.P. French and P.J. Kennedy (Cambridge, Massachusetts, 1985), and *Adventures in Radioisotope Research: the Collected Papers of George Hevesy* (2 vols, Oxford, 1962), especially vol. I, pp. 11–30, and II, pp. 928–60. *Cockcroft and the Atom,* by Guy Hartcup and T.E. Allibone (Bristol, 1984), describes Cockcroft's time at Owens, the Tech and Metropolitan Vickers and his work with Rutherford at the Cavendish Laboratory in Cambridge. *The Fly in the Cathedral (How a Small Group of Cambridge Scientists Won the Race to Split the Atom),* by Brian Cathcart (London, 2005), opens with a lucid account of the experiment in Manchester which enabled Rutherford to deduce the structure of the atom.

William Henry Bragg, 1862–1942. Man and Scientist, by G.M. Caroe (Cambridge, 1978), is a biography by the daughter of W.H. and sister of W.L. Bragg which describes the work and working relationship of father and son. A substantial memoir, 'William Lawrence Bragg', by David Phillips, appears in *Biographical Memoirs of Fellows of the Royal Society,* vol. 25 (1979), 75–143. There is a study of Bragg's Manchester pupil and Cambridge colleague, later a professor at the Tech, by M.M. Woolfson, 'Henry Solomon Lipson', in the same publication, vol. 39 (1994), 229–42.

For Blackett, Lovell and radio astronomy, see Bernard Lovell, 'Patrick Maynard Stuart Blackett', *Biographical Memoirs of Fellows of the Royal Society,* vol. 21 (1975), 1–116. Dudley Saward's biography, *Bernard Lovell* (London, 1984) and Lovell's autobiography, *Astronomer by Chance* (Oxford, 1992) tell the story of Jodrell Bank.

Nobel Laureates

For the lives of other Nobel laureates associated with Manchester, see, for example, *A Time to Remember,* by Alexander Todd (Cambridge, 1983); *A Life in Science,* by Nevill Mott (London, 1986); *Force of Nature. The Life of Linus Pauling,* by Thomas Hager (New York, 1995); *No Ordinary Mike. Michael Smith, Nobel Laureate,* by Eric Damer and Caroline Astell (Vancouver, 2004).

Computing

A History of Manchester Computers, by Simon Lavington, published by the National Computing Centre at Manchester in 1975, is well illustrated. *Electrical Engineering at Manchester University. 125 Years of Achievement,* by T.E. Broadbent (Manchester, 1998), tells the story of the department in which computers were first designed. Memoirs of Manchester's pioneers have appeared in *Biographical Memoirs of Fellows of the Royal Society:* 'Frederic Calland Williams', by Tom Kilburn and L.S. Piggott in vol. 24 (1978), 583–604, and 'Tom Kilburn', by Maurice Wilkes and Hilary J. Kahn, in vol. 49 (2003), 283–97. There are many accounts of Alan Turing and his intellectual achievements. The biography *Alan Turing. The Enigma of Intelligence,* by Andrew Hodges (London, 1985), does justice to his life in Manchester; Hugh Whitemore's play, *Breaking the Code* (Oxford, 1987), draws on this. For an up-to-date bibliography, see *The Man Who Knew Too Much. Alan Turing and the Invention of the Computer,* by David Leavitt (London, 2006).

Medicine and Life Sciences

An important monograph is John Pickstone, *Medicine and Industrial Society: a History of Hospital Development in Manchester* (Manchester, 1985). *The Manchester Regional History Review* is shortly to publish in vol. 18 a special number on *Science and Technology in the Manchester Region.* This will include an article by the editor, John Pickstone, 'Science and technology in Manchester: an introduction to the history'. For recent work on medicine in Manchester, see the special volume of the *Bulletin of the John Rylands University Library of Manchester,* edited by Stella Butler and John

Pickstone, which will appear as vol. 87, part I, in 2007. On botany see *135 Years of Botany in Manchester*, by W.A. Charlton and E.G. Cutter (Manchester, ca. 1986), published at the time when the biosciences were reorganised and botanists went to the new departments of Cell and Structural Biology and Environmental Biology. For Marie Stopes's work as a palaeobotanist in Manchester see the biography by Ruth Hall, *Marie Stopes* (London, 1977).

There are biographical sketches of physicians and surgeons in *The Honorary Medical Staff of the Manchester Royal Infirmary, 1830–1948,* by William Brockbank (Manchester, 1965) and *Some Manchester Doctors. A Biographical Collection to Mark the 150th Anniversary of the Manchester Medical Society, 1834–1984,* edited by W.J. Elwood and A.F. Tuxford (Manchester, 1984). This commemorates several of those mentioned in John Pickstone's chapter, from Joseph Jordan and Thomas Turner to Robert Platt and John Charnley. See also 'John Sebastian Bach Stopford', by Wilfrid Le Gros Clark and William Mansfield Cooper, *Biographical Memoirs of Fellows of the Royal Society,* vol. 7 (1961), 271–9; Robert Platt, *Private and Controversial* (London, 1972) and Douglas Black, *Recollections and Reflections* (Cambridge, 1987).

Law
There is a memoir of Harry Street by J.C. Smith in *Proceedings of the British Academy,* 72 (1986), 473–90.

Economic and Social Sciences
For one of Manchester's great economists, see the *Letters and Journal of W. Stanley Jevons,* edited by his wife, Harriet Ann Jevons (London, 1886) and a modern study by Sandra Peart, *The Economics of W.S. Jevons* (London, 1996). For another, the Nobel laureate Arthur Lewis, see 'The Manchester years, 1947–1958. A tribute to the work of Arthur Lewis', by Barbara Ingham (University of Salford: *Salford Papers in Economics,* Paper no. 10 of 1991) and Robert L. Tignor, *W. Arthur Lewis and the Birth of Development Economics* (Princeton, 2006). The *Proceedings of the British Academy* contains memoirs of the anthropologist Max Gluckman (by Raymond Firth, vol. 61, 1975, 479–96); of the founding Professor of Government and Administration, W.J.M. Mackenzie (by Richard Rose, vol. 101: *1998 Lectures and Memoirs,* 347–66*),* and of another eminent Professor of Government, S.E. Finer (by Hugh Berrington, vol. 90: *1995 Lectures and Memoirs,* 465–85).

Business and Management
John F. Wilson has written *The Manchester Experiment: a History of Manchester Business School, 1965–90* (Manchester, 1993).

Education
The broadest account is *A Century of Change. The Study of Education in the University of Manchester* (Manchester, 1990), by Alex B. Robertson. For extramural and adult education, see Thomas Kelly, *Outside the Walls. Sixty Years of University Extension in Manchester, 1886–1946* (Manchester, 1946).

Residences and Lodgings
Dalton Hall. A Quaker Venture (London, 1963) is a chronicle of Manchester's first purpose-built student residence, by one of its longest-serving wardens, G.A. Sutherland. *Ashburne Hall. The First Fifty Years 1899–1949* (Manchester, 1949) rests on the researches of Mary Tout, edited by M.W. Hughes; its sequel, *Ashburne Hall 1949–1974* (Manchester, 1974) is by Hilary Airey. T.E. Lawrenson, some time Lecturer in French, offers a lively account of *Hall of Residence. Saint Anselm Hall in the University of Manchester, 1907–1957* (Manchester, 1957). *The Story of Ellis 1919–1969* (Manchester, 1969) is a 'scrapbook' of reminiscences of life in Ellis Llwyd Jones Hall, originally a residence in Old Trafford for trainee teachers of the deaf, which subsequently moved to Victoria Park and was joined with Dalton to form Dalton-Ellis Hall.

Manchester University Women
A pioneering monograph is *The Education of Women at Manchester University, 1883–1933,* by Mabel Tylecote (Manchester, 1941). See also 'Manchester, Owens College and the higher education of women: "a large hole for the cat and a small one for the kitten"', by Alex B. Robertson, *Bulletin of the John Rylands University Library of Manchester,* 77 (1995), 201–20. For the lives of some famous women associated with the University, see *Marie Stopes: a Biography,* by Ruth Hall (London, 1977); *Alison Uttley: the Life of a Country Child, 1884–1976,* by Denis Judd (first published London, 1986; paperback, Stroud, 2001); *Ellen Wilkinson,* by Betty D. Vernon (London, 1982). A life of Phoebe Sheavyn, by members of her family, will be published in the near future.

Students' Unions
The University Union marked the demolition of its old buildings by publishing *In Memory of Burlington Street. An Appreciation of the Manchester University Unions 1861–1957,* edited by Ian G. Gregory (Manchester, 1958).

Music, Drama and Entertainment
Important biographies are *Max. The Life and Music of Peter Maxwell Davies,* by Mike Seabrook (London, 1994); *Harrison Birtwistle,* by Michael Hall (London, 1998); Jonathan Cross, *Harrison Birtwistle. Man, Mind, Music* (London, 2000); Adrian Turner, *Robert Bolt: Scenes from Two Lives* (London, 1999). For Anthony Burgess, see above, the section on 'Arts and Theology', and, on the internet, www.anthonyburgess.org/ and the weighty reference at http.en.wikipedia.org/wiki/Anthony_Burgess. Rik Mayall's 'autobigraphy', *The Rik Mayall. Bigger than Hitler Better than Christ* (London, 2005) is written from the perspective of a comedic persona; the Rik Mayall website contains much to interest fans and researchers. See www.orangeneko.co.Rik/ *Wikipedia* contains useful articles on Radiohead, Ben Elton and Adrian Edmondson. Other websites are (for Birtwistle) http://www.boosey.com/pages/cr/composer/composer_main.asp?composerid=2729; for Maxwell Davies http://www.maxopus.com/; for Howarth http.//www.alliedartists.co.uk/artist_page.php?aid=19&tid=1; for Ogdon http:??johnogdon.org.uk/index.php; for Syal http.//www.contemporarywriters.com/authors/?p=auth94; for Tomlinson httpl//www.johntomlinson.org/

Student Protest
This is discussed in several chapters of *A History of the University of Manchester 1951–73* and *1973–90,* by Brian Pullan with Michele Abendstern (Manchester, 2000 and 2004).

Students from Abroad
Alex J. Robertson's chapter in this volume depends to a large extent on original research in the archives of the Vice-Chancellor's Office, the President's Office and the Alumni Office, and on Annual Reports of the Victoria University of Manchester and UMIST. Among his other sources are 'A tale of technological diffusion in the Meiji Era', by G. Saxonhouse, *Journal of Economic History,* vol. 39 (1974), 149-65; *The Economic Impact of International Students on UK Universities,* by D. Greenaway (London, 1995); his own article, 'Trends and strategies in international education: British universities and the wider world since 1980', among the papers of the *International Conference on Cross-Cultural and Educational Studies* (Taipei, 1996), at 27–50, and *The University of Manchester: an Introduction for International Students* (Manchester, 2005).

Acknowledgements

From Professor Brian Pullan:

Innumerable people, not all of them directly connected with Manchester University, have been generous with their time and encouragement during the preparation of this book. I thank them all, but must make particular mention of:

Dr James Peters of the John Rylands University Library of Manchester, the University archivist, for general assistance.

Miss Michelle O'Doherty the Warden of Ashburne Hall, for allowing access to the Hall archives and works of art; also Mrs Sheila Griffiths, the Honorary Archivist, for her valuable assistance.

Dr Timothy Stibbs, the Principal of Dalton-Ellis Hall, for access to and assistance with the photographic archives of the Hall.

Dr Robert Quayle for assistance with images of UMIST and of Manchester scientists.

Dr Michael Powell and Dr Fergus Wilde of Chetham's Library for assistance with visual and other materials from the Library's local history archives.

Mrs Elisabeth Vinaver for a photograph of Professor Eugene Vinaver.

My wife Janet Pullan and my daughter-in-law Anne Pullan for valiant assistance in identifying key locations for photography and for general picture research.

From Michele Abendstern:

I would like to thank Sir Martin Harris, Professor John Garside, and the members of the Dalton Group who were interviewed in 2003 and on whose comments this chapter is based.

From Alex J. Robertson:

I have received invaluable help from a number of people within the University of Manchester. I am particularly indebted to James Peters (University Archivist) and the staff of the Special Collections Department of the John Rylands University Library for their help in identifying and accessing important sources of information. Diana Leitch, Deputy Librarian, graciously loaned me her personal copy of Henry Roscoe's memoirs, and was a mine of information on science in Manchester. Lynda McKean of the President's Office kindly arranged access for me to key files in its archives. In the Alumni Office, David Bradley and Jacky Furby provided me with valuable information about overseas graduates. My old colleague from the Department of History, Brian Pullan, not only lent me a copy of his excellent *History of the University of Manchester, 1973–90*, but also suggested several interesting lines of enquiry. I am very grateful indeed to them all.

From the Publisher:

Third Millennium is delighted to acknowledge the unstinting assistance of the University of Manchester Alumni Development Office and the University of Manchester Communications and Marketing Services team and Design Studio throughout the preparation of this book. Special thanks are due to Donna Prince, of the Alumni Development Office, for Herculean feats of organization and coordination.

Picture acknowledgements:

While every effort has been made to trace and credit copyright holders of images used in this book, the publishers welcome any further information.

t=top, m=middle, b=bottom, l=left, r=right

John Batten, 177b; Russell Bloor, 11, 13t, 14br, 27tr, 30tl+tm, 31, 32r, 34, 50tm, 58, 60, 61br, 63r, 64, 65, 67tr, 71, 79, 80, 81, 83b, 84tl, 87b, 90, 93, 95tr, 98tl, 100, 110, 116t, 119, 120l, 122, 126t, 131r, 134, 135, 141, 142, 144tl+tr+ml, 147, 148, 157, 159t, 160, 162, 165b, 166, 170, 172tr+ml, 189, 191, 192t; Margaret Bramford, 163t; © Chetham Library, 12, 15tl, 17m, 20b, 22, 35b, 36tl+bl+br, 38, 49, 50tr, 54l, 63l, 75tl, 77, 83tl, 84tr, 89, 98tr, 99, 120r, 124, 126b, 138, 143r, 144m, 146, 164t, 179, 182b; Christopher Cockcroft, 35t; Dr J.P. Critchely, 37br; Anna Ford, 167; © Getty Images, 43l (Hans Wild/Time Life Pictures/Getty Images), 87tl (George C. Beresford/Beresford/Getty Images), 160br (Central Press/Getty Images), 176b (Daniel Berehulak/Getty Images), 178 (Dave Etheridge-Barnes/Getty Images); Ian Gregory, 164b (illustration by J. Tynan); Dr Mike Hughes, 73; Irish National Press (1948), 165tl; Sarah Jones, 154–155; Reproduced by courtesy of The University Librarian and Director, The John Rylands University Library, The University of Manchester, 10, 24, 29, 39b, 76, 150t+b, 151tm, 153br; Hilary Kahn, 101–7; © Manchester Archives and Local Studies, 20t+tl, 23, 25tl+tm, 53, 171, 181b; The Manchester Museum, The University of Manchester, 75m, 78; Stavros Mantis, 186; Arthur Merrall, 165tr; © The Nobel Foundation, 96, 130, 131l; *Architects of Wings*, © Harald Penrose, 1985, 40; Jane Pullan, 16t, 92, 149t; G. Roberts, 169; Royal Haskoning, 113; Dr J.B. Taylor, 42; The University of Manchester, 13b, 14bl, 14t, 15tr, 18, 21, 25b+tr, 27tl, 30tr, 32l, 33, 36/37, 39t, 43r, 44, 45, 46, 47, 52, 54m, 57, 59, 67bm+br, 68, 69, 70, 72, 74, 82, 83tr, 85, 86, 87m, 91, 94/95, 94tl, 114, 115, 116b, 118t, 121, 123, 127, 129, 132, 133, 136, 137, 140, 145, 156, 158, 161, 168, 180, 190, 112l, 112r, 118m, 125, 126bl, 143l, 149b, 150m, 151tl+b, 151tr, 152, 153tr+bm, 159b, 163b, 172tl, 173–5, 176t, 177t, 181t, 183–5, 187–8, 192b, 193–5; from The University of Manchester and Professor H.C.A. Hankins collection, 108–109, 112b (illustration by Richard Willson); Mrs E Vinaver, 88